Advanced Sciences and Techn for Security Applications

CW00541059

Series Editor

Anthony J. Masys, Associate Professor, Director of Global Disaster Management, Humanitarian Assistance and Homeland Security, University of South Florida, Tampa, USA

Advisory Editors

Gisela Bichler, California State University, San Bernardino, CA, USA

Thirimachos Bourlai, Lane Department of Computer Science and Electrical Engineering, Multispectral Imagery Lab (MILab), West Virginia University, Morgantown, WV, USA

Chris Johnson, University of Glasgow, Glasgow, UK

Panagiotis Karampelas, Hellenic Air Force Academy, Attica, Greece

Christian Leuprecht, Royal Military College of Canada, Kingston, ON, Canada

Edward C. Morse, University of California, Berkeley, CA, USA

David Skillicorn, Queen's University, Kingston, ON, Canada

Yoshiki Yamagata, National Institute for Environmental Studies, Tsukuba, Ibaraki, Japan

Indexed by SCOPUS

The series Advanced Sciences and Technologies for Security Applications comprises interdisciplinary research covering the theory, foundations and domain-specific topics pertaining to security. Publications within the series are peer-reviewed monographs and edited works in the areas of:

- biological and chemical threat recognition and detection (e.g., biosensors, aerosols, forensics)
- crisis and disaster management
- terrorism
- cyber security and secure information systems (e.g., encryption, optical and photonic systems)
- traditional and non-traditional security
- energy, food and resource security
- economic security and securitization (including associated infrastructures)
- transnational crime
- human security and health security
- social, political and psychological aspects of security
- recognition and identification (e.g., optical imaging, biometrics, authentication and verification)
- smart surveillance systems
- applications of theoretical frameworks and methodologies (e.g., grounded theory, complexity, network sciences, modelling and simulation)

Together, the high-quality contributions to this series provide a cross-disciplinary overview of forefront research endeavours aiming to make the world a safer place.

The editors encourage prospective authors to correspond with them in advance of submitting a manuscript. Submission of manuscripts should be made to the Editor-in-Chief or one of the Editors.

More information about this series at http://www.springer.com/series/5540

Marina Nuciari · Eraldo Olivetta
Editors

Leaders for Tomorrow: Challenges for Military Leadership in the Age of Asymmetric Warfare

Editors
Marina Nuciari
Department of Economic and Social
Sciences, Mathematics and Statistics
University of Torino (Italy)
Turin, Italy

Eraldo Olivetta
School of Management and Economics
University of Torino (Italy)
Turin, Italy

ISSN 1613-5113   ISSN 2363-9466 (electronic)
Advanced Sciences and Technologies for Security Applications
ISBN 978-3-030-71716-2   ISBN 978-3-030-71714-8 (eBook)
https://doi.org/10.1007/978-3-030-71714-8

This Springer imprint is published by the registered company Springer Nature Switzerland AG
The registered company address is: Gewerbestrasse 11, 6330 Cham, Switzerland

Preface

Leaders for Tomorrow: Challenges for Military Leadership in the Age of Asymmetric Warfare is the new title chosen at the end of the research process to enlighten a topic differently defined by Giuseppe Caforio, Coordinator of the ERGOMAS Association Working Group "Military Profession", when in 2014 launched his first call for a new research project named by him "Officer and Commander in Asymmetric Warfare Operations". For those who had the opportunity to know personally and work with Giuseppe, this title has remained the common reference under which to consider a number of topics stemming from a previous research, published in 2013 and titled *Soldiers Without Frontiers. The View from the Ground*, taken by Caforio as a point of departure to deepen a strictly related topic such as the change in what he called *command responsibilities*. In *Soldiers Without Frontiers*, the actors under observation were the rank and file soldiers dealing with unconventional military operations together with their NCOs and Officers, all considered as members of the same institution, the Armed Forces, trying together to cope with diverse, unpredictable and somewhat ambiguous missions. From that project, a new research question arose, asking to explore the ongoing adaptation and expected change as far as *officers with command responsibilities* were concerned. It is somewhat odd that terms like *leader* and *leadership* were never used by Caforio (a retired General!) in the various versions of the research project proposals, to name the very nature of the object, that is adaptation and change in leadership action and behaviours under the pressure of the extremely various and demanding asymmetric warfare operations. To a certain extent, *command* is a true military word, much more than *leadership*, maybe in his view it seemed to refer mainly to a business environment.

After Giuseppe Caforio sudden passing, in summer 2015, members of the research group agreed upon the decision to try to go on with the research, collecting data where such work was not accomplished and presenting some provisional papers based on the available data at the 30th Biennial ERGOMAS Conference in Athens in summer 2017. And step by step, by means of reciprocal confrontation among authors and thanks also to the attention and advice of my co-editor Eraldo Olivetta and several experts within Springer Publishers, the central topic for an original collective volume has found its definition: new military leaders for new military missions, being those missions more and more characterized by 'volatile, uncertain, complex and ambiguous environments' (VUCA), according to the definition given by US Army General George W. Casey, which are "normal" in asymmetric and crises management operations. In a few words, *Leaders for Tomorrow*.

Now the volume is here, and I am sure to express the sentiment and will of all authors in dedicating this new book to its first proponent, our colleague and friend Giuseppe Caforio.

Turin, Italy   Marina Nuciari
November 2020

Contents

A New Kind of Leadership?

Asymmetric Warfare Operations. Research Framework and Some Methodological Remarks

Marina Nuciari

Abstract Since the end of bipolarism the concept of asymmetric warfare, or the more general term of asymmetric conflict, began to be more and more used in connection with conventional armed forces activities and tasks. The term was considered more adequate and inclusive of the wide variety of international missions performed by multinational military units, ranging from classic UN peacekeeping to counterinsurgency operations.

1 Premise

Since the end of bipolarism the concept of asymmetric warfare, or the more general term of asymmetric conflict, began to be more and more used in connection with conventional armed forces activities and tasks. The term was considered more adequate and inclusive of the wide variety of international missions performed by multinational military units, ranging from classic UN peacekeeping to counterinsurgency operations. The term "new wars" coined by Kaldor [1, p. 9] is a classic and well-known definition with no need of explanation or quotation, but the inclusion in the concept of many different types of conflictual and variously armed actors and behaviours (such as "*paramilitary groups organised around a charismatic leader, warlords who control particular areas, terrorists cells, fanatic volunteers like the Mujahadeen, organised criminal groups, units of irregular forces or other security services, as well as mercenaries and private military companies*") opened the doors to many tentatives to find out some common traits able to distinguish from conventional warfare, and to include in a unique definition, this extreme variety of unconventional armed conflicts. Since the time when the "constabulary force" was proposed by Janowitz [2] as the definition of that "*...military establishment*

M. Nuciari (✉)
University of Torino, Torino, Italy
e-mail: marina.nuciari@unito.it

Department of Economic and Social Sciences, Mathematics and Statistics, Corso Unione Sovietica 218bis, 10134 Torino, TO, Italy

© Springer Nature Switzerland AG 2021
M. Nuciari and E. Olivetta (eds.), *Leaders for Tomorrow: Challenges for Military Leadership in the Age of Asymmetric Warfare*, Advanced Sciences and Technologies for Security Applications, https://doi.org/10.1007/978-3-030-71714-8_1

(...) continuously prepared to act, committed to the minimum use of force", seeking for "*viable international relations rather than victory*", too diverse types of use of force became evident and persistent, confronting conventional militaries, and mainly western democratic societies with, as Shultz and Dew [3] wrote, new and brutal types of warfare are performed by non-state armed groups, where asymmetrical tactics are employed often successfully against the larger and technologically superior forces normally expression of independent nation-states.

Deep changes in mind, attitudes and behaviours are thus required to military professionals, and especially to that part of the military organisation composed by officers, to confront these new conflicts conditions. Military professionals, in facts, and military leaders in particular, perceive themselves facing an ambiguous situation, requiring from them some renewal in their professional training, new skills to confront unexpected, unpredictable and uncertain factors. In the words of Abrahamsson [4, p. 13] "*the change from an invasion defence towards a defence based on flexible response puts the military profession under the strain of changing large parts of its expert base, as well as ethical norms and corporate traditions*".

In the discussion of the project to propose the research that has originated this volume, and in the presentation of its final proposal, a general question was posed by Caforio [5, p. 25], in order to ascertain what capabilities were necessary to military leaders to deal with such a new demanding environment, admitting that many scholars, since the last decades of XX century, "*agree in believing that the traditional military preparation for conventional conflicts constitutes the indispensable base also for the vast range of operations in asymmetric warfare* [6–9]. And following Abrahamsson and Weibull, what ethical codes should be adopted, different from traditional military ethics [10]? A conventional military education and training, anyway unavoidable, is questioned by the necessity for other skills to be added within the current geo-strategic scenario (see also Caforio et al. [11]).

These new knowledges and skills cover a wide range of different fields, since they must transmit bases for adequate operative answers to very unusual situations for a military force in asymmetric conflict contexts. The very frequent presence of civilians, to be saved or protected, goes together with the need to reduce the use of force at a minimal level without endangering soldiers' motivations and morale in an anyway dangerous environment [12]. Moreover, political and governance roles, not exactly military functions [13, 14], Nagl [9] played by military leaders require to include managerial and socio-political skills, together with the acquisition of an intercultural communicative approach and the ability to develop "third cultures" features in leadership as well as in negotiation in order to efficiently manage culture clashes [15–19]. This happens not only in the frequent case of relations with many different types of "civilians" but also because of the current multinational nature of expeditionary forces where task forces are formed by units coming from different countries [20, 21].

Going along with a similar process appeared in international business, leaders in the military organisations are experiencing the same needs to develop *new and more adequate leadership skills*.

In the research at the basis of this volume the original scope was rightly on possible changes in the commanding function in military units deployed in asymmetric conflicts theatres, with special attention to low and mid-level commanding roles. The comparative project launched within ERGOMAS Working Group on Military Profession, at that time coordinated by Giuseppe Caforio, began in 2014 with the original title of "Officer and Commander in Asymmetric Warfare Operations", and it can be considered a sort of "spin-off" from a previous research conducted within the same ERGOMAS Working Group on the Military Profession, published as "Soldiers Without Frontiers. The View from the Ground" [5]. But it has taken inevitably an original dimension, because of its specific point of interest, being centred around the military commander, the officer as a leader, in at least three hierarchical levels: platoon commander, company commander and regiment/battalion commander. Here commanding functions are considered in Crises Response Operations, according to the various deployments in asymmetric missions performed by armed forces (mainly the Army) of eight countries, Bulgaria, Cameroon, Denmark, Finland, Italy, Lithuania, Philippines and Spain. If in *Soldiers without Frontiers* actors under observation were rank and files soldiers and their NCOs and Officers, altogether considered as members of the same institution, in the "Officer and Commander" project there was the attempt to grasp from living experiences a better definition of what a new kind of leadership means when leaders must cope with diverse, unpredictable and somewhat ambiguous missions.

Thus, the aim of the volume based on that project is to present and discuss, from answers given by military leaders with strong and repeated experience in the field, their remarks to the existing doctrines on military leaderships, their applicability on the field according to their experiences and their proposals and suggestions towards new directions.

2 A New Kind of Leadership?

Intercultural experiences are part of multinational military operations since early Nineties, when Peace Support Operations (PSOs) or Crises Response Operations (CROs) became routine instead of exceptions for various military organizations. Research data on military personnel's attitudes toward cultural diversity and intercultural encounters ability induce to think that some "third culture" creation process (in the sense given to it by Casmir [15] and by Dodd [16] is at work, which permits to improve cooperation and negotiation activities with many different social actors on theatre. The case of Italian Armed Forces, in this volume compared with six other and different national militaries, is somewhat exemplar of such a revolution in military roles and behaviors, because of their developing of a peculiar ability in cultural diversity acknowledgement and consideration in their performance [19]. But this process can be observed in many other countries whose armed forces have been involved in many different operations other than war. Officers' preparation in sociology and cultural anthropology is provided in first level formal education in many military academies all around the world, and negotiation and intercultural awareness are taught in subsequent learning.

In the research here presented under different topics and goals in the chapters of Part 2, the main subject is *leadership* and the key actor under observation is the *leader* and her/his behavior in those 'volatile', uncertain, complex and ambiguous environments' (VUCA), according to the definition given by General George W. Casey, U.S.A., (Ret.),[1] which are "normal" in asymmetric and crises management operations.

Experiences of intercultural encounters and third culture creation processes are observed by means of in-depth interviews of officers of various countries and in different ranks, describing their activities in CROs, exploring paths of trustful environment creation in different crisis and cultural diversities contexts. The main goal leading the research was to understand reasons of success and failure of trustful cooperation, in order to ascertain what qualities and abilities must be improved in officers' education and training to give rise to a culturally flexible soldier.

3   Some Concepts and Definitions

In order to keep a wide range of topics and disciplinary *stimula* under control, a number of key words can be listed and considered typical and recurrent in scientific research in this field. These keywords are the following:

- Flexibility
- Multiculturality
- Cultural Awareness
- Intercultural competence
- Intercultural encounters and Third Culture creation.

Flexibility began to be used as a concept since the end of the Eighties of past century, taken from firms and transnational companies organizational idioma, to define the main character to be acquired in order to adequately sail in the new global economic order, where turbulent technological environments and unstable and unpredictable new markets signed the generalized crisis of the Fordist model [23, 24] and the rise of the word *flexibility* as a kind of a new *mantra* able to solve those new and risky challenges.

With the end of Cold War, similarly, the same concept was extended to the military organization in general but with specific reference to western armed forces more and more involved in the so-called Peace Support Operations (PSOs), or Crises Response Operations (CROs), or even the Military Operations Other Than War (MOOTWs).[2] If flexibility was the condition of the military organization, then *flexible* was the qualification of the military professional, be him/her an officer, an NCO or a soldier.

---

[1] Wells et al. [22].
[2] Dandeker [25–27].

Generally speaking, "the flexible soldier" became the overriding definition of the military personnel employed in a global world where complexity and unpredictability were the norm in rather every social life phenomena.[3]

Multiculturality is part of the new lexicon, both as a definition of the majority of unconventional missions and of the general quality of global society. Expressions such as *multicultural forces for a multicultural world,* or *multicultural abilities for multicultural environments* are very common in most of the papers dealing with CRO's. Very often the term is considered synonymous of *multinationality*, but it has different uses: multinational are normally military formations made of different national units forming multinational military intervention forces that Soeters and Manigart [28] describe as a type where a *horizontal military cooperation* is working, a traditional type of integration consisting "*...of a simple lining up of individual national units within a battle group (...),* where "*work-related contacts between military personnel from the various national contingents (...) occur only at the level of headquarters*".[4] A *vertical multinationality* is on the other side defined by Soeters and Manigart in those cases where "*...cooperation and interaction between the various national components (...) takes the form of mixed bi- or multinational contingents.*"

This is the case when "*...work-related interactions between personnel occur at the battalion or even company level*". And in these cases cultural differences arise, different military cultures play together with cultural diversities at general levels, thus creating a *multicultural environment*, where cultural diversity very often originates problems and difficulties in mutual understanding, with different and at times positive as well as negative effects on the conduct of operations and their outcomes [32]. Paying attention to the topic under study, leadership styles and behaviors vary with culture, and notwithstanding the often recalled isomorphic character of military culture [33, 34], differences in leadership are well documented [17, 35] with specific reference to multicultural and multinational missions. As noted by many authors (see among others MacIsaac [36], Shamir and Ben-Ari [37]), commanders in multinational units, as well as commanders in units dealing with multicultural theatres, must develop a true flexible leadership capability, trying to apply different styles and techniques. Shamir and Ben-Ari [37] refer to aspects of transactional leadership as well as of transformational leadership that find good exempla in this volume, where Olivetta in Chap. 2 makes explicit reference to field experiences of Italian units junior commanders who, in culturally diverse and often strongly demanding operative situations, report a range of behaviors often unconsciously inspired by *transformational leadership* factors, such as "*...to be role models for their subordinates (idealized influence), and succeed in motivating them by making their work meaningful (inspirational motivation) but, above all, they are attentive to the needs of each of their subordinates (individualized consideration)*" (Olivetta, here, Olivetta [38]), and *emotional intelligence* in Golemanian sense is required in those extreme situations [39, 40] when military leaders must manage with threats of "intolerable magnitude" [41].

---

[3] A good example is Caforio [20].

[4] Soeters and Manigart [29]. See on this also Klein and Kuemmel [30], Klein [31].

This is a sounding topic, on which the research on the military, especially socio-logical and psychological research, is working since the end of XXth century. Shamir and Ben-Ari [37, p. 54], observing the fact that those leadership theories *"may be highly relevant to the military context (...) But they do not deal specifically with leaders in inter-organizational and cross-cultural frameworks"*, sustained the need for *"a new wave of empirical studies of military leadership"*, envisaging the need for *new modes of leadership training and education* [42]. In her Chapter in this volume, Soili Paananen reflects rightly on this need for adequate and new education for young officers, in order to train them effectively as future military leaders, showing how different cultures, but also different experiences and assignments, have a sure effect in orienting and designing different leadership styles and appropriate skills.

Cultural Awareness and *Intercultural competence* thus became two somewhat "magic" refrains giving evidence to new education concepts and skills for the mili-tary. When dealing with asymmetric conflicts environments, many various actors are present (civilians such as local population, refugees, fighiting factions, local politi-cians, international and NGO officials and members, media representatives.). We can say that military culture affects the ability to cope with an uncertain and differentiated theatre where many different actors are present, especially when they are civilians; we can say also that military culture is affected by the mix of experience acquired by officers, and it is pushed to go in a direction where a mixed, flexible, and not simply definitely "peacekeeper" pattern is prevailing. An educational path adequate to the non conventional operative theatres should then be oriented to reinforce these attitudes, reducing without eliminating the warrior-like attitudes: the outcome should be a kind of officer able to refer to more than one pattern, to use more than one code system, so that he or she could understand and behave in an adequate way within the highly uncertain and somewhat ambiguous environments where MOOTW are usually performed.

Intercultural competence, then, and *intercultural sensitivity*, in the sense given by Bennett [43, 44], Hammer et al. [45, 48], and Bennett and Bennett [47], together with crosscultural management techniques, cultural diversity awareness and ability to analyse and solve role conflicts, all these are new skills required to deal with culturally complex and diverse environments [18], Nuciari [19].

Intercultural encounters and Third Culture creation are strictly connected processes. It has been often observed that actors in intercultural situations become able with time to overcome difficulties in communication and to reduce misperceptions. This happens especially when some shared interests and a cooperative outlook permit to reduce cultural distance by adopting an empathetic orientation stressing on similarities and reducing cultural discomfort. From observations of that kind of processes, Fred Casmir developed his theory about a Third-Culture Building Process, defined as "...A mutually beneficial, dialogic communication process which allows for ambiguity and the creation of meaning under chaotic circumstances" [15]. Third-Culture building abilities can be part of individual empathetic personalities, which means that it can be a spontaneous way in approaching the "cultural other". In inter-national and multicultural conflict contexts such spontaneous and occasional talents can find their proper application, but it cannot be enough at all to base successful or, more often, acceptable compromise solutions on randomly distributed skills. Inter-cultural competence and third culture creation abilities should become new skills to be taught to and learned by military commanders in their basic military education as well as along their career advancement, combining a proper consideration of the various operative experiences and practices with theoretical learning and training.

Empirical observations of military leaders in action, comments and evaluations on their reactions and adaptation strategies in asymmetric conflict environments with high presence of cultural diversity are frequent in the following chapters and represent one of the most valuable results of the "Officer and Commander" project.

4 The Research Framework

4.1 Some Notes on Methodology and Research Activity

The aim of the project was oriented to acquire a direct knowledge about leader-ship models and practises applied in asymmetric theatres. For this goal, a semi-directive questionnaire was prepared, written in English and shared with participating researchers, and realized in order to be submitted autonomously by the eight (then seven) country research groups (see Annex 1. The questionnaire, in this volume). Semi-directive interviews were conducted in local languages, registered and then translated into English to permit shared readings by means of a Dropbox virtual place, where all materials were stored and individually accessible by every research group member, who could treat original discursive data by means of the preferred qualitative analysis tool. Thus, the generalized possibility to access empirical data directly by single researchers permitted to propose, select and choose a number of thematic areas from which the various Chapters in this volume took origin.

4.2 National Samples Characteristics

The comparative survey was conducted in different times from the end of 2015 to 2018, mainly because of different possibilities to do empirical research by involved partners, and in selected units, mainly in the Army, according to the various deployments in asymmetric missions performed by the armed forces of the eight participating countries, Bulgaria, Cameroon, Denmark, Finland, Italy, Lithuania, Philippines and Spain.

Notwithstanding the minimum required sample per country counted for **10 platoon commanders, 8 company commanders, and 6 battalion/regiment commanders** with real command experiences in asymmetric warfare environments, the true sample sizes are somewhat different, ranging from the 57 cases of Bulgaria to the 25 cases of Finland, and counting only four cases from Lithuania (see Fig. 1). Rank

Fig. 1 Total sampling

Participating Countries	Number of interviews
Bulgaria	57
Cameroun	34
Denmark	26
Finland	25
Italy	44
Lithuania	4
Philippines	29
Spain	27
TOTAL	246

and variety of experiences were carefully determined by each country research group in order to reflect types and variety of international missions actually performed. Whilst the research in its beginning had a comparative intention, the main goal was to assure diversity and variety of deployments, experiences and solutions actively adopted by military leaders in the various specific assigned tasks and responsibilities. Thus, the high variety in asymmetric/international missions has been recognized to play a fundamental role for military leadership [18], Nuciari [49]) and this turned into a great attention to every single context where missions were deployed, in order to obtain substantial diversity.

Missions deployments, taking into account only those performed since the year 2000, show a rather high level of diversity (many different missions in many different theatres) for all the eight countries, but there is also a recurrent set of missions where rather all countries have been involved, such as Afghanistan, Balkans, Iraq as well as different African countries, as shown in Fig. 2. Two exceptions are Cameroun and The Philippines, currently engaged in Central Africa the former and in domestic counterinsurgency operations the latter.

National samples according to their size and composition are anyway important to show the situational variety where military forces were deployed, and how these diverse deployments implied various adjustments and adaptations of leadership styles also according to cultural diversities involved in the field.

Out of the eight countries, six countries are EU members, even though from a highly different time lapse, and two belong to two different continents. Among the European Union, Denmark and Finland (and The Netherlands, although with different status) are a good representation of Northern Europe, Italy and Spain belong to Southern Europe, Bulgaria and Lithuania are inevitably considered also as representative of the so-called Eastern Europe in the past bipolar era on the one side and for their very recent entry into the European Union on the other. Cameroon and Philippines add not only simple variety to the general sample but they constitute an evident and positive enlargement, presenting two diverse situations of military forces

COUNTRY	PREVAILING DEPLOYMENT THEATRES 2000-2017
Bulgaria	Afghanistan, Iraq, Balkans, Eritrea, Ethiopia
Cameroun	Central Africa since 2006
Denmark	Afghanistan, Iraq, Balkans, Arabian Sea
Finland	Afghanistan, Kurdistan, Lebanon, Balkans, Somalia, Mali, India, Pakistan
Italy	Afghanistan, Iraq, Balkans, Lebanon, Arabian Sea, Sudan, Mozambique, Sinai
Lithuania	Iraq, Balkans, Mali, Central Africa, Somalia, Afghanistan, Pakistan, Turkey
Philippines	Philippines (domestic counterinsurgency)
Spain	Afghanistan, Iraq, Balkans, Lebanon, Arabian Sea, Chad, Mauritania

Fig. 2 Deployment theatres

mainly deployed in South-Eastern Asian theatres, as it is the case for The Philippines, and in Central Africa theatres as it is the case of Cameroun.

5 Leadership and Military Leadership in Asymmetric Theatres. A Cross-National Comparison

The core of the research being the above mentioned "Officer and Commander" behaviour in Asymmetric Conflicts, central consideration is given to leadership styles and behaviours, and to that kind of ground adaptation and individual change perceived and performed by military leaders with special reference to middle and middle-high level ranks, such as captains, majors and colonels. To this organizational side Part One is devoted, particularly the two chapters in this volume by Eraldo Olivetta. In Chap. 2, the question is posed about leadership in a somewhat interlocutory position, bound to find answers to basic questions such as *what leadership is? what's the difference between Authority and Power?* Stemming from organizational sociological literature, the so-called good leader should be able to manage both formal and informal leadership, but "…the way of understanding leadership has changed over time, in relation to the socio-cultural changes of the parent society, and (…) these changes have also influenced military leadership".[5] But the Military is different from any other organization: "…the military organization, due to its particular function, has peculiar characteristics that differentiate it from any other organization

---

[5]E. Olivetta, *Chap. 2—What does Leadership Mean?* in this volume.

(...) although military leadership can draw useful contributions from studies on civilian leadership, the particularity of the military institution influences the styles of command, making it take on particular and distinctive characteristics with respect to the management styles of civil organizations".[6] What does it mean then, to be a military leader? What are the main problems in managing people in the Army and what strategic behaviours should be adopted? Yet these questions are made more difficult to be answered because of the fact that leadership styles have changed not only by means of changes in military organizational format, or even before by means of the changes at a general societal level, but also because of the inner diversity of societies and cultures of which military institutions are a substantive part. And this diversity, whilst reflected within the military institution, it becomes crucial in those operative theatres where many different actors are present: different nationalities and cultures of deployed soldiers in multinational units; variety of actors playing different roles in asymmetric theatres, such as local military and police forces, civil and religious authorities and local populations, NGOs, mass—media, etc.[7] For this reason, a good commander must be able to manage with different cultures, in order to achieve the necessary operative effectiveness, as it is discussed by Olivetta in Chap. 3, dealing with changes in leadership styles and cultural differences management[8] in forces deployed in asymmetric theatres.

5.1   The Many Aspects of a Complex Environment: Voices from the Ground in International Asymmetric Conflicts Operations

In Part Two, eight chapters deal with the core business of the research, how military performances—at all levels but mainly as far as commanding functions are concerned- in the so-called asymmetric conflicts are adjusted and to what extent to the different situations and challenges posed by VUCA (Volatile, Uncertain, Complex, and Ambiguous) conflict environments. Chapter 4 by Soili Paananen deals with a basic and unavoidable topic: how to educate and train young officers so that they could act effectively as future military leaders, and how this task is attained by the various and different national armed forces inasmuch as different cultures, but also different experiences and assignments have a sure effect in orienting and designing different leadership styles and appropriate skills.

Chapters 5 and 6, by Marién Duran & Adolfo Calatrava and by Yantsislav Yanakiev respectively, are based on the very peculiar nature of asymmetric conflicts theatres, their being essentially highly crowded places where many different actors are present and bearing the typical conditions where a cultural shock can take place.

---

[6]E. Olivetta, *ibidem.*

[7]See on this Nuciari [18, pp. 25–53].

[8]E. Olivetta, *Chap. 3—From Culture to Leadership*, in this Volume.

As I stressed in my previous *Coping with diversity* (2007), different military orientations toward operations other than war can affect the perception of difficulties arising from the variety of actors, most of them civilians, active in the operation theatre and bearers of diverse cultures in terms of values, norms, goals, needs and behaviors in general.[9] And it is nonetheless a fact that in asymmetric operations in general (counterinsurgency, constabulary and not only humanitarian missions) the experience of soldiers and officers very often refer about difficulties with civilians, probably ought to the fact that these very diverse types of missions implicate always some kind of relationships with civilians.[10] Diversity is the key element to define the kind of situation facing military personnel in asymmetric conflict situations. At an overall consideration of the various diversities, it seems evident that the main problem for soldiers and officers is to face a high variety of expectations, coming from many differentiated 'others' (being them military or civilians) arising from the many and different situations with whom military personnel has to cope. This variety is felt more or less problematic at the extent to which every actor in each situation is the bearer of a specific culture, that is with values and norms, but also interests, more or less in contrast with each other. At a general level, they can be distinguished according to their specific status and roles in the theatre where the military is deployed. They can be the civil population, local administrative and political authorities, and even fighting factions, who could be defined as *actors within the context*: they are in fact part of the situation for which the mission has been decided. Under certain circumstances, it is normal that problematic relations can arise from these actors, since here the wider cultural gap can be found among each of them and the military force. Of course, they are also differing among themselves: civil population plays often, if not always, the role of the "victim" who must be 'saved', helped and protected by soldiers; it maintains anyway ambiguous relationships with factions in arms (if any), and this ambiguity is also present in its relationships with local authorities; on their side, political authorities and fighting factions have specific goals and interests, and tend to make opportunistic use of the military force presence in a variety of manners according to the overall framework of the mission. Evidence is given on this by Duran & Calatrava, when reporting from answers of Italian and Spanish officers deployed in Afghanistan, that "It is a complex relation, always based on respect and politeness, but often with mismatched interests".[11] If a different language and more general cultural differences are added to this picture, it is evident that the largest part of problematic relationships came from these actors, as openly expressed by Finn and Lithuanian interviewees when addressing to a sort of cultural clash or to explicit cultural differences.[12]

A second type of actor is made by those whose actions are bound *toward the context*, that is those who are directly playing the role of the peacekeeper, even

---

[9]Nuciari [18, p. 34].

[10]Ibidem, p. 35.

[11]See Duran M. and Calatrava A. *Chap. 5—Military Interaction With Local Actors*, in this volume.

[12]See Duran M. and Calatrava A., in this volume.

though at very different levels and with highly different status: international agencies representatives and officials, members of NGOs, and the military itself in its diversity as far as national contingents are concerned; they are all acting in order to settle the conflictual or dramatic situation for which they have been deployed. They should have mainly common goals, and their interaction should give place to some kind of problem solution. Notwithstanding this positive premise, cultural distance is even here a matter of fact, together with at least some conflicting goals and interests. International agencies, such as United Nations, EU, or other mid-level regional agencies, are usually bureaucratic organisations whose representatives act as members of an organisation, following norms and practices according to a well-established and peculiar 'organisational culture'. If they do not differ from the military as far as bureaucratic patterns of thinking and acting are concerned, they differ anyway as far as goals and inner values are concerned. Another source of problems is the relationships with NGOs. The military is an *institution* while an NGO is a '*movement*', authority and hierarchical responsibility are featuring the military while normative commitment under an individual and voluntary basis are the cement of an NGO. Rules and procedural correctness, division of labour, discipline and obedience form the bulk of military organisation, while individual initiative, diffuse and unspecialized roles, critical mind and an antiauthoritarian habit are usually common features of any NGO. Following a well-known conceptual dichotomy in organizational literature, the military is a mechanic system, while an NGO is an organic system [50]. NGOs, furthermore, are very often antimilitaristic, and they are not so well inclined toward armed forces, notwithstanding their need for security and protection. Problematic relationships, thus, are the results of a shared responsibility, stemming both from NGOs themselves and from the military [18]. If this was true already in the recent past, as well documented by Moskos [46 p. 33] when writing "...*it is customary to view NGOs and the military as somehow at odds one another in terms of staff recruitment and organizational styles...The rigidly hierarchical approach to decision making that is the hallmark of the military may not be possible or desirable in humanitarian crises where their help is needed. This contrast is sharpened by the strong national loyalty of military personnel as opposed to the more typical international orientation of NGO staff. And, of course, military efforts may be at odds with NGO objectives and* vice versa", it appears to remain true even now, and well documented in this research by Duran & Calatrava.[13]

Similar observations are proposed by Arcala Hall & Dumpit in their Chap. 11, where the many other types of "locals" are considered in their typical aspects of subjects of the military task in unconventional operations. A peculiar trait is the multiple deployment occurring to the Philippines's troops, normally engaged for internal security where, in order to assure territorial security, they must exert a high level of flexibility trying to build up "...*collaborative, competitive or contested relations with local civilian actors*", according to the case.

Another well-known type of possible problematic relationships, often present in multinational coalitions where military forces are coming from different countries,

---

[13]Duran M. & Calatrava A., in this volume.

are the so-called military-to-military relationships. Here a sort of 'cultural shock' could be expected, even though not of the same relevance as in the previous kind of diversity. But difficulties arising from relations with other units' members of different nationality and language can affect performance, and give rise also to a kind of 'relative deprivation feeling, as 'a sharp perception of many kinds of unfair differences, for instance in wages, equipment, rules of conduct or discipline among contingents.[14]' In one of the first surveys dealing with samples from nine different countries' officers employed in Military Operations other Than War [20], Bernard Boene openly wrote about the fact that there was "...*interesting evidence which, though it is limited in scope and details, is enough to invalidate the most pessimistic hypotheses on the incidence of problems posed by intercultural relations and the deficiencies in professional education and training that might cause them. Indeed, the simple findings (...)point to fewer difficulties than could reasonably be expected*" (in Caforio [20, p. 91]. Only 38% of the total officers sample, in facts, declared difficulties and problems in interpersonal relations with colleagues from other national contingents, and of those, less than three percent declared these difficulties as frequent (remaining 35% declared these difficulties to be intermittent). When difficulties were considered, lower rank officers 'mentioned problematic cross-national relations less often (below 30%) than do senior officers (between 40 and 55%)', and the same was registered for younger officers (25–35 years old). With relation to the source of problematic intercultural relations, the main difficulties arose rightly from general cultural diversity (language, culture) and from diversity in military culture (divided loyalties, mission interpretation, professional preparation, ethical codes of conduct). But the fact that such difficulties were reported to be less frequent than expected does not mean at all that they are not so relevant for units performance. Some fifteen years after, in this volume Yantsislav Yanakiev (Chap. 6) presents situations where military-to-military relations can be highly different according to "*different assessments of the relationships among the coalition partners, some of which are completely controversial*". Among the reasons, the possible variety of experiences of interviewed people, different abilities to work in a multinational environment, together with "...*attitudes towards the different nations and cultures, their specific situation, the personality of the different individuals, the nature of the missions...*" (Yanakiev, in this volume). Asymmetric situations can create tensions among partners in multinational coalitions and negatively affects operational effectiveness. Cultural as well as organizational diversities are at work, but also, as Yanakiev writes: "*lack of trust among coalition partners—including local armed forces—(...) deserves particular attention because it is related to information sharing and the coalition operations' effectiveness as a whole. There is an urgent need for a focused international comparative study on the issue of trust to identify different dimensions of trustworthiness and factors to establish trust in coalitions*".

A substantial part of the research was devoted to consider young leaders' experiences in operative conditions, where they must front up practical problems often asking for immediate solutions. The rules of engagements (ROE) are often a cause

---

[14]Nuciari [18, p. 33].

of stress in MOOTWs mainly because of their ambiguity: normally relating to the definition of the enemy and the use of force (in quantity and quality) against it, in asymmetric conflicts the concept of enemy itself is ambiguous and sometimes not to be recognized as such or de facto inexistent. Because of these reasons, ROE application is among the most demanding questions posed to those in command at every level, and subject to diversity according also to military organizational cultures and rules. As observed by Martinez (Chap. 7 here), ROE in asymmetric warfare "…*become more restrictive because of political and strategic reasons which go beyond the strictly military nature of a mission*", since the neutrality of the international military force must be anyway maintained and the use of force limited. Uncertainty and ambiguity are in fact the main characters recognized in every type of asymmetric situation, and ROE's application is a frequent subject of criticism from interviewed military personnel. As Martinez clearly put it "*Ultimately, they are perceived as recommendations which do not go much beyond common sense and are designed by a 'bureaucrat' oblivious to what the soldiers on the ground will actually face*". For young leaders in particular this is also an area of proper training and education before being sent to act in uncertain and suddenly changing theatres.

Operational experience, logistical problems and solutions, and morale assessment and related problems receive thus a strong attention (see Chaps. 8, 9 and 10 respectively) by Peter Dimitrov, Plamen Petkov and Henning Sorensen. Experiences such as the so-called *baptism of fire*, encounters with armed forces in battles and skirmishes, or with IED, casualties and death of buddies, all these events concur to shape the on-the-field operational experience in asymmetric conflict theatres. Logistic support and related not always adequate equipment are documented to be problematic in many expeditionary units, according to shared views of many interviewed, in a measure inducing "…*to the conclusion that the future involvement of military units in operations to support international peace and security requires improvement in the planning and the delivery of logistical support in missions*" (Petkov, Chap. 10 this volume).

Harsh experiences in operations and unsatisfactory logistic can affect troop cohesion with well-known bad consequences on operative effectiveness. In asymmetric conflict missions, ranging from true peacekeeping to peace enforcement and counterinsurgency operations, the topic of cohesion within units maintains the same crucial importance as in true and "classic" warfare. And it calls for leadership in rather similar ways, as it is documented by Sorensen when considering how and to what extent morale problems are felt by officers more as a responsibility of the organization and less as individual problems of soldiers. "*Perhaps, the most decisive result is the fact that the military leadership, at the same time, is most aware of its responsibility for causing morale problems, and for solving them. Accordingly, it seems as if the burden of no morale problems has shifted from individual to organizational responsibility.*" (Sorensen, Chap. 8, this volume). And some solutions envisaged by interviewed officers address to a peculiar competence of these "new leaders": in order to maintain and improve morale, commanders must appear as a credible example by means of action and attitude and not simply as a superior, being able to explain and convince their subordinates about goals and accomplishments of the mission; for this task, they should develop also adequate communication skills.

5.2 A Deeper Look: Two Country Cases

A somewhat different outlook was chosen to deal with two contributions organized as country cases. Notwithstanding both subjects belong to the same area of interest, Chaps. 12 and 13 are differently organized. In Chap. 12 **Nkfunkoh Ndamnsah** offers a deep analysis of a single case, discussing the experience of Cameroon's armed forces as contributor to peace-keeping operations under the banners of the African Union and United Nations, sending troops to the Central African regional force (ECCAS Standby Force/FOMAC) since 2006, as well as in domestic deployments such as the fight against the Boko Haram threat. The research on Cameroonian military is based on the same open questionnaire, but for a choice of the author the country case format was preferred, in order to better describe and explain roles, competences and needs of an African country bound to promote and maintain peace and socio-economic development also by improving the education level of its armed forces, making them able to contribute in peace keeping operations *lato sensu*. Cameroonian data and findings discussion are therefore presented not under a comparative perspective (being Cameroonian military considered in all the chapters anyway in this volume) but with a deeper and expert insight on a true country case dealing with young officers' education, training and operative experiences. Finally, in Chap. 13 another country case is discussed by Jos Groen, about an original research conducted on Dutch experiences in Afghanistan, dealing mainly with junior officers in their leadership role as platoon commanders. Notwithstanding the fact that origins and research plan were not part of the "Officer and Commander" project, the contribution founds its right place in this volume. The focus is in fact on the field experience of Dutch junior commanders and their behaviors confronting many different aspects of crises situations, in the highly turbulent Afghan theatre. As Groen stresses, *"The objective of the project (…) was no longer simply a matter of recording factual experiences, but also themes such as personal perception, appreciation, recognition, and coping"*, expressed by young officers not only engaged in combat experience but also in Provincial Reconstruction Teams, in Liaison Teams or Psyops Support groups.

Annex 1—The Questionnaire And Interviewer Guide

Open with a brief explanation of the purposes of the research, as well as its cross-national dimension.

As is customary, assure the interviewee that his or her answers will be anonymous and will be used only in a general comparative statistical context.

1. **Record an initial set of information of a socio-demographic nature. In particular**:
    Code number (Country code, Service code, No. of the interview): example ITC20 (*)

Birth year and city:
Gender: male   ☐   female   ☐
Rank (**):
Service and specialty:☐
Years of service:
Marital Status: single ☐   married ☐
Operational experiences:

Theatre	Year	Duration	Role
Example:			
Afghanistan	2009	6 months	pl. com.

(*)The country code is as usual: SL for Slovenia, BG for Bulgaria, etc; The service code is the following: C for Army, B for Navy, A for Airforce

(**)Please indicate the rank in the traditional way: lieutenant, captain, major, lieutenant colonel, colonel.

2. **Training and specific training**:

    2a.   Mastery of languages (what languages?), good training before mission, language problems during the mission, the mission influence of such mastery
    2b.   Received basic training, his correspondence, proposals
    2c.   Specific training received (governance, cultural, socio-political training), its correspondence, the mission influence on your ability in these fields, proposals
    2d.   Suitability of preparation received to acquire intercultural communicative ability in the theater of the mission.

3. **Field experiences**:

    3a.   logistical problems encountered
    3b.   ROEs: Did you have to apply the ROEs in some occasion? If yes, what is your impression on them? Did you face problems in applying them?
    3c.   hierarchical relationships, (degree of autonomy in the field)
    3d.   relationships with other actors in the area (other units of the coalition, the local armed forces, local communities, local civil authorities, local authorities and international organizations, NGOs, mass media)
    3e.   Interoperability problems
    3f.   operational experiences (baptism of fire and other combat situations; non-combat situations such as participation to local committees, governance experiences with and without civilian leaders and the like, humanitarian support...)

3g. experience of particular problematic situations in the field, solutions and results.

4. **Commanded unit**:

4a. training level of the unit to the test of facts, proposals

4b. compliance of the materials, proposals

4c. Unit's morale: trends during mission, influencing factors, cases of defection, possible cases of PTSD.

5. **Personal experiences**: satisfaction with (the) Mission/s; personal assessment of the results, the desire to be sent in asymmetric warfare missions again in future; anything more to say?

References

1. Kaldor M (1999) New and old wars. Polity Press, Cambridge
2. Janowitz M (1960) The professional soldier: a social and political portrait. Free Press, New York
3. Shultz RH, Dew AJ (2006) Insurgents, terrorists, and militias: the warriors of contemporary combat. Columbia University Press, New York
4. Abrahamsson B (2008) Restraint, unbridled emotion and war amongst the people. In: Weibull A, Abrahamsson B (eds) The heritage and the present: from invasion defence to mission oriented organisation. Karlstad, Swedish National Defence College, pp 147–168
5. Caforio G (2013) Officer and commander in asymmetric warfare operations. J Defense Resour Manage 4, 1 (6):9–26
6. Moskos ChC (1976) Peace soldiers. University of Chicago Press, Chicago
7. Blomgren E (2008) Is military praxis in international missions reforming the profession? In: Weibull A, Abrahamsson B (eds) The heritage and the present: from invasion defence to mission oriented organisation. Karlstad, Swedish National Defence College, pp 233–242
8. Gentile GP (2008) A (slightly) better war: a narrative and its defects. World Affairs 171(1) (Summer):57–64
9. Nagl JA (2009) Let's win the wars we're in. Center for a New American Security, Washington, DC
10. Kucera T, Gulpers L (2018) A military ethics for the new missions. In: Caforio G, Nuciari M (eds) The handbook of the sociology of the military. Springer International Publishing AG, Cham, pp 359–376
11. Caforio G (2012) The military profession and asymmetric warfare. In: Kümmel G, Soeters J (eds) New wars, new militaries, new soldiers. Bingley (UK), Emerald, pp 3–18
12. Petraeus DH (2006) Learning counterinsurgency: observations from soldiering in Iraq. In: Military review (January–February), pp 2–12
13. Carafano J (2009) 20 Years later: professional military education. Testimony before the sub-committee on oversight and investigations, Armed Services Committee, United States House of Representatives, published on May 20, 2009. https://www.heritage.org/Research/Testimony/20-Years-Later-Professional-Military-Education
14. Soeters J, van Fenema PC, Beeres R (2010) Managing military organizations. Routledge, Oxon and New York
15. Casmir FL (1999) Foundations for the study of intercultural communication based on a third-culture model. Intercultural Relat 23(1):91–116

16. Dodd CH (1998) Dynamics of intercultural communication, 5th edn. McGraw-Hill, Boston
17. Febbraro AR (2008) Leadership and management teams in multinational military cooperation. In: Soeters J, Manigart P (eds) Military cooperation in multinational peace operations.
Managing cultural diversity and crises response. Routledge, Oxon, New York, pp 49–69
18. Nuciari M (2007) Coping with diversity: military and civilian actors in MOOTWs. Int Rev
Sociol 17(1):25–53
19. Nuciari M (2013) Third culture in multinational military units. some experiences referring to
Italian soldiers, mimeo
20. Caforio G (ed) (2001) The flexible officer: professional education and military operations other
than war, a cross-national analysis, Artistic & Publishing Company, Gaeta
21. Strom M (2008) Cognitive warfighting. In: Weibull A, Abrahamsson B (eds) The heritage
and the present: from invasion defence to mission oriented organisation. Karlstad, Swedish
National Defence College, pp 217–232
22. Wells II, Hailes TC, Davies MC (eds) (2013) Changing mindsets to transform security: leader
development for an unpredictable and complex world, Center for Technology and National
Security Policy-Institute for National Strategic Studies, National Defense University, Chapter 1-
Volatile, Uncertain, Complex, and Ambiguous: Leadership. Lessons from Iraq, pp 7–24
23. Piore M, Sabel C (1984) The Second industrial divide. Basic Books, New York
24. Boyer R, Saillard Y (eds) (2002) Théories de la regulation: L'état des savoirs. La Découverte,
Paris
25. Dandeker C (1996) Flexible forces for a post-cold war world: a view from the United Kingdom.
Tocqueville Rev XVI I(1):23–38
26. Dandeker C (1999) Facing uncertainty: flexible forces for the twenty-first century. Karlstad,
Swedish National Defense College
27. Dandeker C (2000) International security and its impact on national defense roles. In: Boëne B,
Dandeker C, Kuhlman J, Van der Meulen J (eds) Facing uncertainty, Report No. 2: the Swedish
military in international perspective: 2000, Karlstad, Swedish National Defense College, pp
107–112
28. Soeters J, Manigart (eds) (2008) Military cooperation in multinational peace operations. Taylor
& Francis Group. Routledge, London and New York, p 3
29. Soeters J, Manigart P (eds) (2008) Military cooperation in multinational peace operations.
Managing cultural diversity and crises response. Routledge, Oxon and New York
30. Klein P, Kuemmel G (2000) The internationalisation of military life: necessity, problems and
prospects of multinational armed forces. In: Kuemmel G, Pruefert A (eds) Military sociology.
The Richness of a Discipline, Baden-Baden, Nomos
31. Klein P (2003) Multinational armed forces. In: Kallaghan J, Kernic F (eds) Armed forces and
international security: global trends and issues. LIT Verlag, Muenster
32. Soeters J, Poponete C, Page J Jr (2006) Culture's consequences in the military. In: Bratt TW,
Adler AB, Castro CA (eds), Military life. The psychology of serving in peace and combat, vol
4 (Military Culture), Wesport, Praeger, CT
33. Geser H (1983) Strukturformen und Funktionsleistungen sozialer Systeme. Westdeutscher
Verlag, Opladen
34. Geser H (1990) Le forme organizzative in campo militare e in campo economico. Battistelli F
(ed) Marte e Mercurio. Sociologia dell'organizzazione militare. Milan, Angeli, pp 427–451
35. Elron S, Ben-Ari (1999) Why don't they fight each other? Cultural diversity and operational
units in multinational forces. Armed Forces Soc 26:73–97
36. MacIsaac JR (2000) Leadership during peace support operations: "mission impossible."
Canadian Forces College, Kingston, ON
37. Shamir B, Ben-Ari E (2000) Challenges of military leadership in changing armies. J Polit Mil
Soc 28(1):43–59
38. Olivetta E (2017) Leadership, morale and cohesion: what should be changed? In: Holenweger
M, Jager MK, Kernic F (eds) Leadership in extreme situations. Springer, Cham
39. Kernic F (2001) Sozialwissenschaften und Militar. Eine kritische analyse. Dt. Univ. Verlang,
Wiesbaden

40. Holenweger M, Jager MK, Kernic F (eds) (2017) Leadership in extreme situations. Springer, Cham
41. Hannah ST, Campbell DJ, Matthews MD (2009) A framework for examining leadership in extreme context. Leadership Q 20:897–919
42. Shamir B, Ben-Ari E (1999) Leadership in an open army: civilian connections, interorganizational frameworks and changes in military leadership. In: Hunt JG, Dodge G, Wing L (eds) Out-of-the-box leadership: transforming the twenty-first century army and other top-reforming organizations. Stanford, JAJ Press, CT
43. Bennett MJ (1986) A developmental approach to training for intercultural sensitivity. Int J Intercultural Relat 10(2):179–196
44. Bennett MJ (2004) Becoming interculturally competent. In: Wurzel J (ed) Towards multiculturalism: a reader in multicultural education, 2nd edn. Intercultural Resource Corporation, Newton, MA, pp 62–77
45. Hammer MR, Bennett MJ, Wiseman R (2003) The intercultural development inventory: a measure of intercultural sensitivity. In: Paige M (Guest Editor) Int J Intercultural Relat 27:421–443
46. Moskos ChC (2000) The media and the military in peace and humanitarian operations. McCormick Tribune Foundation, Chicago
47. Bennett JM, Bennett MJ (2004) Developing intercultural sensitivity: an integrative approach to global and domestic diversity. In: Landis D, Bennett JM, Bennett MJ (eds) Handbook of intercultural training, 3rd edn. Sage, Thousand Oaks, CA, pp 147–165
48. Hammer MR (2009) Solving problems and resolving conflict using the intercultural conflict style model and inventory. In: Moodian MA (ed) Contemporary leadership and intercultural competence: understanding and utilizing cultural diversity to build successful organizations. Sage Publications, Inc. Thousand Oaks (CA), Chap. 17
49. Nuciari M (2001) Officers education for MOOTW: a comparative research on military and civilian agencies problematic relationships. In: Caforio G (ed) The flexible officer: professional education and military operations other than war, a cross-national analysis. Artistic & Publishing Company, Gaeta, pp 61–88
50. Burns T, Stalker GM (1994) The management of innovation, Oxford U.P.

What Does Leadership Mean?

Eraldo Olivetta

Abstract A study on military leadership in situations of asymmetric conflict must necessarily ask the question of exactly what leadership is. The hypothesis of this study is that the way of understanding leadership has changed over times, in relation to the socio-cultural changes of the parent society. By analysing "the problematic space of leadership", this study shows that military leadership is changing, and the relational aspect takes on ever greater importance, along with the ability to act concerning emotions.

1 Introduction and Theoretical Remarks

A study on military leadership in situations of asymmetric conflict must necessarily ask the question of exactly what leadership is.

The studies on leadership have tried to give an answer to some fundamental questions: who is a leader; what skills and abilities are needed to be a good leader; how can his/her effectiveness and operational efficiency be measured; and how can one become a leader. In the specific military context, one asks whether or not military leadership is different from civil leadership, and what can be done to improve the exercise of the leadership role.

The hypothesis of this study is that the way of understanding leadership has changed over time, in relation to the socio-cultural changes of the parent society, and that these changes have also influenced military leadership. The evolution of the understanding of leadership necessarily involves changes in the role of the leader, the understanding of which is necessary not only for the purpose of understanding the processes in progress, but also for predicting possible future trends. It is only through this understanding that it is possible to train commanders who possess not only the knowledge but also the skills and abilities necessary for the effective exercise of their role.

E. Olivetta (✉)
School of Management and Economics, Turin University, Turin, Italy
e-mail: eraldo.olivetta@unito.it

© Springer Nature Switzerland AG 2021
M. Nuciari and E. Olivetta (eds.), *Leaders for Tomorrow: Challenges for Military Leadership in the Age of Asymmetric Warfare*, Advanced Sciences and Technologies for Security Applications, https://doi.org/10.1007/978-3-030-71714-8_2

However, the military organization, due to its particular function, has particular characteristics that differentiate it from any other organization [25]. Precisely for this reason, from the previous hypothesis, a second result follows: although military leadership can draw useful contributions from studies on civil leadership, the particularity of the military institution influences the styles of command, making it take on particular and distinctive characteristics with respect to the management styles of civil organizations.

The thinking regarding the first hypothesis can be conducted by briefly taking up the most important theoretical contributions. While taking into account the conceptual complexity of the studied phenomenon which, precisely for this reason, may concern different study approaches (psychological, sociological and cultural, and political), [20] this brief analysis will mainly focus on the socio-organizational value, especially paying attention to the behavior of the actors as belonging to a group and an organization. Based on this approach, it will therefore be necessary to take into account the expectations, values, and norms characterizing the role of each actor and, at the same time, how the nature of the system and the structure of the organization influence their actions and their behavior. Leadership could therefore be understood as the ability to influence other actors in view of the achievement of certain objectives [1]. In agreement with Ammendola, it is therefore a form of power, consisting in "making others do things". However, it is possible to induce the other actors to put in place particular actions both in the function of power and by virtue of authority.

Legal authority is to be understood as the faculty, established by an impersonal legal system in force in a community, bestowed on an individual or a group to issue commands that oblige, bind, or in any case, induce one or more subjects belonging to this community to act in a certain way [7]. However, authority can also derive from a certain attribute of a person or group that the reference community evaluates to the point of allowing it to be subordinated to the subject that possesses it, so that this is used in its favor. In the first case, we will speak of legal authority and this will be established by the outside through a formal attribution of a particular *status* to which the specific authority is associated. In the second case, we will speak of functional authority, with the conferring of authority done directly by the *followers*, in an informal, substantial, and often spontaneous way [19, 29].

On the other hand, power refers both to the legally attributed faculty and to the actual capacity of doing, as expressed by the Latin term *potestas,* which means being able to "realistically use a force to enforce one's will" [29]. Therefore, power takes on two different meanings, even though complementary to each other: on the one hand, it expresses "having permission to", as well expressed in English by the verb *may*; on the other, it expresses "being able to", expressed in English by the verb *can*. "Powerful" is the person who has permission, and at the same time, is able to do, the one who has the pragmatic faculty to achieve something, the implementer, the actualizer, the concrete manager of things, the one who does things [29]. Therefore, power refers to a situation of both legal and factual capacity.

The person who is formally invested with legal authority is certainly a "boss", but not necessarily a leader. To become one, he/she must be able to transform authority into power, by obtaining informal recognition from the followers and thus acquiring legitimacy [19].

The "boss" exercises his/her role's authority formally attributed to them by an authority external to the group, without it being necessary that the collaborators who depend on them hierarchically consider them as "the most suitable" to lead the group itself. He/She does not need to "influence" the members, or obtain the legitimacy of his/her work from them, nor to win their loyalty: he/she must only command and expect complete adherence to his/her orders. "The subordinates obey the provisions of the boss because they recognize the legitimate mechanisms governing the organization to which they belong, on the basis of which the boss was chosen and has the authority to issue orders and provisions" [27]. On the other hand, the "leader" exercises his/her influence over the collaborators who, recognizing and accepting his/her power, legitimize him/her. Therefore, he/she is chosen by the group "because they are perceived as the best to meet certain expectations, relating both to the achievement of certain objectives and to the satisfaction of internal needs" [27].

Having thus clarified that the boss is not necessarily and not always also a leader, and having distinguished concepts of authority and power, the verification of the first hypothesis requires, as anticipated, a brief review of the main orientations to which the most important theories on leadership can be traced.

Until the late 1940s, personological or trait orientations prevailed in the study of leadership [5]. At the base of these theories prevailed the belief that the leader was the possessor of particular qualities and abilities that made his/her role more effective.[1] These qualities and characteristics included particular personality traits (intelligence, willpower, honesty, courage, perseverance, industriousness, adaptation, extroversion, self-confidence, etc.) as well as their physical aspect (stature, weight, physical strength, health, voice, etc.). Therefore, the leader would be a special person who differs from other group members.

It is clear that with this approach attention is focused on the qualities of the leader and therefore on the leader him/herself. It was only at the end of the Forties that the attention shifted from the qualities of the leader to the relationship between the latter and the other members of the group. In fact, according to the interactive guidelines [29], the object of study should not be so much the leader him/herself, but rather his/her interaction with the contingent group situation. Examples of these orientations are the approach based on "styles" of Lewin et al. [14] that tends to show that the mood and the efficiency of the group depend on the type of climate that is created following the adoption of different leadership styles and, subsequently, that of Likert [15] which instead will question that the greater return always, and only, depends on the satisfaction of the subordinates and their favorable attachment to the company. For Likert, the leadership style depends on the leader's trust in his/her subordinates, the type of motivation used, the intensity of the interactions, the communication model, the decision-making process, and the formulation of the objectives. In the style-based approach, it is therefore evident that attention begins to

---

[1]Therefore, the ability of a leader would be innate.

be focused not only on the leader, but also on the other actors included in the process, as well as on the relationships that are established between them.

From the late 1960s to the early 1980s, the situational approach in turn drew attention to the fact that in different situations, the leadership styles, more or less adequate to deal with such situations, may vary from time to time. The effectiveness of leadership therefore depends on the ability of the leader to adapt to changes in the situation and characteristics of the group in which he/she operates. Back in 1955, Bales and Slatter [3] and Bales [2] identified two types of leadership: task-oriented leadership (Task specialist) and relationship-oriented leadership (Socio-emotional specialist). Subsequently Blake and Mouton [4] deepened Bales's studies by elaborating a grid that, in combining the two essential dimensions for managerial efficiency, *concern for production and concern for people*, defined five different styles deriving from the combination of the two variables. The result is a model that goes from the lax style (*Impoverished management*) characterized by a low attention given to people and from an equally low attention given to production, to the "team" style or group leader (*Team management*) that instead aims to obtain results of high quality by also paying attention to the creation of a good collaborative climate.[2]

Subsequently, Reddin [23] introduced a third dimension to the two-dimensional model of Blake and Mouton: managerial efficiency or the "tendency to emphasize concrete things".[3] In practice, orientation to the task and orientation to the relation-ship must also be evaluated in relation to the specific situation, there being cases in which the combination chosen between the two orientations can be effective, but also cases in which this can be less so or not at all.

If with Reddin it becomes clear that in the analysis of the leadership process one cannot help but also consider the context in which this process is carried out, contingency theories deepening this aspect have come to affirm that the effectiveness of a style of leadership can change as the situation in which it is expressed changes. Thus, the leadership style becomes dependent (and contingent) on the various internal and external constraints (factors). Fiedler [6], who argued that the performance of a group is contingent, that is, it depends on the relationship between the style of leadership and the situation of the group, identified three determining factors: the quality of relations between leaders and subordinates (good/bad), the degree of the structuring of the task (structured/unstructured); and the position of power of the leader in the organization (strong/weak).

It wasn't until the early Seventies that House's *Path Goal Theory* model [12] also introduced the motivational aspect: the leader must increase the expectations of subordinates and, based on a series of contingent factors that can be summarized in the personal characteristics of the subordinates and those of the environment in which they work, must choose his/her own style of leadership among four possible types (management, supportive, participatory, and result-oriented).

---

[2]The other styles are: Country Club management (low production, high people); Authority manage-ment (high production, low people); Middle of-the-road management (medium production, medium people).

[3]Eight styles derive from the combination of the three dimensions [23].

This attention given to the "motivational" aspect has paved the way, from the early 1980s onwards, to the approach based on a new leadership in which leaders must possess a "vision" [5] and know how to pass it on to their subordinates. Then there is talk about transfomational leadership, in which leaders motivate subordinates to work for very high goals (vision) rather than for immediate interests and for motivation or for safety. Therefore, transformational leaders not only spread their vision, but also promote in their collaborators the development of autonomy of thought and the ability to identify new paths useful both for the optimization of the objectives of the group, and for the personal development of each individual.

Then Goleman [8, 9] went on to state that the greatness of leadership is based on the ability to leverage collective emotions and to orient them in a positive sense. Leaders must be gifted with emotional intelligence, in order to be able to create resonance, positively orienting emotions and bringing out the best in each person. Instead, "dissonance" should be avoided, that is to say, the condition that is created when emotions are oriented in a negative sense, undermining the emotional foundations necessary for the full realization of each individual [8].

From the brief analysis of the main theories formulated in different moments of the history of leadership studies, the evolution of the concept and, consequently, of the role attributed to the leader is evident. Attention has in fact progressively shifted from the characteristics of the leader (personological orientations) to his/her situation and to the contingent group situation, thereby increasingly considering leadership to be a process that involves different actors, each of them able to influence it. In this process, the relational aspect takes on particular importance, and the role of the leader also includes the ability to motivate his/her collaborators by relying on collective emotions and orienting them in a positive sense.

Noting that the concept of leadership has evolved over time towards models in which the relational aspect takes on ever greater importance, at this point it is necessary to ask whether, and to what extent, the models developed by scholars and briefly mentioned here can also be applied to the military organization or if instead it is not necessary to proceed with adaptations, due to the particularity of the military environment. The reflection that accompanies the answer to this question will be conducted by analyzing what characterizes the "problematic space of leadership".

Given that the reality that surrounds us is constantly changing, leadership must be able to allow the organization of which it is a part not only to survive the latter, but also to develop in the changing environment by adapting [28]. As evidently emerged from the theories previously mentioned, in order to exercise this role, leadership must be able to define the direction, share this objective with all the actors involved in the process, and direct and guide them towards the goal by motivating and inspiring them. One could even say that leadership must be capable of generating change. All this happens precisely in what could be defined as "the problematic space of leadership". The analysis of this space can be conducted by studying each of the elements that characterize it:

1. The Leader
2. The Collaborators

3.   The Organization
4.   The Situation.

2   The Leader

As for the leader, in relation to what has just been said about his/her function as a "generator of change" and referring to the theories previously mentioned, leadership must be able to define its own mission. However, in doing so, it must take into account the needs of the global system in which the organization is inserted, not forgetting that the latter was put in place precisely to satisfy the specific needs of this system and that their function derives from this requirement. However, the definition of the mission must necessarily be preceded by the development of a vision that is therefore adequate for that particular type of organization. Otherwise, the objectives would hardly be shared by the other actors involved in the process. The definition of the operational strategy also requires the clear definition of the roles and functions of each member of the organization and this involves another leadership skill: the ability to communicate and share these goals. In defining the mission, as Fiedler [6] pointed out, the leader must also take into account the status he/she occupies within the organization, the position of power deriving from this status as well as the role expectations that are associated with that position. The definition of the mission is also influenced by the individual abilities of the leader who, in carrying out his/her role, will therefore be influenced by what he/she considers his/her "having to be" and his/her "having to do", or by his/her representation of him/herself. This, in turn, will derive both from their individual abilities, and from their cognitive, evaluative, and operational models, that is, from their culture, as well as from their experience, on which both primary socialization and any vocational training interventions on the role of leader (secondary socialization) in which he/she may have participated. Once he/she has joined that organization, he/she would certainly have participated in further processes of socialization regarding the specific role he/she has to play, this time, however, carried out in accordance with the culture of the organization to which he/she belongs and what it considers "being a good leader". His/her behavior or enaction of a role will therefore be the consequence of his/her representation of him/herself deriving from these processes, but also of his/her way of managing relations with collaborators (which, once again, influence the aforementioned socialization processes) and by the system's constraints, or those constraints that the global system imposes on the organization.

3   The Collaborators

As for the collaborators, it has been said that leadership consists in the ability to involve the members of the organization in carrying out the objectives and that, to do this, it is necessary to motivate the collaborators and create the networks of relations necessary for the achievement of the objectives and to deal with and manage change. The quality of the relationship between the leader and the collaborators mentioned above with regard to the leader, therefore also concerns these other actors in the problematic space of leadership. In fact, Fiedler [6] pointed out that the quality of the relations between the leader and the collaborators also influences the leadership [6]. In turn, the collaborators can be more or less easily motivated and more or less effectively put into relation to one another and relate to their leaders, in relation to their personal characteristics, also conditioned by their cultural models. In the exercise of their role in the organization, the collaborators, just like the leaders, will be influenced by their representation of themselves, by their personal culture, and by the socialization processes in which they have participated once they have joined the organization.

4   The Organization

As for the organization, leadership consists in the ability to identify its primary needs, for example in terms of performance, and in the ability to effectively structure the relationships between the actors involved in achieving the objectives [28]. But "structuring relationships" ultimately means defining the roles and this definition by the leader in organizations cannot, once again, not take into consideration both the culture of that organization and the professional cultures of reference. Therefore, also at the organizational level, the leader cannot disregard the organizational culture, even more so than at the level of artifacts and declared values, in terms of shared tacit assumptions [24].

5   The Situation

Lastly, with regard to the situation, leadership must be able to vary its behavior as the latter changes. Therefore its effectiveness depends on the leader's ability to adapt to changes in the situation and on the characteristics of the group in which he/she operates [2–4, 23]. A leadership style can be efficient in one particular situation, but not necessarily in another [23]. In all organizations, it is possible to find relatively different situations that can influence the roles of the actors involved and even the contingent vision and mission.

From the study of the elements that characterize the problematic space of leadership, with regard to each of them, it is evident that both the culture of the organization and the individual's culture influence the perception of their own role and, at the same time, the role expectations towards the other actors present in the organization. However, in addition to these two variables, there is a third one: system constraints. These are the constraints imposed on the organization by the global system in which it is inserted and which determine its chances of survival and development [28]. It is precisely from this third variable that the specificity of the military organization derives. If what has been said about the problematic space of leadership certainly applies to civil organizations, the military organization has characteristics that require some adaptations of what has been said so far.

In fact, the military organization stands out from the other organizations for the legitimate use of force. The specificity of the military organization lies precisely in the possibility of killing and being killed. The soldier's trade differs from almost all other professions because it involves the signing of a contract of unlimited availability from which the subject cannot withdraw unilaterally when he/she wants to. The latter is required to move to any environment when he/she is commanded to do so and is required to place service needs above those of their own families, with commitments that can go well beyond 8 h a day (Segal 1977). A soldier can be asked for extreme personal sacrifices in emergency situations in non-war contexts (for example, in interventions for natural disasters), or to put his/her own safety at risk and/or to threaten others' safety (for example, in combat contexts), or to put personal safety at risk but to limit the counterparty's losses in a non-war operating context in the traditional sense (for example, peacekeeping operations) [28].

How does this particularity of military organization affect the elements that, as noted, characterize the problematic space of leadership?

As for the leader, in the military organization what has been said about the development of the vision and the definition of the mission takes on a very particular relevance: the sacrifice required, which can lead to making one's life available, requires a motivation that is hardly required in other organizations. In this case, in fact, it is necessary to define a greatly motivating vision that is able to share such demanding objectives as those described above. So in the military organization, given its hierarchical structure, the positional power that the leader derives from his/her status is important, without forgetting the role of expectations associated by subordinates to that particular position. Finally, with regard to his/her own role, the military leader will behave more or less in accordance with what was learned in the specific processes of socialization secondary to the leadership role in which he/she participated in their training, but in any case, one cannot forget socialization prior to entry into the organization and their previous experiences.

As for the collaborators, the ability to motivate and involve the members of the organization in achieving the objectives, given the particularity of the latter and the risk associated with them, requires the leadership to know how to create effective networks of relationships between them. There are many studies on the military organization that have recalled the function of cohesion in relation to combative effectiveness: that it is the role of the primary group [16, 26], or the dyadic reactions of buddy relations [17]. But if, in the military organization, horizontal cohesion takes on a particular relevance and one that is often greater than in other organizations, vertical cohesion also presents particular characteristics that differentiate it from civil organizations. The military organization is a bureaucratic organization with a strong formalization of hierarchical levels. Its organizational culture requires a marked differentiation of status among its members. Here, an order is required to be executed, even when this involves the sacrifices mentioned above. For this to happen, the leader must assume a position of strong power, depending on the performance of the contingent group also from this aspect [6]. It follows that here the "collaborator" resource becomes "subordinate". In Italy, even though in their training the officers are taught to call their subordinates by the term "employees", the status differentiation remains strongly marked, the roles are formalized, and the relationship nevertheless remains as that of commander/subordinate. However, the fact that the collaborators who have chosen to be a part of the military organization come from civil society in which there have been more or less significant cultural changes, especially regarding some values, rights and duties, hierarchical relationships, etc., requires, on the one hand, even more effective processes of secondary socialization and, on the other hand, that the commander takes into account this particular aspect, above all in consideration of the motivations, perhaps mainly occupational, which have led the soldier to enlist.

With regard to the organization, we have mentioned the need to identify its primary needs, for example in terms of performance, and the ability to effectively structure the relationships between the actors involved in achieving the objectives. However, in this regard, another problem arises in the military organization: the evaluation of effectiveness and efficiency. In the organization, the leader is called upon to manage human resources and means, as Weber [30] would say, in a rational manner with respect to its purpose. But whereas in civil organizations the effectiveness of leadership can almost always be evaluated in fairly defined terms (for example, greater/lesser productivity, saving/expenditure of resources, etc.), in the military this does not always happen [18, 28]. A commander who manages to reach a strategic goal but with a significant loss of human life may be considered a good officer by superiors and maybe even by his/her soldiers if this goal was particularly relevant but, in the case in which they believed that he/she was unable to avoid unnecessary losses, he/she would lose the esteem of his/her soldiers.

Finally, with regard to the situation, the ability of the leader to adapt to changes in the situation and characteristics of the group in which he/she operates is even more relevant in the context of military organizations. The latter, as we have seen, are in fact called upon to operate in quite different situations: from those that are less operational and of preparation, to those that are operative but do not involve combat, to those of actual combat. Based on what has been said, the leader will then have to be able to vary his/her own command styles in different situations, in relation to the different risk and exercise of the social function carried out by the organization in that specific context. This flexibility, recalling the situational approach and contingency theories, becomes even more relevant if we consider that the operational situations also often tend to vary their characteristics during their course. For example, consider interventions created as peacekeeping operations that, in their course become peace-enforcement or peace-making operations.

From these reflections on the elements of the "problematic space of leadership", the particularity of the military organization is evident. At the same time, from the transversal reading of the specificities of each of the elements, one element that seems to take on particular relevance is also evident: cohesion.

 Given the unique social function of the Armed Forces and the particular sacrifice required by these organizations for their employees, cohesion takes on a fundamental importance, almost always superior to that of other civil organizations. So the primary objective of the military leader must be to promote and develop cohesion within the group that he/she is called to command. Moreover, as already mentioned, the importance of cohesion had already been widely detected by studies carried out since the Second World War and also repeated in the most important subsequent conflicts.

Since cohesion has always been considered a determining factor in operational effectiveness and efficiency, this will certainly tend to take on even greater relevance today if we consider the changes that have taken place in the Armed Forces in the last decades. The changed perception of the threat resulting from changes in the geopolitical situation, the transformations deriving from the advent of technology in the profession of weapons, the socio-economic environment and the socio-cultural changes that have taken place in the parent society have led to significant organizational transformations in military institutions, as well as having changed the professionalism of the actors called to work in them [19]. Moskos [17] already recalled the transition from the institutional model to the occupational one. Today, the Armed Forces are organizations always composed almost exclusively of voluntary professionals, in which their enrollment, although being a vocational choice, is also a professional choice. The target groups tend to be increasingly external to the institution, horizontal rather than vertical [17] and the human resources come from societies in which cultural models are changing and in which some values (for example, "the fatherland") tend to lose the meaning they had in the past, not to mention the idea of nation. In increasingly individualistic societies, whose cultures tend to recognize authority less and less and to reduce the distance index from power, the military leader will necessarily have to develop special skills for promoting and maintaining cohesion. Referring to Bales and Slatter [3], he/she will have to adopt models of leadership that are increasingly geared to relationships: while not neglecting the achievement of the task, the relationship becomes an increasingly necessary condition for effective leadership. In relation to what has been said about each of the elements of the problematic space of action of military leadership, if we consider that the military organizations have changed but, even more so, it is the parent society that has changed and thus the related culture, it is reasonable to think that all the social actors that operate in the military institution have also changed. Therefore, the officers will be changed, as they will arrive at the academy to begin their training course with an idea of the military institution that is probably different from that of those who preceded them in the last century, even with a different conception of their role and what it means to command. In the same way, but with even more relevant consequences, the idea that subordinates will have of their own role, as well as the motivations that led them to enlist in the first place, and to perform their action effectively and efficiently afterwards, will also be different. The models of the past do not appear to be more effective and efficient. The new military leaders must change the way they orient and motivate people. How? While taking into account the diversity of different cultures, a possible answer comes from the experience of Italian Army officers [21] who, in operational situations, tend to be role models for their subordinates (idealized influence), and succeed in motivating them by making their work meaningful (inspirational motivation) but, above all, they are attentive to the needs of each of their subordinates (individualized consideration). The characterizing element of the role of the military leader therefore seems to be the ability to intuit the potential of the emotional factor in those particular environments that are operational theaters. The strong stress that accompanies certain moments in life while on mission requires the ability of the leader to keep the morale of his/her soldiers high and to encourage their motivation and commitment. In order to do this, today more than in the past, the military leader must be able to influence the emotions of the members. In practice, he/she must be endowed with "emotional intelligence" [8].

As has emerged from the same research on Italian officers [21], the characteristics of transformational leadership become all the more necessary the more turbulent the environment is in which the leadership role is exercised. Therefore, it is necessary to distinguish between the "less operational" and the "more operational" situations and, among the latter, to focus on those that it are customarily defined as *extreme situations*. Although there are many similarities between leadership in extreme situations, leadership in dangerous situations, and in crisis situations, the features that distinguish an extreme event are (Holenweger 2017): the threat "must reach the threshold of intolerable magnitude" [10]; the leaders may have a long preparation time, but they can still be extemporaneous when the situation arises; low probability is a characteristic of an extreme situation; the ambiguity of cause, effect, and means resolution.

In extreme situations [11], the events that occur and characterize them (for example, the death of a soldier) have a particular impact both on the leadership and on the behavior of the group [13]. Particularly serious events that generate high stress and can undermine cohesion must be carefully managed by leaders, especially by platoon commanders [21]. In fact, the impact of these events tends to vary between the different ranks [22], and different strategies must be adopted at different levels [21]. These events must be tackled by the lower ranks (team commander and platoon commander), by discussing and relating them adequately with their subordinates. In fact, it is the lower rank officers who have the most contact with the soldiers and it is precisely in these cases that they must relate to their men and women to face the event that characterizes that situation as extreme, by resorting to emotional intelligence [21]. The leadership to be adopted in these situations will therefore tend to come even closer to a model of transformational leadership [8]. Thus the contingent situation of extreme situations would seem to further confirm the model designed with the considerations proposed in this chapter.

In summary, the military leader, even if endowed with an unquestionable authority deriving from their rank and formally attributed to him/her, must necessarily take into account that the way of conceiving his/her own role and that of others by the different actors involved in the leadership process has changed in relation to the cultural changes of the parent society and they must be able to transform this authority into power by also gaining informal legitimacy from their subordinates. In practice, he/she will have to know how to become a leader from scratch. How?

- Given the particular characteristics of the military organization, the commander, here more than in most other organizations, will have to be able to motivate his/her soldiers, to whom significant sacrifices are required, up to the extreme one of life itself. So he/she must possess the vision and know-how to pass it on to his/her men. The leader needs to be able to push his/her soldiers towards a common ideal—that of the institution—by indicating the goal and giving a strong positive orientation to the emotional climate. If everyone is aware of collaborating to reach a common goal, a greater commitment and involvement within the platoon may result and everyone will feel proud to belong to it. Continually reminding his/her soldiers of the broader end to which their work tends, the commander will also give greater importance to the tasks and activities that would otherwise be considered ordinary and prosaic. In this way, the soldiers should come to consider common goals perfectly in tune with their personal interest, doing their work with an inspired mood. But to be able to do this, the commander must endowed with an inspiring leadership [8], thereby inspiring others, showing and describing a shared mission to them in order to encourage them to follow him/her. He/she must be able to convey a sense of common purpose that transcends everyday tasks and makes the work exciting. But all this requires that he/she has the necessary confidence in him/herself, that he/she has adequate self-awareness (assessment of his/her strengths and weaknesses), and that he/she knows how to be sufficiently empathetic by understanding the perspective of others.
- Given the importance of cohesion, the military leader is required to work constantly for its development and conservation. Taking into account the changes in military organization over the past few decades, he/she will need to be able to combine the typical characteristics of task-oriented leadership with those of relationship-oriented leadership. Today, more than in the past, the lower level commander (platoon commander) must pay attention to these aspects, also to keep the group morale high.
- Differently from what happens in civil organizations, in the military one, coexisting with the other styles, there is also the authoritarian one. Especially in extreme situations, this style must suitably be integrated with the style aimed at promoting his/her vision and with the style aimed at promoting the relationships.
- However, the leadership style must always take into account the contingent situation. Therefore, the commander must be able to adapt his/her own command styles both to the characteristics of the different groups and to the different situations and their variation. If the relational aspect tends to take on a greater relevance in combat situations, in the less operational and preparatory ones or in the operative but non-combat ones, the formal aspect tends to prevail. Upon returning after a job in operational theaters, the formal aspect must absolutely be restored, given the particular characteristics of the military organization mentioned above. A good military leader must therefore be able to know how to pass from one leadership style to another according to the contingent situation, managing to adapt him/herself to it.
- Finally, in the context of extreme situations, he/she will have to be able, more than in other situations, to be a role model for his/her soldiers; he/she will have to

be able to motivate them to achieve the objectives by making their contribution significant; he/she will have to stimulate them to be also able to face unexpected situations; the leader must be attentive to the needs of each of his/her soldiers. Precisely with regard to this last point, he/she must be able to flexibly adapt his/her role above all to the occurrence of the most extreme events that characterize these situations, "relating" with his/her own soldiers. Therefore, he/she must be able to manage interpersonal relationships with empathy and by acting on emotions.

From the considerations made so far, it is therefore confirmed that leadership in military organizations is changing in the same way as what happened and is happening in civilian ones. The relational aspect takes on ever greater importance, along with the ability to act concerning emotions. Even though the military organization has characteristics that make it different from civil organizations, the changes that have occurred in the elements of the leadership and action space, and, in particular, the cultural changes that have involved both the actors involved and the organization itself, require ever greater emotional intelligence, so that in fact whoever is already formally a leader, can also be considered a leader by his/her subordinates.

References

1. Ammendola T (2004) Guidare il cambiamento: la leadership nelle Forze Armate italiane. Rubettino, Soveria Mannelli
2. Bales RF (1955) How people interact in conferences. Freeman, San Francisco
3. Bales RF, Slater PE (1955) Role differentiation. In: Parsons T, Bales RF et al (eds) (a cura di) The family, socialization and interaction process. Free Press, Glencoe IL
4. Blake R, Mouton J (1964) The managerial grid: the key to leadership excellence. Gulf Publishing Co, Houston
5. Bryman A (1992) Charisma and leadership in organization. Sage, London
6. Fiedler F (1967) A theory of leadership effectiveness. McGraw-Hill, New York
7. Gallino L (2006) Dizionario di Socilogia. Utet, Torino
8. Goleman P, Boyatzis R, McKee A (2002) Essere leader. Rizzoli, Milano
9. Goleman P, Boyatzis R, McKee A (2002) Primal leadership. Arward Business School Press, Boston
10. Hannah ST, Campbell DJ, Matthews MD (2009) A framework for examining leadership in extreme context. Leadersh Quart 20:897–919
11. Holenweger M, Jager MK, Kernic F (eds) (2017) Leadership in extreme situations. Springer, Cham
12. House RJ (1971) A path-goal theory of leader effectiveness. Adm Sci Q 16:321–328
13. Kernic F (2001) Sozialwissenschaften und Militar. Eine kritische analyse. Dt. Univ.-Verlag, Wiesbaden
14. Lewin K, Lippitt R, White R (1939) Patterns of aggressive behavior in experimentally created social climates. J Soc Psychol 10:271–301
15. Likert R (1961) New patterns of management. McGraw-Hill, New York
16. Little RW (1964) Buddy relations and combat performance. In: Janowitz M (ed) The new military. Changing patterns of organizations. Sage, New York
17. Moskos CC (1975) The American combat soldier in Vietnam. J Soc Issues 31(41):25–37
18. Nuciari M (1990) Efficienza e Forze Armate. Franco Angeli, Milano
19. Olivetta E (2012) Le culture della leadership. Bonanno, Acireale

20. Olivetta E (2012) L'istituzione inevitabile. Bonanno, Acireale
21. Olivetta E (2017) Leadership, morale and cohesion: what should be changed? In: Holenweger M, Jager MK, Kernic F (eds) Leadership in extreme situations. Springer, Cham
22. Padan C (2017) Constructing "Crisis Events" in military contexts—an Israeli perspective. In: Holenweger M, Jager MK, Kernic F (eds) Leadership in extreme situations. Springer, Cham
23. Reddin WJ (1983) Managerial effectiveness and style. Individual or situation (Doctoral). E.U.A: New Brunswick Bussines School
24. Schein E (2000) Culture d'impresa. Cortina Editore, Milano
25. Segal D, Kramer RC (1977) Attitudes toward unions in the ground combat forces. In: Taylor W, Arango R, Lockwood R (eds) Military union: U.S. trends and issues. Sage, Beverly Hills
26. Shils E, Janowitz M (1948). Cohesion and disintegration in the Wehrmacht in World War II, in public opinion quarterly, vol 1, Summer, pp 280–315. Trad. It.: Shils E, Janowitz M (1999) Coesione e disintegrazione nella Wehrmacht nella Seconda Guerra Mondiale. In: Nuciari M (ed) Efficienza e Forze Armate. Franco Angeli, Milano
27. Sola G (2004) Leadership e sociologia dell'organizzazione. In: Ammendola T (ed) Guidare il cambiamento: la leadership nelle Forze Armate italiane. Rubbettino, Soveria Mannelli
28. Striuli L (2004) Leadership e cultura militare. In: Ammendola T (ed) Guidare il cambiamento: la leadership nelle Forze Armate italiane. Rubbettino, Soveria Mannelli
29. Trentini G (1997) Oltre il potere. Discorso sulla leadership. Franco Angeli, Milano
30. Weber M (2005) Economia e Società. (Tubinga, 1922, 1966) Roma, Donzelli

From Culture to Leadership

Eraldo Olivetta

Abstract In the theaters of operations where missions take place and in which international military contingents are used, a plurality of actors belonging to different cultures are operating. The results and the achievement of the objectives of missions also depend on the ability of the military forces involved to establish good relations with the other actors present in the area in which they are called upon to operate and, to do this, it is important to establish effective methods of communication. This work intends to demonstrate, through the experience gained by soldiers from different countries in a plurality of missions, that the ability to relate to cultures that are different from one's own takes on a relevant role for the purpose of adequate operational efficiency.

1 Introduction

Acting with meaning is built on the basis of cognitive models through which the social actor perceives the reality that surrounds him/her, based on evaluation models that allowed them to make a choice between different alternatives of different actions and operational models that have governed the implementation of the action itself. Therefore, behavior is influenced by culture and, in the same situations, in the face of different problems, actors belonging to different cultures can act differently. Knowledge of the cultural models that underlie actions in different cultures makes it possible to manage cross-cultural relationships more effectively.

In the theaters of operations where missions take place and in which international military contingents are used, a plurality of actors, including civilians, belonging to different cultures, are operating. Inasmuch as the culture of the military forces deployed in the ambit of that international contingent is already different, the culture of the latter will be even more so compared to the culture of the local actors (local

E. Olivetta (✉)
School of Management and Economics, University of Torino, Corso Unione Sovietica 218bis, Torino, Italy
e-mail: eraldo.olivetta@unito.it

© Springer Nature Switzerland AG 2021   37
M. Nuciari and E. Olivetta (eds.), *Leaders for Tomorrow: Challenges for Military Leadership in the Age of Asymmetric Warfare*, Advanced Sciences and Technologies for Security Applications, https://doi.org/10.1007/978-3-030-71714-8_3

forces, authorities, population) and/or other civilian actors hosted in those territories (for example, NGOs, the Press, etc.).

However, the results and the achievement of the objectives of a mission also depend on the ability of the military forces involved to establish good relations with the other actors present in the area in which they are called upon to operate and, to do this, it is important to establish effective methods of communication. In turn, communicating and relating with actors from different cultures requires knowledge of the necessary tools in order to understand and interact with these other cultures.

This work intends to demonstrate, through the experience gained by soldiers from different countries in a plurality of missions in different parts of the world, that the ability to relate to cultures that are different from one's own takes on a relevant role for the purpose of adequate operational efficiency. If this were the case, the result would be the need for training interventions aimed at providing those tools necessary for the conduct of good relations and effective cross-cultural communication. The innovative contribution of this study is the proposal of a model of training intervention, that can be adopted in all the countries that make up the international contingents used in the different missions, which is aimed at limiting the critical issues that emerged from the experience of the commanders who operated in those cross-cultural contexts. Equally innovative and useful to the Armed Forces of different countries is the knowledge of the profile of the military leader called upon to operate in these contexts and whose professionalism must also include knowledge, skills, and expertise to manage cross-cultural relations.

2   Theoretical Background

In the territories where international missions take place, there is a plurality of actors, both military and civilian. The military actors include the troops that form the international contingent involved in that mission, the Armed Forces, and the local police forces. The civilian ones include: the local population, the local authorities, journalists present in those operational theaters, and the local and international NGOs, as well as international organizations and private companies and the staff of the local intelligence agencies [4, 13–19]. If the culture of the military forces deployed in the ambit of that international contingent is already different, the culture of the latter will be even more so than that of the local actors [2, 5, 6, 16, 17, 20].

The missions necessarily involve the interaction between these different subjects and their success is often conditioned by the ability of these actors to interact effectively. The need to know how to relate in an adequate manner with each of them will therefore be essential in order to achieve the objectives of the mission and to maintain high levels of operational effectiveness [4, 16, 17]. In turn, the ability to communicate effectively lies at the heart of the relationship. Seeing as the actors belong to different cultures, both communication and the ability to relate could be made more difficult by cultural diversity and communication itself could give rise to ambiguities and misunderstanding.

Culture, which gives meaning, orientation, content, and effectiveness to almost all human actions, represents the major factor in the regulation and control of all types of behavior, social relations, and exchange of resources [7], etc.

Tylor [21] defined it in its broad ethnographic sense as "that complex whole that includes knowledge, beliefs, art, morals, law, customs, and any other capacity and habit acquired by mankind as a member of a society".

Although, from Tylor onwards, almost all ethnologists have given their definition of the concept of culture, in all these variations on the subject the common essential content can be summarized in the words of Geertz [8]: "... [culture] denotes a structured set, historically transmitted, of meanings contained in symbols, a system of hereditary conceptions, expressed in symbolic form by which people communicate, perpetuate, and develop their knowledge and their positions with regard to life". This set given by culture, once it has been internalized by human beings, acts as a real patrimony made up of three types of models: *cognitive models*, which preside over the processes of knowledge, to the point of strictly conditioning the perception of things; *evaluative models*, which guide the subject in dealing with the known reality in a positive or negative way; *operational models*, which organize one's action aimed at achieving a specific end, which is configured in the eyes of the subject on the basis of the aforementioned procedures of knowledge and evaluation.

In the studies of the *Global Leadership and Organizational Behavior Effectiveness Research* (GLOBE) [14], culture is defined as that set of "shared reasons, values, beliefs, identities, and interpretations or meanings of events deriving from the common experiences of the members of a collectivity and transmitted from generation to generation".

Culture, as it has been defined, tends to vary as the community of which it is an expression varies. Numerous research studies [1, 11, 12] have attempted to identify the specific characteristics of different cultures. These characteristics, once measured and quantified, become cultural dimensions. These dimensions are then useful not only for understanding the peculiarities of certain cultures, but also for comparing different cultures, especially when the latter are having to interact. Referring to House and Javidan [14], culture can be analyzed on the basis of nine dimensions [3, 14]: aversion to uncertainty, distance from power, institutional collectivism, In-group collectivism, gender egalitarianism, assertiveness, orientation towards the future, performance orientation, and humanitarian orientation.

Table 1 shows, for each dimension, the values of each of the seven countries involved in the research.

Since the most significant among the most recent missions were held or are taking place in countries predominantly of Arab culture, the characteristics of this culture are also reported, to better understand what is reported below (Table 2).

Hall [9,10] showed that communication also tends to vary among cultures, distinguishing between cultures in which it is High Context and cultures in which it is Low Context. In the former, the information surrounding an event is already largely present in the recipient of the message: therefore, it is not necessary to say things verbally by spelling them out, but it is sufficient to make a few essential references, often using symbols. Conversely, the receiver of the message in the Low Context

Table 1 The cultures of the countries involved in the research

Dimensions	Italy	Spain	Finland	Denmark	Bulgaria[b]	Lithuania[b]	Philippines	Cameroun
Humane orientation (3.18–5.23)[a]	(3.63) L	(3.32) L	(3.96) ML	(4.44) MH			(5.12) H	(4.10) ML
Uncertainty avoidance (2.88–5.37)	(3.79) ML	(3.97) ML	(5.02) H	(5.22) H	H	MH	(3.89) ML	(4.29) MH
Performance orientation (3.20–4.94)	(3.58) L	(4.01) M	(3.81) M	(4.22) M			(4.47) H	(3.92) M
Future orientation (2.88–5.07)	(3.25) ML	(3.51) ML	(4.24) MH	(4.44) H			(4.15) MH	(4.09) MH
Institutional collectivism (3.53–6.36)		(3.68) ML	(3.85) ML	(4.63) H	(4.80) H	(H)	(M)	(4.65) H
Institutional collectivism (3.25–5.22)		(3.68) ML	(3.85) ML	(4.63) H	(4.80) H	(H)	(M)	(4.65) H
Power distance (3.89–5.80)		(5.43) H	(5.52) H	(4.89) MH	(3.89) L	H	M	(5.44) H
Assertiveness (3.38–4.89)		(4.07) M	(4.42) H	(3.81) M	(3.80) M			(4.01) M
Gender egalitarianism (2.50–4.08)		(3.24) M	(3.01) M	(3.35) M	(3.93) H	M	ML	(3.64) H
Cluster score	*Latin Europe*		*Nordic Europe*		*Eastern Europe*		*Southern Asia*	*Sub-Saharian Africa*

House and Javidan [14]

[a] Lower score–higher score

[b] This score is not available in House's research. Where possible, Hofstede's information are reported

Legend: *L* Low; *ML* Middle Low; *MH* Middle High; *H* High

Table 2 The Arab culture

	Performance Orientation (3,20–4,94)	Future Orientation (2,88–5,07)	Gender Egalitarianism (2,50–4,08)	Assertiveness (3,38–4,89)	Individualism and Collectivism (3,53–6,36)	Power Distance (3,89–5,80)	Humane Orientation (3,18–5,23)	Uncer-tainty Avoi-dance (2,88–5,37)
Iran	4.58 H	3,70 ML	2,99 ML	4,04 M	6,03 H	5,43 H	4.23 MH	3.67 ML

House and Javidan [14]

[a]Lower score–higher score

[b]This score is not available in House's research. Where possible, Hofstede's information are reported

Legend: *L* Low; *ML* Middle Low; *MH* Middle High; *H* High communication needs the latter to contain all the information necessary to put in place the action underlying the communication: the failure to explain the details would cause disorientation in this case. Hall draws attention to all those elements that are not part of verbal communication but that are equally important, especially in High Context cultures, and whose meaning can vary from culture to culture. These are the typical elements of non-verbal communication: tone of voice, use of pauses and timing of silence, gestures, facial expressions, eye contact, physical contact, etc. Added to all these elements are the proxemics (personal space) that varies significantly between cultures in which a smaller distance between people is deemed correct and physical contact is not deemed negative, and cultures that instead tend to prefer greater distances between individuals, considering contact to be improper.

Lastly, with the variation of cultures, the conception of time also changes with cultures in which time is considered in a linear and monochronic way and cultures in which a circular and polychronic conception prevails. In the former, time is considered to be a succession of moments that follow one another: the elapsed time is "gone", it is no longer possible to go back in time. Therefore, time becomes a precious resource that must not be wasted and must therefore be planned and managed wisely. For this reason, a moment tends to exist for each activity and that particular moment is dedicated to that—and only that—thing. Hence the conception of the monochromatic time in which one tends to do one thing at a time. Vice versa, in cultures where the conception of circular time prevails, time is considered as something cyclical which tends to repeat itself. Therefore, what has not been done today, can be done tomorrow or at other times. In these cultures, programming tends to be less important and more things can be done at the same time (polychronic).

3   The Study

3.1   Presentation

This study is part of the Officer And Commander In Asymmetric Warfare Operations research conducted between 2014 and 2016 in seven countries, interviewing 246 officers who had participated in various missions in the different theaters of operations.[1]

3.2   The Starting Hypotheses

The starting hypothesis is that leaders called to exercise command roles in mission theaters must possess particular knowledge, skills, and expertise to operate in the

---

[1] For details regarding the research, and for the list of missions and the composition of the sample, see the chapter on the presentation of the research in this volume.

cross-cultural context in which these leadership roles are exercised. In particular, it is assumed that there is a specific training need aimed at providing commanders with the tools necessary to operate effectively in such contexts.

The other particular hypotheses listed below are also connected to this fundamental hypothesis:

– that, in the context of these missions, the cultural approach is indispensable for the purposes of greater and better operational efficiency;
– that the officers interviewed perceive the cultural diversity between themselves and the other actors present in the territories where the missions take place and recognize the importance of knowing how to relate to it, but are not able to frame it in cultural models that allow an understanding and management that is always effective;
– that different kinds of behavior based on different cultural models are considered as "curious peculiarities" rather than scientifically explainable cultural characteristics that can be managed rationally in order to achieve certain goals.

3.3 The Variables Studied

The following variables were studied for the verification of the starting hypotheses:

a.   The perception of cultural diversity.

Studying the problem of cultural diversity in the missions starts first of all from the analysis of its perception by the officers called upon to operate in those contexts, in order to also understand how much they consider appropriate to know about how to manage cross-cultural relations for the purposes of operational effectiveness.

b.   The problems stemming from cultural differences.

The analysis of the problems faced by the commanders in the different missions and referable to the transculturality allows for a better understanding of the cultural dynamics that characterize their reported experiences, to know the characteristics of the training needs better, and to trace the profile of the leader who must operate in these contexts.

c.   The training received.

The comparison between the training received and the training needed that emerges from the study of the previous variable makes it possible to detect any gaps in training, thereby providing useful indications regarding the interventions necessary for providing leaders with the tools to operate effectively in relation to the problem studied.

3.4   The Method Used

The semi-structured interviews conducted in the different countries with the in-depth interview method were reworked taking into account both the cultural characteristics of the interviewed officer and those of the theaters of operations to which the latter referred or the nationality of the actors of he's talking about (for example, military colleagues from other countries within the international contingent). The re-elaboration took place using specific grids, within in the context of a qualitative study approach, considered more appropriate with respect to the research objectives and the way in which the interviews were collected in the different countries.

4   The Results of the Survey

4.1   Perception of Cultural Diversity

The respondents' perception of the cultural diversity among the actors involved in the different theaters of operations emerges first of all in terms of communication. However, the reference population above all highlights the problems related to the spoken languages, by focusing more on verbal communication, rather than on non-verbal communication.

Regarding the language, or better yet, the languages spoken in the different operating theaters, English is the communication tool par excellence, both between the different actors who are guests in those territories and with the local actors through interpreters.

From the interviews, no particular and significant differences emerge with regard to English studied in the Armed forces, although some clarifications are needed. Knowledge of English is usually good and sufficient for operating in theaters of deployment. However, some differences can be noted with respect to: the nationality of the military men; their rank; their experience gained during the mission. As far as nationality is concerned, in addition of course to soldiers who come from English-speaking countries, those from Northern Europe tend to have less difficulty with English, given that, starting with primary school, greater attention is paid to its study than in the countries of Latin Europe. Regarding rank, officers tend to declare less difficulty than those with a lower rank and this is due to their good education obtained in the academies. As for experience, even the lower ranks tend to declare fewer difficulties as the number of missions they participated in increased. Their direct experience in theaters of operations has in fact enabled them to learn the most frequent expressions for operating in such contexts, even replacing possibly poor linguistic bases at the origin.

In addition to communication between armed forces of different nationalities within the international contingent and with other guest actors (NGOs, the Press, etc.), English is used to communicate with interpreters who act as intermediaries with the local actors.

The only thing that was problematic was patrolling with them (Local Forces) *without a language helper. If there was nobody who spoke the language well, interaction was challenging* [FIN14, 1st lieutenant].

Respondents of different nationalities have underlined the problem of the reliability of the interpreters who, in general, do not seem to have problems understanding English but who, when they translate into the local language, cannot be controlled very much and therefore the verification of communication effectiveness is difficult.

On the other hand, the interpreters could also represent important "consultants" regarding the local culture.

The fact that the respondents above all recall the language problem highlights that the latter's attention is mainly focused on verbal communication and the necessary relevance is not given to non-verbal communication (high and low contexts, proxemics, chronemics, etc.) which is more influenced by cultural differences.

Nevertheless, the perception of cultural diversity emerges from the interviews of all the countries of the reference population, both for the various guests and hosts. Among the former, the military recognizes both the cultural diversity and the different organizational cultures of the Armed Forces of different nationalities employed in the different theaters of operations.

We Nordic countries think we can work together, and often do so, and it was even easy to work with the Croats and Serbs in former Yugoslavia. However, I had soldiers from seven different cultures/nations and I had to handle them differently due to their specific discipline, language, norms, and so on. (DKC22, Colonel).

As for local actors, the respondents show that they are aware of the importance of creating social capital with them and that to do so, of the need to relate effectively with them in order to gain their trust. Therefore communication (in the broadest sense of the term) becomes an indispensable tool.

It makes you realize that as there is a cultural gap, you must firstly understand who you are going to relate to, and the culture of these people, and then try to establish a certain kind of relationship [...] maintain contact with the village chief. (ITC30, lieutenant).

Cultural factors were essential to this type of interaction [FIN07, Captain].

The perception of cultural diversity, as well as the importance of knowing how to effectively manage communication for the purpose of developing effective relationships with all the actors involved, clearly emerges from the problems and examples of situations that the interviewees describe. Referring then to the study of the next variable, here we will limit our attention to an aspect that seems to emerge a little in all the countries studied, although less in Italy and in Finland: the superficial level with which cultural diversity is perceived. In fact, in telling stories or describing the problems encountered in operational theaters, the interviewees seem to grasp cultural diversity, thus demonstrating their perception, but without being able to explain and interpret it. This superficial approach does not allow us to fully understand the reason for the social action of the interlocutor, to interpret his/her behavior so as to arrive reasonably to predict future actions but above all to intuit his/her reactions to our actions.

For example, in the following interview, the behavior of local actors is well highlightened, the difference is perceived with respect to one's own, yet without recognizing how it is attributable to a high index of distance from power, and only partially understanding what is most appropriate do in this case, but without exactly knowing why.

With local authorities, however, the goal was to show that we still recognized their authority as leaders and keep a respectful attitude towards them, that ranged from turn-taking in dialogue, talking to one person rather than another, giving them the weight that they were expected to have, etc. (ITC31, Lieutenant).

The knowledge of this cultural dimension, of what it implies and according to what modalities would not only allow a better understanding of the situation, but also to develop more effective strategies of action, as well as predicting the counterpart's responses to the action just taken.

Instead, the superficial perception of cultural diversity can lead to the risks of "labeling" actions different from one's own as "peculiar", "strange", almost something due to folklore alone, when not even falling into prejudice, perhaps based on stereotypes.

In a way they still live in the medieval ages. [LTC04, Colonel].

4.2   Cultural Problems

After having assessed the perception of cultural diversity which, as we have seen, is also useful for understanding the importance of knowing the tools to interact with it, the study of the latter was carried out by analyzing the problems detected by the interviewees in their experience in the different theaters of operations.

Since there are a plurality of actors present in such theaters (military and non-military) with which the soldiers of the international contingents had to communicate and relate, the analysis will be conducted separately for each category.

A common problem with many of the categories examined below is that of interpreters who are used for talking with local actors (authorities, population, etc.). In addition to the problem mentioned of the difficulty in verifying the efficacy of their translation and their reliability, sometimes the interviewees underline their lack of motivation and their standards of professionalism are not always considered adequate.

Interpreters are essential. Employing them makes relations with the population and its leaders more difficult. The poor quality of the interpreters in some cases makes the situation even worse. [BGR21, Captain].

Then there were the local interpreters who you could never rely on fully. Sometimes there were there just for easy money. We maintained a clinical relationship with them. [FIN23, 1st lieutenant].

This could easily be explained by the index of orientation to performance, but even more so by the conception of circular and polychronic time that characterizes, among those of the different theaters of operations studied, above all the Arab culture. In these cases, the role of commanders who should be able to mediate by taking into account the personality of local commanders seems to become particularly important.

The study of problems related to cultural diversity will be conducted in the context of relations with the following categories of actors: the local armed forces; local authorities; local communities; International Governmental Organizations (IGOs), and International Non-Governmental Organizations (NGOs).

4.2.1 The Local Armed Forces

If the cultural diversity has already been grasped by the interviewees with respect to the other military actors within the international contingents in the various operating theaters, the differences with respect to the local military forces are even more evident.

It is a complex relation, always based on respect and politeness, but often with mismatched interests. [SP27, Colonel].

The reference population draws attention to the poor reliability and trust-worthiness of local forces, their poor preparation, and low attitude regarding discipline.

They were very unreliable. They had to be respected, but it was not real respect. We knew their performance was weak and they were not trustworthy. [FIN08, Captain].

Afghans are excellent fighters, but they are not always reliable; their commander said that when his soldiers returned from leave he never knew what was going through their minds. [ITC21, Captain].

The Iraqis as soldiers make the following impression: they are mentally weak, timid and one cannot rely on them. They can be bought easily. (BGR29, Captain).

Iraqi Armed Forces had no confidence. Their esprit de core was broken. Their morale was gone. [BGR03, Brigadier General].

I worked closely with the Iraqi Armed Forces. They were "rag and bobtail" but adapted fast. The Iraqi are much better soldiers than the Afghani ("when something exploded, the Afghani ran away"). [BGR04, Lieutenant Colonel].

I think that the Iraqis are better prepared and more disciplined. The Afghans, I think are more undisciplined.

[BGR07, Brigadier General].

Logistics, for instance, had been provided to them (Afghanistan) by the Americans, but they did not seem able to manage it. The confidence level is low, corruption is widespread. [ITC16, Major].

We have had cases of blue on green (in a while the senior officers of an Afghan unit advised us that it was better than we don't go to the Afghan camp). [ITC16, Major].

Otherwise if an ordinary Afghani soldier cannot do anything he just does not do it at all. But their officers are not like that, they are responsible. [BGR26, Captain].

One of the problems mentioned is the lack of capacity to plan one's work[2] and the slowness with which the soldiers of Arab culture are used to working. This characteristic is interpreted by the respondents as a lacking and is associated with having little willingness to work.

The relationship with locals was business-like and working with everybody. Individuals and their work culture became more important when planning collaborations with them. X (nationality) soldiers have certain qualities you have to work around sometimes. They are a very proud and brave people, but they hate planning. If we plan for a week before an operation they do not do anything. You have to squeeze it out of them. [FIN12, Colonel].

With local forces I have worked as a mentor to the Afghan company. Their desire to work, commitment, patriotism among Afghan soldiers were very low. [ITB2, Captain].

In reality, the Arab culture has a low index of orientation to the future and a more circular and polychronical conception of time than that of the official cultures of the two interviews mentioned above. In countries of Arab culture, less importance is attributed to the planning and scheduling of time, many things can be done at the same time without sticking to a rigid compartmentalization of time and what has not been done today can be done without any problems tomorrow and at another time. Furthermore, for the Islamic religion, the planning of the future is blasphemous because only God has control of time. It also results in a lack of attention to punctuality and all this can be misunderstood as "little desire to work".

The slowness in developing the relationship can be explained by the high index of collectivism: the relationship is completed when trust matures, but it takes time for this to be created.

Well, to have a good relationship, I have seen that it takes time. Because otherwise it is not something that is immediate. At least, in my experience, I have worked very well with certain Afghan departments, but only after we had worked together for a long time. [ITC29, Lieutenant].

Another aspect noted by the interviewees and useful for the study of cultural diversity is the difficulty attributed to local armed forces[3] in understanding the ROEs.

With the ANA a decent relationship, in some cases they are pulled a little back because a very different cultural approach. For them it is very difficult to understand the ROEs and they have applied them only when it suited. [ITC05, Colonel].

This problem, which is interpreted as an indicator of poor professionalism, is easily explained by the low aversion to uncertainty of the Arabs and, at least in part, in the High Context communication. For example, compared to the Italians and above all, to many of the armed forces' cultures used in Afghanistan, the Arabs have less need for rules and it can be difficult for them to adapt to rules that strictly impose that, on the occurrence of a particular situation, certain actions must be performed that are rigorously defined in detail. In Arab culture, communication does not need to verbally describe every part of the message but tends to be reduced to the essential,

---

[2]Particularly in Afghanistan.

[3]Also in this case, especially in Afghanistan.

often using symbols. For an Arab soldier, the fact of dealing with the text of the ROE could perhaps arouse unease or, certainly, difficulties in understanding its meaning and the reason for that way of operating.

Lastly, an image of the local armed forces that emerges from the interviews is that of soldiers still very attached to a tribal conception of society and with a strong attachment to the family, which comes first and whom they wish to protect, perhaps even from the threats of Taliban retaliation.

They are an army still quite tribal. (...) People went on leave and did not come back, the family is deeply felt and comes before the military duty. [ITC16, Major].

The reliability of these troops, however, must always be monitored. They are always in fact blackmailed by insurgents that may threaten their families. Often they have to keep their feet in both camps. So the reliability depends on the area in which they operate. [IT19, Captain].

If this characteristic is also seen by the reference population as an indicator of poor professionalism, implying the need for the good soldier to keep work and family affections separate and, in case of a conflict of roles, to make the interest of the military organization prevail, in reality this peculiarity is also easily explained in the high index of Collectivism of the Arab culture. Within it, the individual is inserted into cohesive groups (Family, tribe) since birth that protect him and that he is called on to protect and towards which he must be careful to "never lose face", nor make other group members lose face.

In particular, when our soldiers are called upon to act as mentors to colleagues in local military forces, "face maintenance" becomes essential in collectivist cultures with a high index of distance from power such as the Arab one, as demonstrated by the experience of this officer:

When I was on my first mission in Afghanistan, having noticed, in my capacity as a mentor of an Afghan company, that a soldier related to his company commander in an insolent manner, I said to the captain that it would be well-advised to require more discipline. After two hours, that soldier was presented to me with his tongue cut lengthwise. Facts like these, having lived them, give you a different perspective of the Afghan culture. [Captain, age 37].

Nor is there any lack of negative judgments related to the personal hygiene of the military colleagues of the local armed forces:

It is extremely difficult to work with Iraqi military. They have poor hygiene and they are lazy. [BGR59—Captain].

In reality, a kind of behavior that for the interviewee should be judged harshly, takes on a completely different meaning in the Arab culture. Body odors are not considered as negatively as in most Western cultures and the sense of smell takes on a different importance and different meanings in personal relationships.

4.2.2 The Local Authorities

The respondents agree on the importance of establishing good relations with local authorities in all the theaters of operations in which they operated. The creation of good relationships represents the *conditio sine qua non* for obtaining their trust (Collectivism) and therefore to be able to operate more effectively in the territory. All this cannot be separated from the knowledge of the characteristics of the local culture and the most effective ways of relating to it.

They also agree on the need to distinguish between formal authorities that formally hold power and informal authorities whose power is in fact also recognized spontaneously by the population.

A fundamental role seems to be played by religious leaders who can greatly influence the more or less positive attitude towards the international contingent deployed in those territories, representing important and influential socialization agencies.

If the reference population recognizes the cultural peculiarity of the local authorities and seems to express the perception of the differences with respect to their culture, in this case too, the interviewees show that they know how to grasp the differences but rarely know how to explain them, going beyond stereotypes or simply considering them as "particularities".

As an example, we report the awareness acquired a bit by all the interviewees of the need to show particular respect for the authority of the person in front of them, whether they be a formal or an informal authority.

With local authorities, however, the goal was to show that we still recognized their authority as leaders and keep a respectful attitude towards them, that went from the turn-taking in dialogue, talk to one person rather than another, give him the weight that this person was expected to have, etc. [ITC31, Lieutenant].

Instead, with the local authorities, we had to show that, in any case, we recognized their authority as leaders and therefore we had to maintain an absolutely respectful attitude towards them, which meant respectfully taking turns in a dialogue, talking with one person rather than another, giving them the importance that this person expected, etc. [ITC30, Lieutenant].

Although this need is recognized by the interviewees, the latter seem to explain it simply as "the importance that is given to the hierarchy" in those countries, sometimes even in a somewhat critical way, almost considering it as an indicator of poor modernization. In reality, in many of the operational theaters where the reference population has matured its experience, local cultures present a high index of distance from Power. In particular in Arab culture, status and the power that corresponds to it are not hidden, but flaunted. For the formal authority to be transformed into real power, this authority must also be recognized by other subjects. The symbols (gestures, attitudes, etc.) represent valid instruments for this recognition. Therefore, with regard to the authorities, it is necessary not only to express their recognition of their power in front of everyone, but also to be very careful not to assume attitudes that could in some way question their authority, thereby causing the "loss of face".

This recognition can take place by participating in any sessions of local councils, religious ceremonies, events in which the authorities play an official role, as well as simply with courtesy visits to which all the necessary time must be devoted in that specific context (circular and polychronic time), and by avoiding a refusal of the drinks or foods that are offered and showing appreciation for these, because their convivial consumption takes on a symbolic meaning and is functional for knowing each other, recognizing each other's status, developing trust and therefore, consolidating the relationship necessary for good operational efficiency. All this would also prove to be useful in creating the relationship and gaining trust within the Arab culture with a high index of Collectivism.

I attend sessions of the village council, so we have open communication. [PHC12, Lieutenant].

I'd arrive at the village, the village leader would come out, I'd approach him, we'd chat, and everything seemed all right. Then maybe he would say, "Come with me, I offer you tea." If I say no to something, if I refuse maybe because I really don't want anything, that's normal for me. But there, if you do that, such a thing is not regarded well in their culture. Perhaps they think they have been offended. So if they feel offended, then the next time ... [ITC30, Lieutenant].

Therefore, with regard to local authorities, the good commander, being the one who interacts with them more or less as "peers", must be aware of the cultural characteristics of their interlocutors, know their meaning and implications, relate to them by demonstrating to recognize their authority (Distance from Power), and to adapt with regard to their uses in order to create the relationship and gain their trust (Collectivism), without ever making them lose face. Precisely because of the high collectivism, another problem is created in the missions: the periodic rotation of the commanders of the deployed forces. This change produces negative effects in collectivist cultures: when, after a more or less long time the commander and the local authorities have finally come to know each other, so trust has matured and the relationship has developed, the commander is replaced as part of normal turnover measures, it is therefore necessary to start over. Since it is not possible to imagine an alternative solution to the normal shifting of troops in the operational theaters, it would be desirable that, at the level of military leaders, there be a period that is not too short of co-presence and support in which the outgoing commander presents his successor to the local authorities.

4.2.3   The Local Community

Like local authorities, respondents also reiterate the need to establish positive relationships and maintain a good relationship with the local population.

We must learn to build relationships, not just with fellow soldiers but be open to civilians. There is a need to develop the capability to reach out. [PHC12, Lieutenant].

The relations with the local population depended very much on the area. In principle, they consider the various coalition forces in the same way. In my area I have established good relationships with the inhabitants of the nearby village, always with due diffidence because, as the old local saying goes, "you can rent the Afghan but you cannot buy him. [ITC 01, Captain].

However, the interviewees repeatedly stated that one way of consolidating the relationships is by "giving" or "doing something" useful for those local communities.

Local communities, for the most part, see us positively. Because, however, both at the level of security and at the economic level the presence of foreign forces bear economy.

It takes some exchange: they give you a little information and you give them something else. The more reports, more information came in countries where there has been a collaboration. Maybe we have given something. In one village we brought a generator that they needed. We get our information that interest us and the local leader of course increases his prestige. [ITC29, Lieutenant].

I invited the elderly to a "shura" every fortnight. It created a network that resulted in sound info from them to us. I opened emergency and medical clinics and in the camp for the locals. In the beginning only men approached, later on women with children, as well. [DCK11, Major].

The tool for creating good relationships once again becomes communication, even though it can be risky for the local population if seen by the insurgents.

But, as we have seen when dealing with the previous variable, in the context of the different theaters of operations, communication is of a cross-cultural type.

In fact, the interviewees seem to capture the diversity between their own culture and those of the theaters of operations in which they operate. In certain territories, for example in Afghanistan, the perception is also that culture and behavior change from village to village, even though in this case, we should talk more about sub-cultures and it is a normal fact in societies where the different tribes retain their historical baggage of traditions, customs, and traditions.

We did often meetings with the chiefs and elders of the local communities. There is a strong difference in behavior according to location. The area, for example, of Bala Murgab is contaminated by insurgents and therefore local authorities have to juggle to survive. For example, in May 2012 I had gone to distribute humanitarian aid in a village. A week later we went back there, convinced to find a good reception by the people of the village and instead we were met with gunfire. [ITC19, Captain].

However, the greater diversity perceived by the interviewees concerns the different religions that significantly influence the different cultures.

With respect to the population, even though the interviewees also recognize the cultural diversity through the observation of diversity of behaviors, beliefs, customs and traditions, traditions, etc., it is however necessary that the social actors involved and oriented to creating a good relationship with it know, also in this case as in the previous one, how to understand the meaning and the implications of these differences. Only through this understanding can the creation of a good relationship and, at least a partial acceptance by the local populations be made more probable. We mustn't forget that, for the latter, even if they were not seen as invaders, they would still be considered out-groups, the "others", who are different, not belonging to their own culture and therefore, as such, perhaps potentially enemies.

When he finds himself interacting with the local populations, after having tried to obtain legitimacy from the authorities (formal and informal) present in that territory (remember the high index of distance from power), the good commander must take into account of all these aspects related to high collectivism, know how to adapt his own communication methods by moving towards the High Context, and try to overcome his natural prejudices, in order to create a good relationship and above all, to be accepted. The stones thrown by children at the passing convoys of armed forces used on a mission are a sign of the need to intervene in this regard.

You must know the local culture norm. A child throwing stones is a "up-bringing" problem, not a warrior. [DK13, Lieutenant].

However, the overcoming of prejudice in local populations necessarily passes before overcoming the prejudice of those who are employed in those missions: any ethnocentric or superior attitude must be avoided. Once again, the tools provided by cross-cultural studies to understand and manage cross-cultural relationships are useful.

4.2.4 The NGOs

Lastly, a brief mention should be made of relations with the various organizations (governmental and non-governmental) present in the territory.

Non-Governmental Organizations are not military organizations, they are not local organizations and therefore, they have more or less the same cultural problems as the armed forces employed in those territories, and usually present characteristics of internationality, operating precisely at the international level and often composed of people of different nationalities.

Although the cultures of the members of these organizations are certainly closer to the culture of the parent society than the military men in the international contingents present in that particular operational theater, their organizational culture (the culture of the organization itself) is certainly a lot different from that of the military organization and this often generates problems.

I've had relationships with NGOs in Lebanon, especially as escorts. Less in Afghanistan. The problem of NGOs is that not having a minimum of military training do not always perceive the danger. Their function is still positive. [ITC19, Captain].

Respondents show that they perceive these differences, also interpreting them as an attitude of distrust, when not downright hostile towards the military.

NGOs with whom we have worked within the PRT were not willing to cooperate with the military, even trying to keep well separated and distinct. [ITC01, Captain].

In Kosovo, I had relations with NGOs; in some cases I have observed an attitude ruling against the military, but then to turn to us when they needed. [ITB01, Lieutenant Colonel].

At other times they do not seem to be sufficiently aware of being in theaters of operations and the possible consequences of their actions.

I had a film crew visiting us to follow our patrolling. However, there is a risk that they do not give the right picture and they may harm more than they inform. Media are not always aware of the responsibility of filming soldiers/interpreters and the risk those people may run being compromised later on. [DKC 13, Lieutenant].

Whilst aware of the differences, synergies may nevertheless arise that can be useful to both parties.

We have worked a lot with the UNIAMA to provide protection especially in case of attacks. Even there, it was still all a work of trying to understand what their needs, make them coincide with our needs and also with the limits of jurisdiction. No problem, indeed: you can develop synergies. [ITC 31, Lieutenant].

What the commanders are called upon to do also in this case is to establish good relations with these organizations in the area, aware of the not always positive attitude towards them, but also of the fact that they need the military to be able to operate in certain situations. It is therefore necessary for the officer to possess good diplomatic skills and the ability to overcome prejudices deriving from cultural and, in these cases, often ideological diversity. It is necessary for them to know how to adopt a positive attitude, as in the case of the Italian officer cited in the last interview, aimed at provoking an equivalent attitude on the part of the other party, without forgetting that, in any case, it is the NGO that needs an escort, protection, etc. and it is the military organization that offers it. The dialectic of bargaining must prevail over prejudice.

4.3 Training

As for the training received by soldiers of different nationalities before being employed in the different missions, this tends to vary from country to country. For the purposes of this study, however, it concerns specific training aimed at developing relationship and communication skills with cultures that are different from their own.

Aside from the aforementioned language training, an adequate formative intervention in this sense does not seem to emerge from the interviewees' experiences. Except for the Finnish and Italian officials who seem a bit more able to analyze the differences in cross-cultural relations, the training interventions in this area are almost always limited to providing the departing military with advice on what is good to do or not do in the culture of the destination country, without providing them with the tools for analyzing the behavior of the actors in that culture, for understanding them, and for their subsequent management.

In most cases and in all countries, the interviewees declare that they have learned, mission after mission, how best to behave with the local culture, often making use of the advice of colleagues who had already participated in missions in that particular country and therefore, with more experience. "Learning by doing" is a very widespread and, to some extent, is an effective way of learning, as is coaching by more experienced colleagues. However, these modalities provide superficial knowledge that is limited to learning behavior on the basis of what has been personally experienced in previous situations or based on what others have experienced in other situations.

But there is no guarantee that situations are always the same, nor that the model of behavior that is effective in one situation can be the same in another. Likewise, the experiences lived by others are in some way interpreted by them and, in this case too, there is no guarantee that the analysis made always corresponds exactly to the reality. So, once again, what is needed is the mastery of the tools for understanding and interacting with other cultures, in order to relate to them effectively.

The Italian case confirms this. In Italy, since 2012, the officers of the Military Academy, in the last two years of their university training course for obtaining a master's degree in Strategic and Military Sciences, have been attending a course in Sociology in which a special part is provided for cross-cultural relationships. In this part one learns: the cultural dimensions that allow one to interpret and understand the different cultures, the ways of interacting with them and above all the different modes of communication with High Context and Low Context cultures, etc. Among the Italian respondents, there was a young lieutenant assigned to a mission a few months after finishing his studies. In his interview, this man, the only one among the Italian officers, who had attended the course of Sociology after 2012 and thereby had acquired knowledge offered by that particular part, shows a greater and better understanding of the cultural differences compared to his colleagues, does not give any signs of stereotyped or prejudice-based attitudes and even seems more capable of dealing with problems arising from cultural diversity.

5   Conclusion: A New Model of Training

The analysis of the studied variables seems to fully verify the starting hypotheses. Not only must the commanders on a mission deal with the cultural diversity in the different countries in which it takes place (local armed forces, local authorities, population), but the subcultures of the other actors present in those operational theaters are also often different (armed forces of the international contingent, NGOs).

The importance of the cultural approach and the confirmation of its usefulness is also demonstrated by the attitude of the respondents with respect to the different problems described in the interviews and regarding relations with other actors. For example, Italians and Spaniards seem to know how to relate more easily to local cultures and this could be explained by the higher index of Collectivism in their cultures.

On the part of the commanders employed in the different missions, the need for adequate training for the acquisition of the possession of effective tools to relate to actors belonging to cultures different from their own is evident from the narration of the interviewees' experiences and the problems they encountered in the different operating theaters.

The fact that cultural diversity is perceived by the reference population, but limited to the simple observation of diversity, often considered as something special, sometimes strange, in some cases "backward" or belonging to a culture less evolved than one's own, confirms the need to have the tools for understanding and the consequent effective interaction with this diversity.

As we have said, it is not enough just to grasp cultural differences: we need to understand them (the reason why those people behave like this), interpret them (what their cultural models of reference are), and know how to predict the consequences of their actions on the interlocutors. Only in this way will it be possible to relate to the different actors present in the various theaters of operations of the missions in an effective and efficient manner and, as the research has unquestionably demonstrated, "relating" with the other actors (especially the local ones) is the necessary condition for obtaining high levels of operational effectiveness.

Relations are based on communication. Research has shown the need for useful tools to communicate effectively with cultures other than one's own, by going beyond the use of the language (English, local languages, interpreters), and also to consider the non-verbal communication typical of High context cultures such as those in most of the countries in which international missions have been held or are taking place.

The importance of a training intervention in this sense is also confirmed in the current ways of learning the strategies of interaction with the other cultures used by the officers today (learning by doing and coaching), despite the limits that these entail and which we have already mentioned.

On the other hand, the research confirmed that the officers who participated in a greater number of missions appear to be more able to operate in cross-cultural contexts, and this confirms that these skills can be learned.

The research study also revealed the inadequacy of the training interventions carried out in the different countries and provided indications for a more effective training model for the management of cross-cultural relations. It would be desirable for this model to include:

a. different training interventions with respect to the grade and role played in the mission;
b. the use of qualified trainers, experts in relationships and cross-cultural communications;
c. an intervention at three different levels:

1. At the level of the basic training of the commanders (Academy/University), the fundamental tools for the understanding of the cultures and the consequent interaction with them, as well as for transcultural communication should be provided.
    Therefore, the concept of culture in the anthropological sense should be acquired, its characteristics, the modes of transmission (Socialization), the processes of acculturation and, above all, the cultural dimensions (Hofstede, House) that allow us to interpret the differences between different cultures. Particular attention should be paid to cross-cultural communication, especially between High Context and Low Context cultures, with particular attention given to non-verbal communication, proxemics, and chronemics (Hall).
2. Before setting off on a mission, experts should investigate the characteristics of the specific culture of the country in which the mission takes place (taking into account the cultures of the different actors present in the operational theater). This in-depth analysis would represent an application of the tools learned in the previous level of training to that specific culture. In this phase, in addition to presenting, with appropriate practical examples,

the characteristics of this culture with respect to each of the previously studied cultural dimensions and the methods of communication, it would be appropriate to make extensive use of operational tools such as role-playing, in order to "train" the commanders to operate in that particular cultural context.

3. On a mission, once they arrive at their destination, a further intervention would be appropriate, this time by officers chosen from those already present in that operating theater and deemed most suitable as to their experience and communication skills, aimed at transmitting the know-how acquired in the experience gained up to then in mission and relating to that particular operational context (territory, military forces of other countries, local armed forces, local authorities, population, etc.). In practice, it would be a matter of formalizing what is already happening, in part spontaneously, with an assistance in the handover from one contingent to another.

These three levels of intervention should ensure greater and better effectiveness of the interventions by the commanders in cross-cultural relations.

6 What About Leadership Concerning Cultural Diversity?

What is the role of the leader who is called upon to command a platoon, a company, etc. on missions such as those studied? What knowledge, skills, and expertise must he possess to exercise his leadership role in contexts in which relationships are necessarily transcultural?

The study reveals a complex profile that can be summarized as follows:

- He must be an officer with an open mind who does not judge based on stereotypes, someone who is free from prejudice and not afraid to face diversity, considering it as completely normal. The ability to relate to cultural diversity is an element of his professionalism.
- He must be a flexible leader, able to promptly adapt to different situations characterized by cultural diversity, able to pass from one "register" to another, to vary cultural models with the same naturalness with which he can pass from one to the other of the different languages that he is able to speak.
- He must be aware of cultural diversity and that the different "acting with meaning" can also be explained in the different cultural models of the social actor with which he is relating.
- He must know and be able to use the tools that are useful for understanding and interpreting different cultures, as well as being necessary to act and communicate effectively in them.
- He must be able to relate to the different social actors present in his operative context. In particular:

- With regard to the Armed Forces of different nationalities that make up the international contingents used in each mission, in addition to understanding their cultural diversity, he must also be able to grasp the different organizational cultures that characterize them. For example, the diversity perceived by Italian officers with regard to their US counterparts is almost always explained by their higher Index of Performance Orientation, their higher Individualism, their conception of time which, compared to Italians, is more linear and monochronic, and their type of Low Context communication.
- With regard to the local armed forces, the commander must be able to: know how to give public recognition to the leadership of local colleagues; never make the mistake of belittling the figure of a colleague (to lose face), especially in the eyes of his subordinates; know how to read their way of operating with respect to the culture they belong to; consider the high distance from the power index of their culture (for example, Arab culture) and how this affects their behavior; take into account the high collectivism (for example, regarding the role of families); adapt to communication, usually more High Context in the areas of the current missions.
- With regard to the Local Authorities, it is necessary first of all to be able to recognize their leadership publicly. The commander will then also be able to identify, alongside the formal leaders, the informal ones, paying particular attention to the religious leaders. In dealing with these local leaders, it is necessary to take into account the high distance from power index, even more so than with colleagues in the local armed forces because the latter, being soldiers, are peers, whereas civil authorities cannot be considered as such. It will be of fundamental importance for the commander to earn (I would say win over) the authorities' trust. The creation of the relationship can take place in many ways, which can be different as the situation changes. However, it may be useful to participate in events, initiatives, and public ceremonies (secular or sometimes even religious), thus showing interest and respect for local traditions, customs and habits.
- Also with regard to the civilian population, the commander must try to create and maintain a good relationship. To do this, it is necessary to relate to it by taking into account its particular cultural characteristics, as already mentioned for the previous actors. In particular, above all for the populations of Arab culture, one should never forget their high Collectivism, Low Context communication, low Orientation to the Future, and their conception of circular and polychronic time. It will be necessary not to fall into the error of several officers interviewed who interpreted certain kinds of behavior by the local populations[4] (and also by their colleagues in the local armed forces and other actors) as an implication of having "little desire to work". Arab culture has a high index of performance orientation: that way of acting is explained above all by the different conception of time. But as well as being superficial and wrong, the judgment made tends to refer to stereotypes and risks laying the basis for ethnocentric attitudes. An attitude of this kind can in itself be prejudicial to the creation of the relationship with the local

---

[4]In the case of the Arab culture.

populations and to the construction of that good relationship that the interviewees consider indispensable.

- Lastly, with one's own men, when necessary to obtain from them a kind of behavior aimed at greater operational efficiency, the good commander must be able to explain the kinds of behavior that can be traced back to different cultures. Also within the platoon, prejudice and ethnocentric attitudes must always be fought in order to avoid, in the case of contact with other local actors, that the relationship may be affected. It should not be overlooked that the good commander who is able to demonstrate to his men that he is able to work at this level (of transculturality), can acquire esteem and consideration among them, and this contributes to the recognition of informal leadership.

The leader who demonstrates that he knows how to work effectively in a cross-cultural context will not only be able to relate to all the other actors present in that mission but will receive their esteem and respect. This demonstration of profession-alism will make their job easier. By also attributing informal leadership to him, in addition to his authority, his own men will also recognize his power, and from being the "boss", he will become a true "leader" [18].

References

1. Bollinger D, Hofstede G (1989) Internazionalità. Le differenze culturali nel management. Guerini, Milano
2. Clemmensen JR, Archer EM, Barr J, Belkin A, Guerrero M, Hall C, Swain KEO (2012) Conceptualizing the civil-military gap: a research note. Armed Forces Soc 38(4):669–678
3. Dale C, Gupta V, Javidhan, M (2004) Power distance. In: House RJ, Hanges PJ, Javidan M, Dorfman, PW, Gupta V (eds) Culture, leadership, and organizations. Sage, Thousand Oaks USA
4. Durán M, Ávalos A (2013) Culturas cruzadas en conflicto. Militares poblaciones locales en misiones internacionales: los casos de Afganistán y Líbano. Editorial Universidad de Granada, Granada
5. Egnell R (2013) Civil–military coordination for operational effectiveness: towards a measured approach. Small Wars Insurgencies 24(2):237–256
6. Franke V (2006) The peacebuilding dilemma: civil-military cooperation in stability operations. Int J Peace Stud 11(2):5–25
7. Gallino L (2006) Dizionario di Sociologia. Utet, Torino
8. Geertz C (1966) Religion as a cultural system. In: Banton M (ed) Anthropological approaches to the study of religion. Tavistock Publications, London
9. Hall ET (1960) The silent language in overseas business. Haward Business Review, XXXVIII, 3
10. Hall ET, Hall MR (1990) Understanding cultural differences. Germans, French and Americans, Intercultural Press, Yarmouth
11. Hofstede G (1980) Culture's consequences: international differences in work-related values. Sage, Berverly Hill CA
12. Hofstede G (2001) Culture's consequences: comparing values, behaviors, institutions and organizations across nations. Sage, Thousand Oaks, CA
13. House RJ, Hanges PJ, Mansour J, Dorfman PW, Gupta V (2004) Culture, leadership, and organizations. Sage, Thousand Oaks CA

14. House RJ, Javidan M (2004) Overview of globe. In: House RJ, Hanges PJ, Javidan M, Dorfman PW, Gupta V (eds) Culture, leadership, and organizations. Sage, Thousand Oaks USA
15. Münkler H (2005) Viejas y 'nuevas guerras'. Asimetría y privatización de la violencia. Siglo, Madrid
16. Nuciari M (2001) Officers' education for MOOTW: a comparative research on military and civilian agencies problematic relationships. In: Caforio G (2002) The flexible officer: professional education and military operations other than war: a cross-national analysis. CEMISS Publications Series, Gaeta, Artistic & Publishing Co., pp 61–88
17. Nuciari M (2007) Coping with diversity. Military and Civilian actors in MOOTW. Int Rev Soc-Rev Internationale de Sociologie 7(1):25–54
18. Olivetta E (2012) L'Istituzione Inevitabile. Bonanno, Roma
19. Pouligny B (2003) UN peace operations, INGO, NGO, and promoting the rule of law: exploring the interaction of international and local norms in different postwar contexts. J Human Rights 2(3):359–377
20. Schein EH (1985) Organizational culture and leadership. Jossey-Bass Publishers, San Francisco
21. Tylor EB (1871) Primitive culture. Harper, New York (1958)

Leadership Problems for Armed Forces in Asymmetric Warfare Operations

The Education and Training of Military Leaders for Crisis Management Environments: Perceptions of Its Suitability for Adaptive Expertise

Soili Paananen

Abstract The chapter analyses military leaders' perceptions of the military education and training they receive for their missions. Officers are professional experts on leadership. The question of how to prepare and train leaders to meet the challenges posed by the complexity of their work environment is crucial both for their survival and the success of their mission in a crisis management context. The chapter focuses primarily on military leaders' own experiences of how training facilitates their adaptive expertise for crisis management environments. It argues that in complex, demanding and unfamiliar situations adaptive experts can adapt their knowledge to novel situations and become accustomed to change. The results also allow us to suggest the kind of training and preparation is necessary to meet and overcome the challenges inherent in crisis management environments.

This chapter analyses military leaders' perceptions of the military education and training they receive for their missions. The chapter focuses primarily on military leaders' own experiences of how this training facilitates their adaptive expertise, and its development for crisis management environments.

Officers are professional experts on leadership. Although countries differ in their ways of organising military education, officers' professionalism is shaped and enhanced through formal and informal learning, as well as on-the-job training. However, the question of how to prepare and train leaders to meet the challenges posed by the complexity of their work environment is crucial both for their survival and the success of their mission in a crisis management context. Moreover, this gives rise to a number of closely-related questions: How do we manage to update and expand their skills, knowledge- and culture-based competences, as well as prepare them to adopt new practices in continuously changing environments and in the face of unforeseen challenges? How do we prepare them to manage situation-specific

S. Paananen (✉)
Department of Leadership and Military Pedagogy, Finnish National Defence University, P.O. Box 7, 00861 Helsinki, Finland
e-mail: soili.paananen@mil.fi

© Springer Nature Switzerland AG 2021
M. Nuciari and E. Olivetta (eds.), *Leaders for Tomorrow: Challenges for Military Leadership in the Age of Asymmetric Warfare*, Advanced Sciences and Technologies for Security Applications, https://doi.org/10.1007/978-3-030-71714-8_4

cases and to work and negotiate with local people in uncertain conditions? In short, how do we help them to cope with the new challenges and demands they are likely to confront in their mission, and how do we manage to develop their professional expertise so that it is more than adequate for their work environment?

This chapter seeks to address two main questions: (1) What are military leaders' perceptions and understandings regarding their experiences of military education and training for their crisis management missions? (2) How do they evaluate the suitability of this preparation for their adaptive expertise? Answering these two questions will enable us first of all to determine whether a new kind of definition of leadership is needed, but it will also allow us to suggest the kind of training and preparation that is necessary to meet and overcome the challenges inherent in crisis management environments.

1   Adaptive Expertise

Meeting and surmounting the challenges in crisis management environments requires interaction and different forms of cooperation between education, (pre)-training and the work environment. Theoretically, this reflects how the education and training system fosters leaders in becoming adaptive or even proactive experts in their own contextualised settings. Hatano and Inagaki [1] initially conceptualized and differentiated between routine and adaptive expertise. Routine experts are highly efficient in a specific domain due to their habitual use of knowledge and extensive experience [2]. They are fluent in applying known schemas or procedures to familiar problems or situations in a stable environment, but lack flexibility and adaptability to new problems ([1], 266). Adaptive expertise builds on these skills, but the difference between routine experts and adaptive experts is that the latter can adapt their previous knowledge to novel situations and quickly become accustomed to change [1]. Adaptive experts' metacognitive skills, ability to remain cognitively flexible and solve analogical problems, as well as their ability to meet challenges, be innovative and learn continuously are evaluated as being at a highly developed level. Consequently, they are better than routine experts at acting in complex, demanding and unfamiliar situations [3].

Adaptive expertise is particularly linked to knowledge transfer and the development of expertise. From the education and learning perspective, it is crucial to know how the previously acquired know-how will be applied in a new situation, and how it will transfer to demanding situations. This traditional definition of transfer is restricted, however, to the efficient use of knowledge of one's own domain. On the other hand, a broader understanding, so-called dynamic transfer, refers to one's ability to use that know-how to learn in new situations or create a novel perspective on, or solution to, a problem [5]. In addition, transfer can take place later and allow one to learn a new task domain quickly [6]. An extensive and integrated knowledge base is also positively related to adaptive expertise because it forms a solid foundation for a leader's ability to navigate novelty and complexity. From the pedagogical perspective, adaptive expertise is enhanced by activated learning and problem- and case-based learning environments in which participants are encouraged to build their own knowledge and reflect on this knowledge as they assimilate it [7]. This deepens their understanding of their domain. Finally, supportive persons or mentors combined with task variety in the work context also have a meaningful role to play in the development of adaptive expertise [3, 8, 9].

Adaptive expertise is generally regarded as highly important in the military profession [10], but its development is not well understood. It is usually studied by means of think-aloud strategies, interviews and surveys [2]. The present study is based on interviews in which military leaders assess for themselves the suitability of their education and training for adaptation to their crisis management missions. The interviews focused on officers with practical command experiences in an asymmetric environment at a platoon, company or battalion level. The interviews (N = 247) were conducted in eight countries—Bulgaria (N = 60), Cameroon (N = 33), Denmark (N = 26), Finland (N = 25), Lithuania (N = 4), Italy (N = 43), the Philippines (N = 29), and Spain (N = 27)—by a native researcher using an identical interview protocol in each country. The interviews consisted of six themes: socio-demographic factors, operational experiences, basic and specific training, field experiences, commanded unit and personal experiences. This chapter is based on analyses of the training theme. The results are presented in tables, which facilitates a comparison between leaders' experiences of their education and training, and its suitability for their work. Direct quotations from the interviews are also used to support the central arguments of the chapter.

The results comprise three parts: The first part describes the national differences between the basic and specific education and training for missions. Each leader's perception is categorised as being either 'good' or 'inadequate'. The second part analyses the leaders' individual experiences of their basic training and military education, while the third part focuses on their specific training. These parts are based on the perceptions of those leaders who provided arguments or comments concerning the nature of their training. At the end of the chapter, the significance of the education and training received and its role in developing adaptive military leaders are discussed. Based on the results, brief reflections are also included on the kind of leadership that is needed in these extreme contexts.

2   Results

2.1   National Differences Between Basic and Specific Training

Basic military education and training refers to skills and knowledge—such as countering Improvised Explosive Devices (IEDs), and tactical procedures—that are acquired either during the formal education that officers receive at official military academies, institutions or universities, or in pre-deployment training for each mission. Specific training, such as cultural training, relates to supplementary know-how that will enable leaders to succeed in a particular mission area.

Overall, the informants were relatively satisfied with the basic military education and training they had received (Table 1). However, some country-specific features were evident: For example, 39% of the Cameroonian informants said that they had received no basic training for their mission. Similarly, 58% of the Italian informants were only partially satisfied with their basic training, and many of them would have preferred to receive more training about asymmetric conflicts. 27% of the Bulgarian informants were partially satisfied with the basic training, although many of them would have liked to receive training tailored to their specific position or task in the mission.

The informants were also fairly satisfied with the specific training they received, although in this respect slightly more variation is seen in the way they assessed their specific training compared to the basic training they obtained (Table 2). According to the Spanish interviewees, they were provided with specific training, but 30% of them were only partly satisfied due to the fact that it inadequately reflected the real needs of the mission. For 38% of Danish respondents, the reason for dissatisfaction was the apparent discrepancy between theoretical knowledge and practice in the mission area. In contrast, 67% of the Cameroonian informants either received no training at all, or reported that it held no significance for them.

2.2   Experiences of Basic Training and Military Education

Experiences at the individual level

Missions differ, and hence the training for each one has to be customized. Pre-deployment training takes into account the characteristic features of the mission, and changes according to the activities and threats in the area of operations. Many informants responded positively when it came to describing how the pre-training for missions had developed over the years. They gave very detailed accounts of each of the pre-training sessions and evaluated how they had corresponded with the reality of a mission (Table 3).

Table 1 National differences concerning basic training received for missions

	Bulgaria	Cameroon	Denmark	Finland	Italy	Lithuania	Philippines	Spain
Good	14 23%	0 0%	5 19%	16 64%	6 14%	2 50%	5 18%	4 15%
Satisfactory/Adequate	25 42%	16 49%	14 54%	6 24%	10 23%		19 66%	20 74%
Partly Satisfactory	16 27%	0 0%	5 19%	1 4%	25 58%	1 25%	1 3%	3 11%
Insufficient	2 3%	4 12%	2 8%	2 8%	2 5%		1 3%	0 0%
No training	3 5%	13 39%	0 0%	0 0%	0 0%	1 25%	3 10%	0 0%
Total	60 100%	33 100%	26 100%	25 100%	43 100%	4 100%	29 100%	27 100%

Table 2 National differences concerning specific training received for missions

	Bulgaria	Cameroon	Denmark	Finland	Italy	Lithuania	Philippines	Spain
Good	10 17%	3 9%	3 11.5%	16 64%	17 39.5%	3 75%	6 21%	5 19%
Satisfactory/adequate	35 58%	3 9%	8 31%	3 12%	17 39.5%		13 45%	12 44%
Partly satisfactory	11 18%	2 6%	10 38%	4 16%	7 16%		2 7%	8 30%
Insufficient	3 5%	3 9%	2 8%	2 8%	2 5%		4 13.5%	2 7%
No training/No meaning	1 2%	22 67%	3 11.5%	0 0%	0 0%	1 25%	4 13.5%	0 0%
Total	60 100%	33 100%	26 100%	25 100%	43 100%	4 100%	29 100%	27 100%

Table 3 Experiences of basic training received for missions

BASIC TRAINING	Good/satisfactory	Partly satisfactory/insufficient
Individual level		– No competence for mission M = 1 – More information about asymmetry M = 22 – More room for adjustment M = 3
	M = 48	M = 26
Unit level	M = 11	M = 7
Total	M = 59	M = 33

M mentions

As a rule, however, the question concerning leaders' basic skills for the mission was interpreted in two interconnected ways (M = 48). First, basic skills were understood as individual leadership and battle skills for which formal officer education and training provides adequate preparation. Officers could have acquired such skills from different national educational institutions and universities or from international training centers. Added to this, long-term experience in different leadership positions, different kinds of commanding jobs and working with people forms a good basis for performing the mission. As one officer put it, "All the basic training and experience in the background consolidates professionalism" (FIN09). Only in one case did a leader say (see ITC31) that his friend had been sent on a really challenging mission almost straight from school and that he lacked the competence for it.

"The warrant officer school provided a sufficient basis for addressing the role of platoon commander without any problems" (ITC17).

"Potentially, you arrive at the regiment and, after two months, you're thrown in at the deep end in Afghanistan. Not Albania or Kosovo but Afghanistan, where, if things go wrong, you're the commander on the ground and you have to ask a plane to drop a bomb. Or you have to manage a MEDEVAC, or an IED event. So, it is true that school cannot provide everything, but it can provide a lot more in terms of technical and tactical preparation. But [...] to put an officer in command just two months after leaving school isn't good. It happened to my course mate who went to Afghanistan, and after two weeks men died, which is just awful" (ITC31).

Second, the pre-mission training provides the basic skills needed for that specific mission. The training focuses directly on the objective and purpose of the mission to be accomplished. This training might also include international training periods where, for example, multinational staff procedures or multinational operational planning procedures were practiced. According to the informants, training consisted of vehicle training, convoys, medical training, stress management and the rules of engagement. Besides general weapon training, night fire drills, basic combat approaches, specific activities for countering IEDs, procedures in the event of mines, tactical procedures and drilling goals for the units prepared everyone adequately for the worst situations. Even though officers in crisis management missions maintain peace and try to work for and help the locals, they have to be prepared to operate in the most perilous situations possible, as well as be able to defend themselves.

"My last participation was in Afghanistan in 2010. Although there was a major change in the orientation of the mission, the training was perfectly standardized and organized, and well oriented to the mission" (SPO27).

However, some informants (M = 22) said that officer education and training was dominated by the idea of conventional warfare rather than asymmetric conflict. As one officer pointed out, "The basic training is not useful for asymmetric warfare missions" (ITB10). Most of the skills that officers learn in basic training are for the purposes of defending one's own country, but the missions were quite different from the usual role of a soldier: They can display their power but they do not use it in normal situations. Their role might be "More to talk to people, and not to wear your helmet and shield" (DKC20). The threat is also completely different. It could originate from civilian crowds in the form of blocking vehicles and stoning. But it could also stem from old explosives and mines. All of these have elements of military threats, but they are quite different from defending one's country.

In addition, asymmetry is a complex phenomenon. One officer crystallized it by saying, "The asymmetric environment continually creates new challenges and problems, for which the training is never enough" (ITB01). In asymmetric conditions, one needs to be able to combine theoretical knowledge with the mission, its context and situation. This gives a leader "A bigger 'frame' in which to use his knowledge" (DKC26), and at the same time apply that knowledge in new situations. Keeping this in mind, it is important that training is not too mechanistic and that it leaves room for adjustment (M = 3). Training should provide opportunities for adjustment because circumstances in the field are often so different from formal training, and leaders have to apply their knowledge and ways of working to new situations.

"Always when there is a situation they have a learned procedure according to which they react. It does not work perfectly in that you always do the same thing. First you have to think whether your actions might provoke the opposing side. That is something which leaders have to be taught, to construct mental images of different situations. That is the challenge of leadership training anywhere" (FIN14).

Experiences at the unit level

Officers' basic skills are often understood to be individual, but officers always operate as a part of a team (Table 3). A team may be for example a patrol consisting of a few people, a section, or a platoon. This may well be why informants (M = 11) considered unit-building to be a crucial aspect of basic training. Team-building consisted of being and practicing in, as well as overcoming, difficult situations together. In this way team members got to know one another and each other's strengths and weaknesses. This shaped their ability to work together and trust one another. The underlying aim is to amalgamate the various components so that officers can enter the theatre of operations as a cohesive unit and can then act efficiently in field operations. Team spirit is also important because it binds the troops together, particularly through difficult times. From the leaders' point of view, it is important that the team members know their leader and his way of working. At the same time, the leader gets to know his soldiers' competences and can take these into consideration when planning how to deploy them in the field.

"I would really strengthen the team-building phases to allow people to get to know each other better. It is crucial to be able to trust what the other person is doing. As each man is specialized in his own sphere, it is very important when engaged in a task that I'm assured that the area is covered by the expertise of my fellow soldier. If I know him, this gives me a lot more confidence in dealing with all kinds of activities" (ITC27).

"Of course what I would have wanted as platoon leader would have been more team-building exercises because there are different special training sessions at the beginning before the platoon is assembled as whole, and I get to practice things with them. Out of the three weeks that the company was being formed, there were only a few days when it was together in its entirety and we got to perform platoon exercises. That was something I would have liked more of so that I could get to know the men better before they head off to the location. I would be able to get acquainted with everyone's challenges and good sides beforehand, and I could take them into consideration better" (FIN16).

From the other perspective (M = 7), however, some said that they "Did not get to know each other before leaving" and "had no time for tactics and battle strategy" (FIN08). One leader said, "I would have wanted to train my company more freely. The exercises were very strictly planned beforehand" (FIN21). "For one, the training was inadequate because the pre-deployment should be conducted in a manner that simulates the mission as closely as possible" (ITC09), but he did not have the whole unit available that would work together in the field. Moreover, two leaders were of the opinion that the official basic training did not provide them with the tools they needed to handle everyday life in the unit.

"The preparation provided by educational institutions is inadequate in practical terms because it doesn't give the young officers the tools to face everyday life in the unit, both from the point of view of the management of a company, and operationally. We had to learn everything in the unit with the help of the company commander, or of older lieutenants" (ITC08).

Basic skills training was understood by the informants in the first instance as their professional battle and leadership skills. These comprise the general and universal military skills that every soldier is taught and gets to practice in the course of their military education and work, and which they should be able to perform in every context ([11], 3). These can also be defined as their routine skills because soldiers should be highly efficient and become habituated into using them in a stable, familiar and practiced environment [1, 2]. Secondly, the informants also highlighted the importance of unit-building so that teams become interoperable. The embedded social nature of their profession requires adaptation to team members' personal characteristics and competences, so that they do not need to negotiate existing practices in crisis situations; instead, they would be able to cooperate with others based on the known principles and choreographies [12]. This builds professional cohesion [4], which in turn increases predictability in crisis situations.

However, asymmetry as an operational context is complex. Informants highlighted two important issues related to it. On the one hand, basic training should leave room for adjustment or even for innovativeness so that leaders can demonstrate flexibility in handling a multitude of complex situations. On the other hand, they need to understand the grand scheme or big picture of the situated context in which they have to adjust their work and decisions. Overall, this reflects a gradual transition between routine and adaptive expertise [1], or between the modern and postmodern soldier [11], where the latter implies the ability to understand and handle uncommon, situated and contextualized challenges creatively.

2.3 Experiences of Specific Training

The analysis revealed three characteristics of the types of experiences related to specific training—Communication, collaboration and networking, Cultural awareness, as well as Mission-specific training (Table 4).

Communication, collaboration and networking training

Specific training was seen as being insufficient in general (M = 6), or too short (M = 3) in that more time would have been needed to prepare for the mission. But the informants were particularly satisfied (M = 35) with the exercises that prepared them

Table 4 Experiences of specific training received for missions

SPECIFIC TRAINING	Good/satisfactory	Partly satisfactory/insufficient
General		– General M = 6 – Too short training M = 3
		M = 9
Communication, collaboration and networking	– With locals M = 35 – With local army, police, multinational forces M = 17 – With local NGOs M = 3	
	M = 55	M = 11
Cultural awareness		– More information about culture M = 2
		M = 2
	M = 57	
Mission-specific	– General M = 25 – Task M = 12 – Area M = 11	– General M = 45 – Task M = 25 – Area M = 6 – Materiel M = 6
	M = 48	M = 82
No basic training N = 13 No specific training N = 27		
Total	M = 160	M = 104

M mentions, N numerus

for meeting, communicating and negotiating with the locals. In these exercises, they tried to simulate different situations, as well as practice basic vocabulary and the appropriate cultural etiquette. They also learned to stay calm under pressure and in extreme situations.

In order to communicate with the local people, mastery of languages becomes essential. In the data from the Philippines in particular, knowledge of local languages was considered of paramount importance. Officers might be placed in groups to learn Tagalog or Ilocano, for example, and a candidate could be assigned to an area which corresponded with a specific language. Pre-training is often too short a time to learn local languages such as Dari, however. Nonetheless, officers often learned the basics so that they could exchange greetings and pass the time of day in the local people's own language. These "opening words" helped them to start a conversation, which was usually appreciated. After this, they often transferred the dialogue to an interpreter or switched into English, if possible. This was not without its challenges, of course. As one officer aptly explained:

"We used interpreters, such as the X (nationality), who we spoke English to and who translated back and forth between languages. Their language skills were quite good but we always had to make sure our skills were good enough for the interpreter to understand. This was one of the most irritating aspects of the mission. For about three or four hours we would negotiate with an X (nationality) commander about anything and everything, and also just generally about football and such matters so as to get to know them. It was interesting to try and maintain eye contact and get to know another person while talking through an interpreter. I do feel that I got to know the X (nationality) commander through the interpreter, but it was challenging nonetheless. All the tea drinking and tobacco smoking and chit-chat is an important part of their culture. Rarely did we take notes on the discussions, but that was a question of language skills. Of course, the best thing would have been to have had an X (nationality) interpreter who could have spoken X (language) to us. There was always English in between" (FIN17).

The interpreters often doubled as cultural advisors, who helped officers to better understand what the locals were trying to explain, and to acquire a better cultural understanding of the situation. Communication through interpreters naturally depends on their availability as well as their language competence. If the interlocutors did not share a common language, then sometimes the only option was to use sign language.

"But we used interpreters with the locals, such as the security authorities, who were our collaboration partners and who did not speak any English, of course. Local interpreters were not always available, however, in which case we had to resort to primitive sign language. Dari basics would have been helpful then" (FIN02).

Hence, language skills are critical for officers' basic work. As one informant said, "The truth is that it is always difficult to communicate, to collect data and intelligence when you have language problems in operation areas" (CMRC30). But it is also necessary for leaders to relate to key figures and build a relationship with them. One platoon commander said that, "It makes you realize that as there is a cultural gap, you must firstly understand who you are going to relate to, and the culture of these people, and then try to establish a certain kind of relationship [...] maintain contact with the village chief" (ITC30). Establishing a relationship with key people is crucial because it is through them that leaders can extend their influence while trying to stabilize the situation in the mission area.

"I ask religious leaders, priests and imams for help on how best to express our concern and sincerity [...] I go to schools, small vendors in the marketplace, and the people directly to make them understand the importance of peace" (PHC17).

For leaders, specific training means adaptation to the local languages and collaboration. This enables them, firstly, to create trust and hence to communicate with local leaders in particular. Secondly, it helps them to gather information, to tackle and resolve local problems, and pay attention to the security concerns of the village. At the same time, they can convey their message—like the importance of peace—either directly or through the village elders to the locals. A leader should be "Someone that can be the battalion's face in linking up with partners and stakeholders, able to talk face-to-face with the mayor" (PHC2) and be aware of "How to present ourselves to the locals as soldiers in a peacekeeping area, namely how to adopt the all-important operational posture" (FIN09). This skill exerts a major influence on their ability to carry out the mission because asymmetry "is more about establishing relationships and language is the key" (PHC10). "The goal is to win hearts and minds" (PHC12).

In addition to cooperation with the local population, the respondents emphasized the importance of collaboration with the local security forces as well as with the multinational forces (M = 17). They are the actors with whom they have to communicate and collaborate on a daily basis. In joint multinational operations the reference language is English. As one officer put it, "Certainly the language is a fundamental aspect. At the level of platoon commander, not knowing at least basic English is really problematic because a number of assets (air support, MEDEVAC, etc.) are often provided by partners who are not Italian" (ICT31). At the battalion commander level, English is needed for planning and dealing with difficult scenarios. Apart from general or technical language skills, some informants reported that they also received training in how to work with militaries from different countries because they might adopt different military cultures when going about their daily business. Only three informants claimed to have practiced how to conduct joint operations with governmental and international agencies.

"We Nordic countries think we can work together, and often do so, and it was even easy to work with the Croats and Serbs in former Yugoslavia. However, I had soldiers from seven different cultures/nations and I had to handle them differently due to their specific discipline, language, norms, and so on" (DKC22).

Communication, collaboration and even networking skills seem to be vital for leaders. For this reason, some leaders (M = 11) were slightly dissatisfied with the communication training. Leaders have to adapt to joint, multinational and multicultural collaboration in which languages play an essential role. Leaders have to appreciate and be in active cooperation with key actor groups in particular—locals, local security forces and multinational joint military communities—and to establish an operative network with them. This reflects a broader understanding of the operational environment ([11], 14).

Cultural awareness-specific training

Cultural awareness training was one of the most important aspects of specific training, which the leaders appreciated and found beneficial ($M = 57$). Two respondents would have preferred to have even more training of this type. Among other things, it included the operational area's (cultural) history, socio-political situation, geopolitical environment, juridical system, religions, governance, demographics, ethnic groups and their tensions, local flora and fauna, as well as gender issues. In the data from the Philippines in particular, the subjects to be taught were broader, embracing such topics as seasonal preparation for disaster, corruption, wildlife preservation, election laws, their review and monitoring, peace-building, and public and civil affairs. Moreover, training usually dealt with everyday life, such as getting accustomed to local time-keeping behaviors, and tips on how to meet and interact with the local people. The leaders were given lectures on cultural knowledge and behaviour by professionals and experts who had lived in the mission area. They also received handbooks, guidelines and other supplementary materials as well as lists of important references and online resources for studying the subject independently. In particular, role-playing based on real cases was evaluated as being a good way to learn. However, this type of training was also considered to be "insufficient; it was a starting point that we then tried to complete in the field" (ITC17).

"During the first week of rotation training, we were taught the necessary skills when meeting local leaders: When we meet a local, how should we handle the general arrangements? How to secure the area, how to be seated, how to use an interpreter, establish eye contact? Related to that, we talked a lot about the cultural side. We learned the basics of the culture and scenarios for different meetings which had cultural considerations, such as a female participant. We practiced the special features" (FIN19).

From the leaders' point of view, this knowledge is essential because "You cannot arrive at a new scene without knowing the social, religious and cultural reality. That opens doors and helps you avoid misunderstandings, which could have implications for the mission" (SPO23). This cultural knowledge helped the leaders to obtain a reasonable picture of the local situation and to understand the socio-cultural environment in which they would operate. It improved their knowledge and capability about how to behave, how to respect local customs like certain religious practices, and to be sensitive towards dos and don'ts. This cultural sensitivity helped the officers to avoid mistakes which would otherwise have the potential to undo all their civil-military efforts.

"Your action could result in the breakdown of the peace process. You can potentially be a peace spoiler if your actions are misinterpreted. We are very cautious in that regard […] We don't want to violate anything" (PHC21).

Adaptation means learning to take on board cultural as well as contextual and situational knowledge and to be prepared to act and work accordingly. From the leadership point of view, this means that when equipped with cultural knowledge, leaders should be able to make sense of small incidents and avoid provocation with their behaviour. But from a broader perspective, cultural knowledge allows leaders to understand the big picture from different angles. In this sense, both communication and cultural know-how enable leaders to increase their operability and achieve their operational goals [11].

Mission-specific training

For the mission in general

Of paramount importance when it comes to education in general is its suitability and relevance for the mission and the way it enables leaders to fulfil their duties. Training should "correspond to the tasks and meet mission requirements" (BRG16), as in most cases it did (M = 25). In some cases, the training was viewed as slightly inadequate, however, because it did not reflect the needs in the mission area. In other words, the training had not been in sync with the mission, and it did not give the trainees the know-how they would have needed in missions (M = 45). Four reasons were given by the informants for this shortcoming. First, the training "was common sense we could figure out ourselves" (DKC05), or it was too theoretical. In the latter case, the informants found it challenging to integrate the things they had learned into the concrete situations. For example, one officer stated that "Getting the locals on your side was the solution. But I don't know the means by which this can be achieved. I would have maybe needed training for that" (FIN02). Second, the sessions focused on the last mission and not on the mission they had to face. This meant that "their knowledge reflected the past and did not correspond to the real situation" (BRG31). In other words, the knowledge was outdated and people could not make use of it at the operational level of the mission (SPO13). Third, "Due to a lack of information, they were not able to draw up an adequate training agenda" (BRG48). This was particularly visible when a mission was new and there was no real-time information about either the mission or its tasks, or "when a mission got underway in a new setting, and the preparation didn't reflect the new theatre of operations accurately" (SPO09). Fourth, sometimes the mission tasks were much broader than the preparation. One officer said that, "For example, in Kosovo, I found myself having to deal with police dog units, managing private contractors in Iraq, and having to collaborate with armored army units elsewhere; and I had to learn everything on the ground" (ITB02). In any event, "when the training organization gains information from the previous contingents about what they have experienced during the mission, they can better adapt the programs to the mission and its objectives" (SPO23).

Task-specific training

However, it is more important for leaders to receive training according to their role, task and/or rank (M = 12). At first, they usually received the same training as everyone else, but the training was subsequently differentiated according to team, platoon and company levels. Battalion commanders might have had more freedom to tailor their training specifically to their own needs. For example, one commander described his training in the following way:

"Apart from the five-week rotation training period, which was compulsory for everybody and which I as their commander took part in about 80% of the time, I also got to know about leaving for the operation well in advance, so I took part in a civilian crisis management course in X (city), which focused on the so-called comprehensive approach, which took the civilian actors in the area into consideration. I also attended a one-week commander's course in X (country), which focused on commanding and leadership matters and the Islamic culture. In X (country), I took part in the NATO School's ISAF operation course, which also lasted for a week. The three courses plus the rotation training formed the homeland part, and then there was one week for the changeover between commanders, which can be seen as training on location" (FIN12).

One issue which raised concerns was that the training was not tailored to an officer's forthcoming position (M = 25). In such cases, the training was deemed to be too general. In a few cases there was no qualified person to conduct specialized training or to relay experiences from the field. In such cases, the knowledge for their special positions was acquired by studying the subjects independently, by taking online courses, or by gaining it through hands-on tasks. Capitalizing on the experiences of previous commanders and leaders was considered to be particularly useful.

"If we are going to be doing CMO (Civil-Military Operations), it will be difficult because the training we receive is not for that specifically" (PHC14).

"Personally, I didn't receive specialized training for my position. I was the first one to go there so I had to learn on the move. I had to accomplish tasks at the same time as I was learning how to do them" (BRG3).

"Training had not yet been defined for battalion commanders at that time, only for soldiers. So I had no training before deployment. It was only with the deployment of PRT 3 that commanders, officers and soldiers started to be trained systematically. Officers who came before or with me did not have any basic training either" (LTC04).

Area and materiel-specific training

Training should also correspond to the mission area (M = 11). This could entail proper acclimatization to the climate (ITC18) or getting used to living and working at a high altitude (ITC14), as well as in the desert (ITC32). But it also implies that leaders need to familiarize themselves with the area and "imitate the performance of tasks with real vehicles in the real terrain" (BRG8), in order to be able to "start the mission tasks without any difficulties" (BRG7). However, in some cases (M = 6), the officers could not train with identical equipment because they had a shortage of materiel, or they received the materiel so late that training was almost non-existent. In the same way, training was not always customized to the area or environment where the officers would be assigned (M = 6). As one officer pointed out, "we were trained to live in the desert, but had to operate in the city" (DKC22). Another officer reported that "They practiced IED disposal in no inhabited areas, without any traffic or people. However, it turned out that when they needed to do it in practice in Kabul with huge crowds and traffic jams, the training procedures were impossible to follow" (BGR57). This naturally reduced the quality of the training because it did not support officers' capabilities to fulfil their tasks.

In the case of mission-related and special leadership tasks, as well as area and material-specific know-how, adaptation means that training should be adapted specifically to these issues. However, it seems that more needs to be done to link theoretical pre-deployment training with the practical work environment and its corresponding tasks. Moreover, this reflects leaders' efforts to extend their skills in order to prepare and adapt to changing and transforming professional practices.

No basic or specific training

Some of the leaders did not receive any basic (N = 13) or specific training (N = 27). These respondents can be divided into three groups. One group thought that they did not need such training because they were involved in a local operation, or because they had received that knowledge during their basic military education and career in different work positions. In only two cases were individuals ordered to take up posts at the last moment, and so they did not receive any training for the mission. Be that as it may, they all received training in the mission area through observation, through sharing experiences with the previous commander, or just "trying to adjust" (PHC01) and using their common sense.

2.4   Conclusions and Discussion

This chapter has examined military leaders' perceptions of how the education and training they received prepared them to become adaptive experts for crisis management environments. The results indicate, firstly, that education and training were quite highly valued by the military leaders. However, there were some country-specific features in both the basic and the specific training that was received. These could be discussed in each country, and the available quality standards could be of great benefit in developing military education. Second, when it comes to special mission and leadership tasks, as well as area- and materiel-specific know-how, it seems that more needs to be done to establish deeper connections between the theoretical pre-deployment training and the operational environment [13]. At present, too many leaders found that they were unable to transfer the know-how imparted in mission-oriented special training to their work in a crisis management environment. Third, the gap between training and mission was particularly wide when a mission was new and there seemed to be neither enough information about the mission nor experienced experts who could have supervised the new leaders. Fourth, leaders would have liked to receive more training tailored specifically to their unique tasks. Finally, more experienced and competent leaders, as well as training on the real crisis management environment, appear to play a crucial role in developing adaptive expertise. This could be developed further by creating a cognizant pedagogical practice that could be planned as part of the official training curriculum [14, 15].

On developing adaptive expertise through education and training

Nevertheless, the leaders also emphasized the traditional individual and unit characteristics [11] as important dimensions of adaptive expertise. These skills cover the basic expert routines and are adapted by practicing the specific requirements of the mission. In this context, adaptation means that everyone provides one's expertise for the benefit of others in the mission context. However, cultural awareness as well as communication, collaboration and networking with different key actors emerge from the interviews as being characteristics of the utmost importance for leaders' work. Leaders should be communicatively and culturally savvy to adapt and use this soft power in different practices to win the hearts and minds of local people (cf. [16]). For this reason, cultural understanding and the requisite skills to communicate and negotiate for operative purposes should be embedded in the military education system and developed as a career-long process ([17], 135–136).

Developing adaptive leadership through education calls for increased integration of professional and scientific knowledge of asymmetry and leadership's role in that context. This extensive and integrated knowledge base would help leaders to build the mental models that they need in order to be flexible in novel and complex situations. These mental models could be enhanced by practicing realistic and complex cases that include many multidisciplinary conflicting elements [3, 8]. In the same way, real emergent crisis experiences can be used to help to reflect and define one's own leadership in new terms. Emergent and successful experiences can provide good opportunities to reflect on, share and abstract one's leadership and action models, and help to build flexibility with others [18, 19].

On military leadership in the crisis management context

In the light of these findings, three further implications for understanding military leadership arose. First, along with the psychological and cognitive view, a communicative perspective on leadership [20] seems to be important in crisis management environments. Leaders build up relationships and create networks with key local leaders [21]. Via this network, they can disseminate information about their role and task and win over the hearts and minds of the locals. To succeed at this, leaders need languages and cultural understanding to make sense of the situations and convey their meanings. This brings us to the second point, namely how leadership is distributed [22]. The key local leaders become strong co-leaders because, as religious and spiritual individuals, they are in a powerful position to influence the local people. Finally, the results indicate that leadership occurs as a practice [23]. Meetings with key leaders are day-to-day experiences in which participants jointly negotiate to achieve an outcome. They try to coordinate their activities with one another and to advance their organizational or individual aims. This view of leadership-as-practice directs attention away from individual abilities towards micro-level everyday actions and interactions.

References

1. Hatano G, Inagaki K (1986) Two courses of expertise. In: Stevenson H, Azuma H, Hakuta K (eds) Child development and education in Japan. W. H. Freeman, New York, pp 262–272
2. Pierrakos O, Anderson RD, Welch CA (2016) Measuring adaptive expertise in engineering education. Paper presented at 2016 ASEE Annual Conference & Exposition. Louisiana, New Orleans
3. Bohle Carbonell K, Stalmeijer RE, Könings KD, Segers M, van Merriënboer JJG (2014) How experts deal with novel situations: a review of adaptive expertise. Educ Res Rev 12:14–29
4. King A (2015b) The future of cohesion. In: King A (ed) Frontline. Combat and cohesion in the twenty-first century. Oxford University Press, Oxford, pp 309–323
5. McKenna AF (2014) Adaptive expertise and knowledge fluency in design and innovation. In: Johri A, Olds BM (eds) Cambridge handbook of engineering education research. Cambridge University Press, Cambridge, pp 227–242
6. VanLehn K, Chi M (2012) Adaptive expertise as acceleration of future learning. In: Durlach PJ, Lesgold A (eds) Adaptive technologies for training and education. Cambridge University Press, Cambridge, pp 28–45
7. Hoffman RR, Ward P, Feltovich PJ, DiBello L, Fiore SM, Andrews DH (2014) Accelerated expertise. Training for high proficiency in a complex world. Tailor & Francis, New York & London
8. Bohle Carbonell K, Könings KD, Segers M, van Merriënboer JJG (2015) Measuring adaptive expertise: development and validation of an instrument. Eur J Work Organ Psychol 25(2):167–180
9. Mustonen V, Hakkarainen K (2015) Tracing two apprentices' trajectories toward adaptive professional expertise in fingerprint examination. Vocat Learn 8:185–211
10. Murray W (2011) Military adaptation in war. With fear of change. Cambridge University Press, Cambridge
11. Sookermany A (2012) What is a skillful soldier? An epistemological foundation for understanding military skill acquisition in (post)modernized armed forces. Armed Forces Soc 38(4):582–603
12. King A (2015a) On cohesion. In: King A (ed) Frontline. Combat and cohesion in the twenty-first century. Oxford University Press, Oxford, pp 3–23
13. Hytönen K, Palonen T, Lehtinen E, Hakkarainen K (2016) Between the two advisors: interconnecting academic and workplace settings in an emerging field. Vocat Learn 9:333–359
14. Billett S (2001) Co-participation: affordance and engagement at work. In: Fenwick T (ed) Sociocultural perspectives on learning through work. Jossey-Bass, San Francisco, pp 63–72
15. Billett S (2004) Learning through work: workplace participatory practices. In: Rainbird H, Fuller A, Munro A (eds) Workplace learning in context. Routledge, London, New York, pp 109–125
16. Ragies IA (2017) Formulating public diplomacy on PKOs. Paper presented 29.6.2017 at the 14th ERGOMAS-conference. Athens, Greece
17. Durán Cenit M (2013) Training and military education in asymmetric warfare. In: Gaforio G (ed) Soldiers without frontiers: the view from the ground. Experiences of asymmetric warfare. Bonanno, Rome, pp 121–139
18. Allen N, Keyes DC (2012) Leader development in dynamic and hazardous environments: company commander learning through combat. In: Mc Kee A, Eraut M (eds) Learning trajectories, innovation and identity for professional development. Innovation and change in Professional Education 7. Springer, London, New York, pp 93–111
19. Keyes DC, Allen N, Self N (2012) Integrating learning, leadership, and crisis in management education: lessons from the army officers in Iraq and Afghanistan. J Manage Educ 37(2):180–202
20. Fairhurst GT, Connaughton SL (2014) Leadership: a communicative perspective. Leadership 10(1):7–35

21. Knoke D (2013) "It takes a network": the rise and fall of social network analysis in U.S. Army counterinsurgency doctrine. Connections 33(1):1–10
22. Bolden R (2011) Distributed leadership in organizations: a review of theory and research. Int J Manag Rev 13:251–269
23. Raelin JA (2016) Introduction to leadership-as-practice. Theory and application. In: Raelin JA (ed) Leadership-as-practice. Theory and application. Routledge, New York & London, pp 1–17

Military Interaction with Local Actors

Marién Durán and Adolfo Calatrava

Abstract The relationship between soldiers and local actors is key to the successful development of Peacekeeping Operations (PKO). In the last decade, an emphasis has been placed on these actors mainly local authorities, populations and NGOs-acceptance of the international missions in order to ensure greater effectiveness. Thus, the purpose of this study is to explore military actions in PKO from a micro-level, focusing on the multiple forms of interaction with those local actors from the point of view of the PKO officers. The most important conclusion drawn is, to these officers, relationships were mainly positive; which in turn provides more information on two important issues: it is possible that positive perceptions add trust to international missions and it shows a general acknowledgement of the army's leadership role and its empathy towards local populations.

1 Introduction

Contemporary conflicts and Peacekeeping Operations are characterized by interaction of a wide variety of local and international actors who must be considered for the development and success of the mission: local populations, local Armed Forces, local authorities, international troops, International Organizations, local and international NGOs, political and army advisers, journalists and private companies [1–7]. The choice of local partners is critical when it comes to stabilization and peace-building operations [8, pp. 333–341, 9]. This shows the return of the local, specifically the importance of the local ownership in recent times [10].

M. Durán (✉) · A. Calatrava
University of Granada, Granada, Spain
e-mail: mduranc@ugr.es

Complutense University of Madrid, Madrid, Spain

A. Calatrava
e-mail: acalatrava@ucm.es

© Springer Nature Switzerland AG 2021
M. Nuciari and E. Olivetta (eds.), *Leaders for Tomorrow: Challenges for Military Leadership in the Age of Asymmetric Warfare*, Advanced Sciences and Technologies for Security Applications, https://doi.org/10.1007/978-3-030-71714-8_5

The significance of focusing work at the micro level, underlies how local intercultural relations and international interactions shape daily practice in Peace Operations [11, 12, p. 2]. The relational effort on all sides is also remarkable and the prioritization of relationships has enhanced the intercultural sensitivity needed to build trust. The conduct of the peacekeepers at local level can be a key factor to explain the success or failure of the operation.

This fact has driven armies to increase and maintain relationships within their context and to build up solid social skills to conduct Peace Support Operations, deepening the doctrine of civilian-military relations in Peacekeeping Operations. Different factors such as familiarity, leadership, empathy, understanding, cultural awareness, gender awareness and cultural competence, are essentials for the army to prevent conflict situations. It is precisely what we call "don't touch without an advisor" [1, 13].

In order to study these interactions in the relationship between local actors and the army during Peacekeeping Operations, we analyzed the results of interviews, carried out to officers of these missions. This analysis would also serve to extract data on the army's perception in complex situations, a micro-analysis of operations. The study analyzed the interactions between different army contingents and local societies, which comprise the following three groups of actors: (i) local authorities, (ii) local population and (iii) local NGOs. The countries included in the study were: Spain, Italy, Denmark, Lithuania, Bulgaria and Finland. The results show two main issues: (i) how international actors (in our case, the military mission) and local actors are linked in multiple forms of interaction that help in building trust [12] and (ii) a general acknowledgement of the army's leadership role and its empathy towards local populations.

On this basis, the results obtained were categorized into the following sections. Firstly, a theoretical outline is given of the relationships of soldiers from the different countries that comprise the Peace Operation or international mission, including the different doctrinal developments and instruments of those armies, and any other theoretical aspects that should be considered. The purpose of this is to define the context within which the relationships under study occur. Secondly, relationships with the principal local actors with whom the army interacts are analyzed: local authorities, local populations and NGOs. Finally, the conclusions drawn are used to answer these questions, focusing on two key aspects: building trust and changes in leadership.

2 Local Actors and the Mission: A Theoretical Approach

The significance, consideration, complexity and even theoretical treatment of issues related to the relationship of soldiers participating in international missions with local and non-state actors such as NGOs, began to emerge during the nineties and has continued to grow since then. In the last decade, it has even been more notorious. It entailed new tasks in the field of civil governance known as the ancillary tasks, consisting of: strengthening the legitimacy of institutions, monitoring elections, demobilizing and reintegrating combatants, building up its security sector, promoting economy, managing the territories and even engaging on diplomacy tasks. To do so, it required an arduous effort of adaption for militaries, in order to perform properly a set of unknown and unusual tasks up to those days. It also required a great effort of adjustment to interact with other actors which were already familiar with these sectors in the field. In consequence, as Mitchell notes, citing from the work by Beatrice Pouligny, the success of Peace Support Operations becomes even more complicated when we analyze it from a micro perspective and perceptions level, from the analysis and perceptions of the soldiers interacting with local societies and from the perceptions of local actors [9, 11].

However, despite the complications, there are facilitators in coordination such as socialization, deformalization and flexibility that improve civil-military coordination. For the military, it is essential to build relationships of trust with local personnel. These can be built through continuous personal contact thanks to a variety of activities. These processes imply to establish relationships through networks, improve the perceptions, develop empathy [14] and build trust between actors. Specifically, when the actors of international operations are interrelated, an extensive network of agreements and transnational contacts is interwoven between civilians and militaries which can alter the way we perceive each other [15, p. 73] and might even open opportunity windows for future collaborations.

Recent studies have also explored this situation and found that some armies tend to give more importance to auxiliary tasks, as it helps to build relationships of trust with local communities [16]. This entails hard work that results in the creation of multiple forms of interaction and numerous actors with whom to interact. The multiple forms of interaction refer to the points of connection, meeting, liaison, concurrence, appointment, agreement and conciliation between people from different institutions working in the same context of operations.

It is certain that when a mission of this kind is being planned, the natural or appropriate local interlocutors must be found. These would usually be local authorities, as well as religious leaders who we will include as local authorities because of the role they play as intermediaries and their use in mobilization and as political allies [6, p. 115, 8, p. 350]. However, there are many more actors: local populations, civil (mayors, governors) and religious authorities, teachers, NGOs, businessmen and representatives of minorities, among others, that the Peace Force must manage and lead within convulsive, changing and, therefore, highly complex contexts. Because the Peacekeeping could be perceived as a colonizing power or imperialistic policing [17], exceptional leadership under these circumstances is required to ensure those perceptions are redirected to facilitate relationships with local entities.

Considering local perspective and needs is not always an easy task, quite the contrary. Factors such as familiarity, empathy, understanding, awareness and cultural competence are fundamental, to such an extent that it is currently believed cultural awareness should be integrated into military education [18, p. 664]. Peace Operations require peacekeepers maintain intense interaction with civilians, that can lead to creation of formal and informal networks, negotiation skills and persuasion, acquisition of skills in conflict management, transparency in action and even work with potential adversaries [17, p. 462].

Local actors, and essentially local populations, often comprise Peacekeeping Operations' Center of Gravity (CoG). Thus, "winning locals' hearts and minds" is crucial for the success of the mission. This would result in the army being involved in projects and activities of a social nature, psychological operations and would allow them to use "minimum force", which is usual in Peacekeeping Operations [19, pp. 358–359]. Relationships with the environment are so crucial to security that both the North Atlantic Treaty Organization (NATO) and the United Nations (UN) carry out a doctrinal development that includes concepts such as CIMIC (Civil-military cooperation), a Comprehensive Approach and Comprehensive Missions. They have also been concerned with training and education in cultural and gender issues [20, 21]. Indeed, it has been actual experiences in international missions that have provided the feed-back on what needs must be addressed. The Spanish and Danish armies, among others, have highlighted the need for cultural awareness and to dedicate time to building relationships with local actors.

The ultimate objective of all those tasks should be to get *local legitimacy*, a success factor in peacekeeping. This legitimacy "empowers peacekeepers because it provides reasons for local actors to comply and cooperate" [22, p. 312]. What's more, these operations' stabilization and reconstruction objectives have involved in prolonging the missions for years, and even in some cases by longer than a decade. On the one hand, this has allowed those armies to gain experience in human relations and in scholarly studies in this area.[1] On the other, it has shown that for support to consolidate, the demands of society must be addressed permanently, through a better knowledge of those demands and its needs. Contemporary wars are closely aligned with winning the war of beliefs and perceptions and local legitimacy. It is fought in the population's environment and the results are determined by the perceptions and support those people give. Therefore, the narratives used are also fundamental.

In this sense, military forces must have the appropriate instruments, both theoretical and practical, to be able to manage diverse situations in daily interaction with local communities, i.e. specific tools that provide them with sufficient cultural awareness, understanding and competence to predict reactions and prevent possible conflicts, and to establish the most appropriate and positive relationships possible. For this the army requires support and advice. Having trained and experienced staff allows for a more professional assessment of the danger and better identification of cultural divides. Armies address this requirement by enlisting Gender Advisers—used by both NATO and the United Nations; Cultural Advisers (CULAD)—used by the Marines and the British and Australian Armies and Human Terrain Teams (HTT)

---

[1] Evidence of this can be found in the variety of studies carried out on Peacekeeping Operations and the Armed Forces and society. Academic journals such as *International Peacekeeping, Armed Forces and Society, Small Wars and Insurgencies* or *Security Dialogue* and studies carried out by a variety of research groups dedicated to these issues are clear examples of the interest in this area. It is even considered that civilian-military relationships in international missions can have an impact on domestic civilian-military relationships.

(multidisciplinary social sciences human resources teams)—used by the US Army for their mission in Afghanistan. The latter ceased to exist in 2014.

Nonetheless, and considering the variety and diversity of the advice teams that has emerged over the last decade, what is common to all armies are the units/sections in the Civil Affairs/Civil military cooperation groups (CIMIC). These units constitute the principal interface between the mission and local societies; they have the most experience in this area and take the pulse of the state of the relationships with these communities. The CIMIC doctrine has developed over the last few decades within the framework of relations with civilian populations. CIMIC serves as a function and a resource for the armies that are operating in conflict situations [23]. Thus, CIMIC serves three purposes: (a) force support, (b) Civilian-military liaison to coordinate planning and (c) assistance and support to the civilian populations (expertise, information, infrastructures, safety, capacity-building, etc.). As a resource, CIMIC is manifest in the training that soldiers received (NATO 2013).[2] The mission of CIMIC soldiers is to be in contact with the local context, maintain cordial relations with the local population, and ensure that this work is reflected through order and security in the mission. Their activities are very diverse: from carrying out Quick Impact Projects (mainly infrastructure or certain one-off humanitarian aid tasks) that influence the economy and project a positive image of the Peace Operation mission, to boosting the prestige of local leaders, or maintaining contact through coordinated meetings with local actors. Therefore, they are required to have significant knowledge of geography, language, religion, culture, ethnic composition, economics, politics, and more salient social problems, such as issues of displaced persons [24, p. 11].

Consequently, another important activity in this area is that of Key Leader Engagement. The contact with key leaders, in the political, military, intellectual, religious or social sphere, is considered essential to ensuring messages reach to those key figures. It is an essential tool, since the mission relies on an officer to manage contact with key actors. Thus, it is also vital that all key actors and their inter-relationships are identified. Having detailed knowledge of key leaders' personalities, leadership styles, ambitions, motivations, objectives (short and long term), current stances, dependencies, psychological profiles and personal histories will be essential to provide the context to plan appropriate information activities.

However, managing these relationships on the ground is significantly complicated. This is why, the leadership capacity of army leaders is such a significant variable. Officers and the rest of the army are expected to fulfill a wide range of functions: security, logistic, humanitarian aid, providing assistance to local authorities, with a series of required skills: knowledge of the local geography, local culture, protocols and customs, economy, politics, social relations, local languages, etc. [25]. This implies that military should be trained in soft skills of communications, gender awareness and cultural awareness [3]. Of all of them, especially that of managing human relationships, requires a great capacity for leadership. Field research has shown how army leaders are able to manage relationships with actors as diverse

---

[2]NATO, 2013, Allied Joint Doctrine for Civil-Military Cooperation AJP-3.4.9 Edition A, Version 1 (Ratification Draft).

as authorities, teachers, religious and political leaders, local entrepreneurs, anonymous citizens and NGO workers while also receiving a positive assessment from them. But also, different research and the experience has shown how actions by non-commissioned officers and troops, in what is known as the "strategic corporal" [26, 27], also count. The need for a soldier to fulfill multiple functions has created the "hybrid warrior" figure, who, in addition to traditional army training must also receive sufficient training in social sciences and humanities to understand and interpret cultural differences and to prevent cultural clashes when carrying out interviews and local contacts.

In any case, the degree of knowledge of cultural issues within the scale of command, levels of responsibility or positions within the General Staff, is variable. While for a soldier, it may be sufficient to know how to avoid misunderstandings or offensive behaviour towards the population, for an officer it will be necessary to have additional and deeper knowledge, such as knowing how to act correctly with key local leaders (KLE, Key Leaders Engagement) or how to incorporate cultural factors in the decision processes.

Cultural understanding implies a more advanced level or step in cultural knowledge. This level of analysis leads us to understand cultural dynamics, cause-effect relationships, changes and the study of potential consequences of actions resulting from decisions made by the head of the Force in a given context. This level could be more reserved for the members of CIMIC (higher education) or Key Leader Engagement and mission chief. Therefore, the experience showed that there was enough room for an adaptive process to take place, which implied some changes in actors' practices, in spite of having diametrically opposed speeches, principles and values, world perceptions, cultural and historical frameworks, and identities.

3 Local Actors and Soldiers in Interaction

An analysis of the relationship between the army and local civilian actors throws light on interesting points which we have categorized into three sections: first, the importance of the relationships in each context and the multiple forms of interaction; second, in what areas should the army coincide, interact or coordinate with local actors; and finally the results emerging from a qualitative analysis of the interviews, where the most relevant issues are highlighted. But while the points or areas of agreement in each case for each actor are crucial or almost determinants when identifying how relationships develop, we cannot forget two other variables that are common to relationships with Local Authorities, Local communities and Non-Governmental Organizations: (i) the nature of the mission and the duties and mandate of the officers involved and (ii) the country or region the mission is being carried out. The missions carried out in Afghanistan in the initial years, or even today, are very different from the one being carried out in Lebanon (UNIFIL) since 2010.

a.   Soldiers and the Local Authorities

Relations with Local Authorities are key to success in the Operating Theatre. In the conducted interviews, the relationship develops on a tactical level, usually with majors, governors, district governors or religious leaders. Enjoying accessible and hospitable relationships with these authorities results in a secure mission. These relations influence a key issue, information: access to information sources, information exchange and knowledge of the local populations' everyday problems. Many of the basic and vital activities must be coordinated with them: (a) Humanitarian Aid; (b) infrastructure reconstruction i.e. hospitals, schools, power grids, public roads and water supply; (c) ceremonies, community events, or others acts; (d) basic services; (e) veterinary, agricultural, engineering and medical services; (f) training programs, languages courses. All of this shows that there are many forms of interactions. In addition, these relations are a very important source of networking for building trust for the whole mission, both for the military and civilian structure. As a result, these interactions have become the norm, and involve small steps which each gain trust for the mission and a better perception.

The results of the interview analysis shed light on three significative elements: (1) identifying the local authorities to contact is important; (2) there is a high percentage of relations with Local Authorities; and finally (3) the assessment of relations is mostly positive, although there are some nuances we will detail further below. We can classify the relationships as: positive because they are polite and enriching and positive because they allow military to detect threats.

We also find some differences between the intensity of the relationships and the authorities with whom the officers interact. It is important to note that the aforementioned general norms must be followed: the relationships with local actors depend on the nature of the mission and the place where it takes place. Beyond these two considerations, the interviews have allowed us to identify that in the missions in Lebanon and Bosnia, contacts with the local authorities were more intense and broader, and included actors in defense groups and the police (in some Lebanese towns, also with religious leaders).

Firstly, an issue that the soldiers emphasize is the correct identification of the authorities they must interact with: "(Lebanon Local Authorities) varied a lot, not only according to religion but also for more specific aspects. Sometimes the mayors of the villages do not live in the village itself" (FIN07). "(Afghanistan) (…) There are so many interested parties, such a tribe elders, warlords, among others (…)" (LIT04). "(Afghanistan) There was a constant turnover: police commander, governors …, they changed regularly. We didn't always have the same partner (…) They were there for a short period to build strong relations (…)" (ITC27). This multiplicity of actors sometimes hinders becoming familiar with local authorities and, especially hinders achieving the stated objectives of the relationship. We must remember that most officers believe that local authorities are driven by a very simple interest: all of them expect to take advantage of their relationship with the army, either for personal reasons or for the community. In the words of a Lithuanian officer "what you give, we take" (LIT03). In one way or another, this situation is always present in the interviews carried out by all armies and can be seen in the different missions to some extent, whether "all of them expect small gifts" (BGR13), referring to Afghanistan or "we had a constructive cooperation with sheiks, teachers and others officers to reconstruct schools, canals, playgrounds and infrastructure" (BGR15), referring to Iraq.

Relationships with local authorities are normally formal and professional, which in many cases emphasize the need to follow cultural guidelines: "(Afghanistan) We had meals with the locals, sometime the food did not taste good, but you had to eat it if you wanted to be welcomed back again" (FIN04); "Good, the relationship was good, normally when one arrives on a mission or is deployed to the area, during the first few days the logical thing is to present yourself to the authorities in your OZ [Operations Zone] and introduce yourself, so that they know you, I am the new boss of …, and you tell them a little bit your position, what the relationship will consist of, they know it by heart because for them it is one face after another, they know our relief structure and know you are relieving someone (…)." (SP16). Although a high percentage of officers in Afghanistan also indicate having maintained different contacts, they have been more infrequent or intense than they were in previous missions. The presence of religious leaders and elders within the consideration of local authorities in these last missions are worth mentioning. There is less information about Iraq or Kosovo than other missions. In any case, as we will also see what happens with the other actors, a relationship with local authorities should be strengthened, especially at the beginning of the mission: "(Lebanon) it was harder to meet the civilian authorities of the villages or the religious leaders, especially at the beginning. Finally, it worked" (FIN09).

Generally speaking, as mentioned above, the officers said that relations with the Local authorities were basically positive and cordial. Although there were some negative aspects and some difficult elements due to divergent interests, parasitism (in reference to the dependency of the mission and its projects), cultural clashes, and even fear. Starting from the last one, the Italian officers point out several times the reluctance of Local Authorities in Afghanistan to have close relations with the mission because they were afraid of retaliation from Taliban: "We had relations with the local populations, in particular with village leaders. The attitude was very positive in some areas, in others they avoided us because of fear of retaliation: there was an awareness that sooner or later we would leave, and they would be alone left alone" (ITB06); "(…) there was often the fear of retaliation by the insurgents (…)" (ITC10).

There have been only a few caveats to this positive assessment: certain cultural clashes during interviews with Lithuanian officers in Afghanistan and, to a lesser extent, Finnish officers in Lebanon. Although communication with local authorities was good, at the initial stages, "there were cultural clashes in communications (…), it is very hard to gain their trust. In a way they still live in the medieval ages" (LTC04). The Finns had little contact with local authorities in Afghanistan, but in Lebanon it was easier to deal with the authorities from Christian populations than Muslims ones (FIN09), also indicating that cultural factors were essential to this type of interaction (FIN07 and FIN05).

Although in general, relations with local authorities were considered proper, there was a difference of perspective between the officers of different armies. The most optimistic of these relations were the Bulgarians, who almost unanimously considered these relationships to be positive (obviously when the officer had contacts with a local authority), regardless of the context of the mission: whether Afghanistan, Iraq, Kosovo or Bosnia.[3] Italian officers also assessed their relationship positively, although they gave detailed information on a more complicated episode, specifically in Afghanistan, regarding fear of retaliation by the Taliban. In any case, they express that these relationships should be positive: "with local authorities, however, the goal was to show that we still recognized their authority as leaders and keep a respectful attitude towards them, that ranged from turn-taking in dialogue, talking to one person rather than another, giving them the weight that they were expected to have, etc." (ITC31). A similar opinion is offered by a Spanish officer: "Yes, it has always been appropriate with mayors, police chiefs, etc., to maintain the same conditions that you try to with the local population: respect and politeness" (SP35). Spanish officers have a quite positive approach to these relationships, although there are criticisms in both directions, mainly arising from cultural differences and suspicions related to insurgency and information (especially in the case of Afghanistan): "It is a complex relation, always based on respect and politeness, but often with mismatched interests." (SP27). For the Finns, relationships were positive, but in some cases, they highlighted the aforementioned cultural clash (especially on the mission in Lebanon). For their part, the Danes do not make many valuable references to relationships with local authorities. They acknowledge that more time should be devoted to fostering relationships with key local actors in the case of Afghanistan (DKC07); and that it is common for interactions to be cordial when there are benefits: "We had a good relationship with authorities and the population thanks to a medical clinic that opened" (DKC11). The Lithuanians are possibly the most critical officers, not because they do not consider relationships to be good, but because of local authorities' attitudes: "Good relationship, constructive. They were constantly asking for something and if we were not able to supply it, they complained. We had cultural differences (they understand promises differently, after the promises were kept on our side, they would try to renegotiate before fulfilling their side) (…)" (LIT01). It should be noted that Lithuanian officers' comments refer exclusively to Afghanistan.

Definitely, contacts with local authorities are considered very important for the mission and for this reason, international armies try to have a formal and proper contact whenever possible. The intensity of these contacts depends on the scenarios of the missions. In the cases studied, the scenarios with the highest intensity of contacts were Lebanon and Bosnia. The officers interviewed consider that relations with local authorities have been generally positive, although in many cases there was a culture shock. In the few cases that have been evaluated as negative relationships, it has been for parasitism (considering that the local authorities want to obtain benefit from the mission) or conflicts of interest. In some cases, international forces have had to work hard to overcome this. We have to underline the case of Afghanistan, where there were fewer contacts and where the local authorities could also fear retaliation from the insurgents (Taliban).

---

[3] Perhaps the most negative reference is to the relationship with Serbs in Bosnia (BGR46).

b.   Soldiers and the Local Populations

Army relations with local populations is also another important topic in the study of civilian-military relations in Peacekeeping Operations [1, 13, 16, 28–32]. These studies highlight that the type of relations is also key to the success of a mission. So, what it known as "winning hearts and minds" and making contact with the local population is crucial to a mission. These interactions have been addressed from various aspects such as pragmatic, moral, emotional and cultural perspectives [32].

As it was indicated above, there are multiple forms of interaction with local communities: (a) sporting events; (b) organization of educational and cultural activities or community events; (c) direct and indirect humanitarian aid; (d) relations with local workers on the bases; (e) during support for reconstruction; and (f) during training and educational tasks. In any case, all the activities are aimed at establishing cordial relations with local populations to facilitate a climate of stability and, therefore, safety.

These forms of interactions can be classified into three types: generic, restricted and auxiliary [33]. Many of the officers in the interviews indicated that contact with the local population was *generic*. This type of relationship is developed mainly through patrolling or acting as CIMIC officers. Through daily contact at shops, bars or restaurants. There is a second type of contact called *restricted*. It refers to contact maintained exclusively through contracted local workers who live on the base: suppliers, contractors and local interpreters. Finally, there is a third type, *auxiliary* contact. This includes relations maintained through the provision of direct or indirect humanitarian aid, or through the protection of CIMIC activities. The results of the analysis are interesting: the highest percentage of *generic* and *auxiliary* contact is to be found in the missions in Bosnia and Kosovo; while *restricted* contact is more usual in Afghanistan and, specially, Iraq. In these last cases the reasons are mainly security, relations are more closely linked to contacts with workers at the base.

It is also important to clarify that relations with local populations, as with other actors, are dynamic and constructed throughout a mission, which often includes several rotations of soldiers who relieve each-other. We should note the two stages that always occur and which influence the construction of these relationships: first, what is known as the beginnings of the mission, when the relationship may not be very fluid and, second, the stabilization stage, the moment the relationships begins to be more fluid and relaxed. It is also important to clarify that even in missions that have lasted many years, relationships of trust have developed between the populations and the army, which have survived the many rotations. An example can be the case of resettlements. In these cases, the bonds of friendship with the resettled population are evident: after providing them with security for months, the locals invited the soldiers into their homes for tea or coffee. These relationships can be seen in the missions in Kosovo and Bosnia.

Regarding *auxiliary contact* and specifically humanitarian aid, CIMIC officers validate the need for humanitarian aid and try to solve these issues with the means at their disposal. Receiving information is important, either directly through the information and liaison teams that are deployed in the territory, or through intense contact with the United Nations agencies, humanitarian aid agencies and NGOs. All of them comprise a humanitarian aid or cooperation community, which the army uses to carry out its mission. These are collateral missions that have a double effect, firstly, they take responsibility for the civilian population needs, and secondly, they are a facilitator in the fulfillment of the mission: "In all missions, in one way or another, humanitarian aid, together with civilian-military cooperation, has always been a continuous and priority task. These tasks were mainly focused on health care, the distribution of basic necessities and infrastructure support projects for the benefit of the communities in whose zones the forces acted" (SP48). In all the cases studied; this distribution of aid was an essential part of the relationship with local populations. It was considered by officers as mainly instrumental, used to gain the trust of these communities: "During the patrols, when crossing populated areas, we made gifts to the locals - balls, clothes, books. That gained the locals' trust" (BGR26); "before, when a local saw a soldier they hide or run away. Now they ask for help with things such as basic needs, heath, education or to take them to an NGO that can assist them" (PH11). In any case, as explained by a Finnish soldier: "the primary actor in humanitarian operations is the local leader" (FIN12). Basically, "little projects were implemented (wells, fences, small footbridges or walls) or humanitarian aid was delivered (food or clothing) to win over the population of a village where the army had an interest" (SP47). Besides this, there was sometimes a personal interest or curiosity: "no official contact with local communities. I did visit a school once, but it was a personal initiative" (FIN05).

Finally, and entering now the evaluation stage, the overall assessment of the relationships can be considered positive. This assessment is evident in many of the responses given by the officers interviewed: they agree that relations are normalized and, on the whole no hostile attitudes are detected. An element that is repeated and must be underlined is that some officers from the Spanish, Italian and Bulgarian armies consider their armies to have a "good reputation" and to be well regarded by the local population: "The people in both Lebanon and Afghanistan were friendly. The Italian forces were particularly well regarded in Afghanistan. The Americans were generally seen as more aggressive" (ITB05).

Beside these generic considerations, this example given by another Italian officer can be illustrative of the relations with these actors: "local communities, for the most part, regard us positively. Because the presence of foreign forces brings both security and economic benefits. It takes some exchange: they give you a little information and you give them something else. The most reports and information come from countries where there is this kind of collaboration. Maybe it is because we have given them something. In one village we brought a generator that they needed. We received the information that interested us, and the local leader of course, increased his prestige" (ITC29). "Bulgarians have a good reputation among the local Afghani population in the mission area" (BGR17). "In Lebanon, we, initially assumed law and order tasks; being from outside ... well, at first it was complicated, but I think that one of the qualities we have is that we are very friendly and with time, as we interact more with the local population, I believe we have good intentions, and in the end, we become familiar to the population" (SP22).[4] Without doubting that certain national idiosyncrasies facilitate relationships with local populations, there are other aspects that also help strengthen relationships such as the type of mission and the specific characteristics of the population. Ultimately relations improve when local populations get what they want and the aforementioned *"what you give, we take"* (LTC03) principle works. Or as another Lithuanian army officer put it. "They judge you according how you act, whether you are afraid or not, whether you are brave enough to eat their food, etc. That is how you earn their respect. You are judged not only by local authorities, but also by insurgents" (LIT01).

Beyond the attitudes and idiosyncrasies of certain officers or armies, culture and cultural similarities are mentioned as elements that help establish better relations with local populations. For example, certain Bulgarian officers believed that the good relations they had with the local population in Bosnia were due to the following reasons: "They had excellent relations. He believes that to a great extent these good relations were due to the similarity of national languages and idiosyncrasies. There was very good level of communication and trust there" (BGR02). Or as a Finnish officer mentioned, the relations with local populations varied from town to town, "it was clearly easier to work with Christian villages than Muslim ones. The difference was obvious" (FIN07). As a Finish officer said: "in missions in Lebanon we had closer ties to local population and organizations that than those in Afghanistan - but there could also be differences between villages according to whether they had "a history" with international troops, and maybe they did not want the troops there again" (FIN09).

Regardless of these affirmations, what is most essential is that which we have already pointed out: the attitude of the local populations towards the armies. When a population considers that the army carrying out the mission are occupying forces, or supports the insurgency for any reason, relations will always be difficult, especially when there are warring local ethnic or religious groups: "We had good relations with the Bosnian people, there were no problems. It was characteristic in Bosnia with the two nationalities – Serbs and Bosnians. They had a different attitude toward the mission and international forces there. Serbs were reluctant to communicate with Peace Keeping Forces. They did not accept the mission. The Bosnians welcomed the mission, and we had good relations with them" (BGR46). "(Lebanon) The relations with Shia communities were never easy. They thought everybody was a spy. The relations were much welcoming with the Christian minorities" (FIN09). "(Afghanistan) The relations with the local population depended very much on the area" (ITC01).

In summary, for most of the officers interviewed the relations maintained with the local population have been positive and, generally, without any hostile attitudes detected, beyond some specific cases. The scenario of the International Mission is very important in this regard: in the missions of Bosnia, Kosovo or Lebanon, the contact with these local populations was greater (either generic or auxiliary, delivery

[4]In the Spanish case, it is particularly significant that up to 12% of the officers interviewed indicated that "Spanish cultural idiosyncrasies" were important elements in fostering relations with local populations.

of humanitarian aid; while in missions at Afghanistan and, especially, Iraq, contacts were mostly of a restrictive nature. Lastly, officers determine several factors that somehow influence these contacts: cultural affinity (for example, Christian populations for the Finns); the idiosyncrasy of the nationals of the armies (in the case of the Spanish, Italians or Bulgarians, who consider themselves to be more open); and finally it is important the memory of these populations of past foreign armies actuations in the past would be positive.

c.   Soldiers' Relationship with NGOs

For at least three decades the army has been forced to interact with all kinds of civil agencies: United Nations agencies and international and local NGOs to the extent that the civilian-military relations in Peacekeeping Operations field of study has been widened [34–36]. In fact, local NGOs play a very important role in post-conflict reconstruction. Its members have first-hand knowledge of local needs and it is important that they receive external support. Similarly, they seek to build longer-term relationships.

These relationships become necessary as security and stabilization operations unfold [37–39] particularly because both parties share certain objectives, especially in the field of reconstruction. However, these interactions are also sometimes controversial in certain situations due to the different organizational cultures and objectives [15, 40–43]. Considering the principles of neutrality, independence and impartiality governing NGO activities, any relationship and interaction with them will be difficult and complicated [44, pp. 363–364].

The reasons behind the interactions between armies and NGO are several: to coordinate safety and logistics issues, for example to give support displaced people and refugees or to provide security for the distribution of humanitarian aid; to exchange information in general; and even project detention [45–52].

Any general conclusions should be put into the context of different missions and armies. Regarding the lack of contact manifested by the officers, it should be noted that, when studying it on a per mission basis, there was more contact in the missions in Bosnia, Kosovo and Lebanon than there was in the missions in Iraq and Afghanistan. This may be due to political or security issues. If we analyze it on a per army basis, Bulgarian officers more generally indicated that they did not have any contact with NGOs, followed by Finns, Italians (who only make reference to an escorting convoy), and Spanish. The Lithuanians stated having more contact with NGOs, as well as with local authorities and communities, as mentioned above, they bond more to the nature of the mission (LTC02).

In general, it can be argued that this relationship is conditioned by three fundamental factors: cultural, institutional and contextual. Organizational culture in NGOs and the Armed Forces is very different, so it must be taken into account when analyzing the relationship. Institutional issues also need to be considered, i.e. the legitimacy effect of the mission in general, and its mandate in particular [23]. Lastly, the environment context is also a key element: we can find benign or favorable environments, fragile or volatile and conflictive. In first ones, it is easier the interaction between the military and NGOs; in second ones, this interaction diminishes and finally, in conflict environments relationships are scarce for evident security reasons [53].

The organizational culture is a factor that remains stables in the different cases studied but institutional and environmental context varied, In fact we can draw two generic conclusions from the data extracted from the interviews, which we will briefly mention now but clarify later: First at all, in general contact with the NGOs in missions such as Afghanistan and Iraq is scarce for reasons of security and legitimacy (or perception of legitimacy). Many officers mentioned that they had no contact with NGOs during their missions. As some officers stated: "sometimes it is very difficult to communicate with (international) NGOs because their policy is to not communicate with armies" (LTC04); or "Civilian organizations do not want to work with army personnel" (FIN09). "The problem of NGOs is that because they have no military training, they do not always perceive the danger. Their function is still positive" (ITC19). So, without a doubt, NGOs are perceived as being hostile to foreign forces. From the officers' view, tensions are attributed to NGO's idiosyncrasies and behavior.

The second general conclusion is that in a significant number of cases where interactions were necessary, especially in the missions in the Balkans, so that armies could provide security for NGOs to carry out their work. Therefore, security is a need that NGOs have to cover, and they have no choice but to outsource, either by hiring private security companies or through the Armed Forces. Hiring the former involves an expense in resources; however, having peacekeepers implies a saving and also obtaining a series of benefits such as information. Generally, armies provided security to NGOs with escorting convoys, trying not compromises its neutrality. In this sense, we can provide the following examples from the interviews conducted: "(Our interactions with NGOs) were seldom, only if they got in some sort of trouble" (LTC03); "civilian organization do not want work with army personnel in any way except for minesweeping activities" (FIN09) or "few relations with NGO, only a few escorting missions" (ITB02). Undoubtedly, security is a determining factor in establishing relationships between aid workers and the army. While the protection of NGOs was traditionally carried out through International Humanitarian Law, and even through contracting private security, today, collaboration, coordination and cooperation with the army has been important in some contexts, especially considering NGOs' principles of independence, neutrality and impartiality [23, 54, 55].

Lastly, beyond stating that the lack of contact was due to the positioning or interests of NGOs, the officers do not mention bad relations with NGOs, only cordial. There were no negative comments about the role of NGOs or about these organizations being an encumbrance to the missions. Among the soldiers, it was the Lithuanians who mostly valued these relations.

4 Conclusions

The results of different studies and reports, some of them cited in this chapter, confirm that, in areas of conflict, peacekeeping and reconstruction, interaction with local actors is key to the success of the mission or at least to making those missions less hazardous for armies. The multiple forms of interaction that occurred build networks through which resources and key supports in the development of the mission can be exchanged.

What can we conclude from the interviews with officers regarding these issues? We can draw two general conclusions, with different implications: first, that contact with local actors, local authorities and local communities occurs regularly, while contact with NGOs is a bit more incidental. Second, that the assessment of these relationships is positive, and go beyond reservations of these actors' generic behavior. Some officers believe that local authorities often demand that the army resolve their problems. There are also criticisms of how NGOs behave. In any case, these criticisms are not generalized and are often justified through structural difficulties such as cultural or political issues.

In any event, the interviews show that the officers from the different armies, all of them experienced in international missions, have internalized the need to create these contacts, giving local actors, especially local authorities, an essential role in their missions. The interviews do not reveal criticism of the relationships themselves, there are only criticisms of certain elements that hinder it or the behavior of actors. What is somewhat criticized is in the role of NGOs, especially in regard to the security issues mentioned above. On several occasions, it is stated that they do not want to act together with armies and that they do not properly consider effective security measures.

Despite these general considerations, there are relevant factors that determine the relationship with local actors. They can be categorized into two groups. The first group would include the types of army activities that are carried out. The second, the context in which the missions are carried out, and would consider spatial and temporal variables. The study found that relationships with local actors were less difficult to maintain in the missions in Bosnia, Kosovo, and even Lebanon, than they were in Afghanistan, and Iraq. Furthermore, it would be necessary to analyze whether relationships within these countries were created with certain populations or others, highlighting cultural or religious (for example in Bosnia, with Bosnian Serbs, or in Lebanon, with Christians or Shiites) or even political (the threat of reprisals by the insurgency in Afghanistan) factors. But we must also remember that trust in these relationships is built up throughout the missions and through the interactions these communities have with the army; as indicated by a Finnish official, an important pillar for these relationships is whether the population have had "a history" with peacekeeping troops (FIN09).

Another element that needs to be highlighted and which is necessary to establishing good relations with the local populations and authorities, is humanitarian aid and the provision of services for populations: delivery of food, clothing, sanitary services, construction and repair of civil infrastructures, etc. Some officers mention that the authorities demand too much, and that sometimes these demands are even gifts. In any case, this benefits the armies in the form of security.

References

1. Durán M, Ávalos A (2013) Culturas Cruzadas en Conflicto. Militares poblaciones locales en misiones internacionales: los casos de Afganistán y Líbano. Editorial Universidad de Granada, Granada
2. Gippert BJ (2016) The sum of its parts? Sources of local legitimacy. Coop Confl 51(4):522–538
3. Holohan A (2019) Transformative training in soft skills for peacekeepers: gaming for peace. Int Peacekeeping 26(5):556–578
4. Kaldor M (1999) New and old wars: organized violence in a global era. Stanford University Press, Stanford
5. Münkler H (2005) Viejas y 'nuevas guerras'. Asimetría y privatización de la violencia. Siglo XXI, Madrid
6. Pouligny B (2003) UN peace operations, INGO, NGO, and promoting the rule of law: exploring the interaction of international and local norms in different post-war contexts. J Hum Rights 2(3):359–377
7. Rietjens SJH, Bollen M (2008) Managing civil-military cooperation: a 24/7 joint effort for stability. Routledge, London
8. Kingston P (2012) The pitfalls of peacebuilding from below: governance promotion and local political processes in post-conflict Lebanon. Int J 67(2):333–350
9. Mitchell C (2016). La naturaleza de los conflictos intratables. Resolución de conflictos en el siglo XXI. Institut Català Internacional per la Pau (ICIP), Barcelona
10. Leonardsson H, Rudd G (2015) The 'local turn' in peacebuilding: a literature review of effective and emancipatory local peacebuilding. Third World Q 36(5):825–839
11. Autesserre S (2014) Going micro: emerging and future peacekeeping research. Int Peace-keeping 21(4):492–500
12. Boege V, Rinck P (2019) The local/international interface in peacebuilding: experiences from Bougainville and Sierra Leone. Int Peacekeeping 26(2):216–239
13. De Graaff MC et al (2015) Emotional reactions and moral judgment: the effects of morally challenging interactions in military operations. Ethics Behav 26(1):14–31
14. Glenn J (2009) Realism versus strategic culture. Competition and collaboration? Int Stud Rev 11(3):523–551
15. Dandeker C, Gow J (2000) Military culture and strategic peacekeeping. In: Schmidl EA (ed) Peace operations between war and peace. Frank Cass, London, pp 58–75
16. Ruffa C (2017) Military cultures and force employment in peace operations. Secur Stud 26(3):391–422
17. Rubinstein RA (2010) Peacekeeping and the return of imperial policing. Int Peacekeeping 17(4):457–470
18. Michael K, Ben-Ari E (2010) Contemporary peace support operations: the primacy of the military and internal contradiction. Armed Forces Soc 37(4):657–679
19. Dixon P (2009) 'Hearts and minds'? British counter-insurgency from Malaya to Iraq. J Strateg Stud 32(3):353–381
20. Durán M (2013) Interests, identities and norms in peace operations: Spanish army and NGOs in Kosovo. Rev CIDOB d'Afers Int 104:181–200
21. Robles Carrillo M (coord) (2012) Género, conflictos armados y seguridad. La asesoría de género en las operaciones. Editorial Universidad de Granada, Granada
22. Whalan J (2017) The local legitimacy of peacekeepers. J Interv Statebuilding 11(3):306–320

23. Durán M (2015) Cooperación y conflicto entre Ejército español y ONG Internacionales: Factores culturales e institucionales en las misiones internacionales de Afganistán, Líbano y Kosovo. Rev Relac Int 28. Universidad Autónoma de Madrid
24. Jenkins L (2003) A CIMIC contribution to assessing progress in peace support operations. Int Peacekeeping 10(3):121–136
25. Sookermany AM (2012) What is a skillful soldier? An epistemological foundation for understanding military skill acquisition in (post) modernized armed forces. Armed Forces Soc 38(4):582–603
26. Martínez R, Durán M (2017) International missions as a way to improve domestic civil-military relations. The Spanish case: 1989–2015. Democr Secur 13(1):1–23
27. Ruffa C et al (2013) Soldiers drawn into politics? Civil-military relations hybrid military spaces and the future of the interventions. In: Giegerich B, Kümmel G (eds) The armed forces: towards a post-interventions era? Springer, Potsdam, pp 29–40
28. Azari J et al (2010) Cultural stress: how interactions with and among foreign populations affect military personnel. Armed Forces Soc 36(4):585–603
29. Blocq D (2010) Western soldiers and the protection of local civilians in UN peacekeeping operations: is a nationalist orientation in the armed forces hindering our preparedness to fight? Armed Forces Soc 36(2):290–309
30. Durán M, Ávalos A (2016) Detecting conflictive cultural factors in complex scenarios of intervention: military and local actors in interaction. UNISCI Discuss Pap 41:9–28
31. Pouligny B (1999) Peacekeepers and local social actors: the need for dynamic, cross-cultural analysis. Glob Gov 5(4)
32. Schut M et al (2014) Moral emotions during military deployments of Dutch forces. Armed Forces Soc 41(4):616–638
33. Durán M et al (2016) Experiencias de la participación militar española en misiones internacionales: el caso de los oficiales del Ejército de Tierra (1993–2015). Rev Esp Cienc Polít 42:125–145
34. Rosén F (2009) Third-generation civil-military relations. Secur Dialogue 40(6):597–616
35. Weiss TG (1999) Learning from military-civilian interactions in peace operations. Int Peacekeeping 6(2):122–128
36. Williams MC (1998) Civil-military relations and peacekeeping. Adelphi Pap 321:9–11
37. Yalçinkaya H (2012) The nongovernmental organizations-military security collaboration mechanism: Afghanistan NGO Safety Office. Armed Forces Soc 39(3):489–510
38. Holmberg A (2011) The changing role of NATO: exploring the implications for security governance and legitimacy. Eur Secur 20(4):529–546
39. Krahmann E (2005) From state to non-state actors: the emergence of security governance. In: Krahmann E (ed) New threats and new actors in international security. Palgrave Macmillan, London, pp 3–19
40. Miller LL (1999) From adversaries to allies: relief workers attitudes towards US military. Qual Sociol 22:181–197
41. Rubinstein RA (2003) Cross-cultural considerations in complex peace operations. Negot J 19(1):29–49
42. Rubinstein RA et al (2008) Culture and interoperability in integrated missions. Int Peacekeeping 15(4):540–555
43. Winslow D (2002) Strange bedfellows: NGOs and the military in humanitarian crisis. Int J Peace Stud 7(2):35–55
44. Spearing C (2008) Private, armed and humanitarian? States, NGOs, international private security companies and shifting humanitarianism. Secur Dialogue 39(4):363–364
45. Braem Y (2004) Les relations Armées-ONG, des relations de pouvoir? Caractéristiques et enjeux de la coopération civil-militaire française: le cas du Kosovo. Centre d'études en sciences sociales de la défense, Paris
46. Byman DL (2002) Uncertain partners: NGOs and the military. Survival 43(2):97–114
47. Harris A, Donbrowski P (2002) Military collaboration with humanitarian organizations in complex emergencies. Glob Gov 8(2):158–177

48. Joëlle J (2001) Civil-military cooperation in complex emergencies: finding ways to make it work. Eur Secur 10(2):23–33
49. Mockaitis TR (2004) Reluctant partners: civil-military cooperation in Kosovo. The future of peace. Small Wars Insur 15(2):38–69
50. Pugh M (2001) The challenge of civil military relations in international peace operations. Disasters 25(4):345–357
51. Rietjens SJH (2006) Civil-military cooperation in response to a complex emergency. Just another drill? Gildeprint Drukkerijen B.V., The Netherlands
52. Rietjens SJH et al (2013) Learning from Afghanistan: towards a compass for civil–military coordination. Small Wars Insur 24(2):257–277
53. Dobbie C (1994) A concept for post-Cold War peacekeeping. Survival 36(3):121–148
54. Studer M (2001) El CICR y las relaciones cívico-militares en los conflictos armados. Rev Int Cruz Roja 842:367–390
55. Van Baarda TA (2001) A legal perspective of cooperation between military and humanitarian organizations in peace support operations. Int Peacekeeping 8(1):99–116

Relationships in Multinational Missions and Operations: Military-To-Military Dimension

Yantsislav Yanakiev

Abstract This chapter is based on an analysis of the experiences in multinational missions and operations of the military from eight countries: Bulgaria, Cameroun, Denmark, Finland, Italy, Lithuania, Philippines, and Spain. It is expected the analysis to further deepen theory and expertise on managing multinationality in coalition operations to successfully meet the desired end state of these operations. Some of the conclusions might be useful also for improving professional military education and training, as well as leadership skills to work in a multinational environment. The following key issues are discussed in the chapter: (a) Coalition hierarchy and degree of autonomy for making independent decisions; (b) Command relationships within coalition forces and patterns of everyday personal relationships among coalition partners; (c) Interoperability issues in multinational coalition forces; (d) Interactions of coalition forces with local militaries. In conclusion, some implications for practice regarding the planning and execution of multinational military operations, as well as professional military education and training of the participants in such operations are summarised.

1 Introduction

During the post-Cold War era there has been a significant increase in the number of military operations that involve many nations willing to contribute forces as part of multinational coalitions in the framework of the United Nations (UN), the European Union (EU), North Atlantic Treaty Organization (NATO), etc. These coalitions have to execute a variety of operations that differ notably in their nature and scope: some include the provision of military training and assistance, others provide humanitarian assistance, or perform peacekeeping or even peace-enforcement tasks. Operational theatres, also, vary considerably, both geographically—from North Africa to the

Y. Yanakiev (✉)
The Bulgarian Defence Institute "Prof. Tsvetan Lazarov", 2 Prof. Tsvetan Lazarov Blvd., 1592 Sofia, Bulgaria
e-mail: y.yanakiev@di.mod.bg

© Springer Nature Switzerland AG 2021
M. Nuciari and E. Olivetta (eds.), *Leaders for Tomorrow: Challenges for Military Leadership in the Age of Asymmetric Warfare*, Advanced Sciences and Technologies for Security Applications, https://doi.org/10.1007/978-3-030-71714-8_6

Balkans, from the Middle East to Central and South-East Asia—and functionally, involving e.g. land forces only, air power or, when fighting piracy, naval forces.

The process of internationalization of the military, participating in coalition operations and multinational formations is among the most important distinctiveness of the post-modern defence organisations [1].

Researchers and practitioners agree that the political legitimacy of a given military operation, the acceptance by the local population, the cost-effectiveness of the mission and the opportunity to encourage better mutual understanding and team work among the military and civilians from different troops-contributing countries are the most important advantages of the multinational coalitions.

At the same time, the effectiveness of the multinational coalition operations has been a controversial issue over a long period of time. Contemporary studies show that differences in national and organisational cultures, different information sharing norms, lack of individual, organizational and national trust, as well as language barriers are among the main turbulences that could impact the overall operational effectiveness of the multinational force [2].

In addition, different national and organisational structures and decision-making processes, concepts of tactics and mission planning, different disciplinary codes, different command and control systems, equipment and armament, and payment differences can be viewed as challenges to the coalitions' effectiveness [3].

Moreover, Sutton and Pierce identified national cultural behaviours associated with high power distance and high uncertainty avoidance to clearly impact team performance in the areas of situation assessment, coordination, assigning roles and responsibilities, and support behaviour [4].

To summarise, multinational coalition forces are complex assemblies of people, both leaders and followers, structured in teams of teams and networks, representing diverse national and organizational cultures, with various education and training level, different doctrines and concepts, organizational structures, decision-making procedures, level of technological advancement, etc. The factors described above operate as organizational and cultural barriers to effective collaboration in multinational settings.

There are some under-researched questions in the area of enablers and impediments of successful military cooperation in multinational coalitions that ask for additional multinational research efforts. Therefore, the topic of military-to-military dimension of the relationships in multinational missions and operations is of high scientific and policy-making interest.

This chapter is based on analysis of the experiences in multinational missions and operations of the military from 8 countries: Bulgaria, Cameroun, Denmark, Finland, Italy, Lithuania, Philippines and Spain. Data was collected via semi-structured interviews in the period 2015–2016.

The analysis of the results from this international comparative survey is succeeding the tradition in the study of military-to military relations in multinational coalition operations [5]. It is expected to further deepen theory and expertise on managing multi-nationality in coalition operations to successfully meet the desired end state of these operations. Some of the conclusions might be useful also for improving professional military education and training and leadership skills to work in multinational environment.

As far as the context of operations is quite different, as well as the national experiences, it is not possible to formulate common criteria for candid comparative cross-country analysis. Instead, groups of typical experiences are presented and analysed to identify common issues that deserve attention. When it is possible, commonalities and differences among the national cases are also commented. Finally, in order to de-personalize the interviewees, no names of the countries will be mentioned in the text when quotes are provided. The quotes are presented in their original without editing.

The following key issues are discussed in the chapter:

- Coalition hierarchy and degree of autonomy for making independent decisions;
- Command relationships within coalition forces and patterns of everyday personal relationships among coalition partners;
- Interoperability issues in multinational coalition forces;
- Interactions of coalition forces with local militaries.

In conclusion some implications for practice regarding planning and execution of multinational military operations, as well as PME and training of the participants in such operations are summarised.

2 Results

2.1 Coalition Hierarchy and Degree of Autonomy for Making Independent Decisions

The coalitions hierarchy and the ability of commanders to make autonomous decisions, assert them, and implement them when solving contingent tasks are being explored in this paragraph. Recent studies show the importance of proper coalition hierarchy (flat vs. hierarchical) and adequate decision-making process (centralized vs. distributed) as one of the most important organizational challenges in multinational coalition operations [6].

Most of the respondents assigned to command positions in different coalition formations confirm that they have had a high degree of autonomy within the framework of their duties and responsibilities for making independent decisions and asserting them in the coalition and the national formations. Regardless of the limitations, the majority of commanders say they have had the necessary flexibility to manage their formations.

Analysis of data shows that the degree of autonomy depends on the person's rank and role in the mission, as well as mission type—whether it is a traditional peacekeeping, operation, peace-enforcement, search and rescue, counter-insurgency, etc., and the specifics of the operational context: "I gave wide autonomy to the companies' commanders, because given the situation in the theatre, it is not possible to do otherwise". In addition, the level of autonomy depends on the composition of the coalition forces and the level of civilian actors involved: "In more complex operations, with the participation of other than military components, you must be more flexible and provide them more freedom to decide". Moreover, the level of autonomy is related to how experienced the subordinates are: "I gave myself a high autonomy to the squad leaders, because they were people who already had a good operational experience and they were older guys". Furthermore, the organisational architecture of the coalition command (hierarchical vs. flat) is an important factor regarding the level of autonomy in coalition operations. In addition, the level of autonomy depends also on the management style and specific leadership abilities of the command of the coalition forces. For example, many respondents provide arguments like the following: "It is Western leadership management style where if you know your task then it is up to you how you fulfil it". "The hierarchical as well as subordination relationships were bit complicated. From the beginning I had problems with subordinates (police, civilians, and military) as they did not obey my command, but later I managed to strengthen my leadership. You really need to have some specific skills if leading not only military personnel. You need to be more flexible. Flexibility and cooperation goes first"; "Given that responsibility in such missions is clearly defined for every actor, a commander has all the autonomy that possible regarding the limits. Undoubtedly, this autonomy is linked to the character of the Chief who is the final authority to increase or reduce this initiative due to his character and leading style". Finally, the level of autonomy depends also on the different patterns of military cooperation in building a coalition: vertical (lead or framework nation), bi-national (parallel) or multinational (horizontal).

The analysis of the data made so far gives an opportunity to identify some common patterns for the countries under scrutiny:

First of all, the respondents undoubtedly understand the need for strong military hierarchy in the international missions and operations. Some typical examples are answers like: "Chain of command must be observed at all times, so the actions below can create a big effect on the overall goal". In the same time, they share the opinion that the situation that they have worked in during multinational coalition operations is significantly different from the traditional hierarchy in defence organisations. This is certainly a challenge for the military personnel. Some typical arguments provided by the respondents are: "The hierarchies also challenge the balance of the operation, because the military is only a small part of the operation"; "I should say these were not typical relations of military subordination"; "If it was a very traditional military hierarchy, I know how to prepare myself for it. But within the coalition forces in which I was it was not really a clear one, or it was perhaps slightly hidden. The people with their own selves or their presence gained their own hierarchy. It was not necessarily based on the military rank".

Second, the analysis identified important cultural differences in the perception of autonomy in multinational operations depending on the national traditions, different organizational architecture of the national armed forces and diverse leadership styles of the counterparts in the coalition. Some examples are the following: "The X nation is definitely different than us. Our (national) flat hierarchy was met with hard resistance. You don't discuss the information and decisions made by a superior, if he/she is from the other nation"; "There is an immense difference between our hierarchies. In our Army we lived up to principle of the mission command: You are told what to do, not how to do it"; "I asked one of the lower ranking officers if something could be done better leading to another decision. The reaction was: "WHAT!?!"; "Our national military has a flat low anti-authoritarian leadership. With the X nation, the officer is upper-class and the soldier is a worker on ground".

Third, the analysis recognised the double subordination (national vs. multinational coalition command) as an issue related to the effectiveness of coalition operations. Some experiences frequently referred to are the following: "As a battalion commander I was under control of two commanders – the one was our national commander (Joint Headquarters Commander) who sent me to Afghanistan; the second was ISAF operational commander who was a chief commander in charge over a whole West region in Afghanistan"; "I was under double subordination which brought a particularity. Usually, I used to get orders from the coalition commander, and seldom from X nation commander; however, reports needed to be written to my national command"; "Our national commanders observe our national chain of command but the company is subordinate to foreign commanders, which goes beyond our national limitations."

One should add here also the issue of national restrains on information sharing in multinational coalitions: some difficulties with proceeding information. There was a requirement that we proceed with information to certain level of classification in order for it to be shared."

2.2 Command Relationships Within Coalition Forces and Patterns of Everyday Relationships Among Partners

2.2.1 Positive Experiences and Enablers of Operational Effectiveness in Multinational Environment

The majority of respondents evaluate the relationships with coalition partners during the missions and operations that they have participated as "correct", "honest", "benevolent", "frank", "collegiate", "professional", "business-like", "cordial, based on good manners" and even "friendly". In addition, the military counterparts in the coalitions, in most of the cases demonstrate "understanding", "sympathy" and "readiness for help". The organisational climate is described as an atmosphere of "mutual respect", "good sense", "rationality" and "calmness". In a situation where necessary assistance is needed within the coalition (supply of resources, technical maintenances, medical services and evacuation, etc.), the colleagues from the other nations are usually "supportive", "responsive" and "correct".

A smaller group of interviewees express the opinion that in their interaction with coalition partners, relations are rather "formal", "polite", based on "mutual respect", "observing the necessary subordination without seeking greater closeness" and "good, despite the different perspectives of each country in the military operations".

The analysis made so far gives an opportunity to identify some distinctive characteristics of everyday relationships among coalition partners.

First of all, there is a tendency of positive development of the relationships in the coalition over time. A significant part of interviewees says that there is an initial stage of examining each other in the beginning of the missions, and after that positive relationships have been developed based on professionalism and mutual understanding. These are some typical answers: "In the course of missions, after they got to know us and had assured our good military standards (morale, discipline, devotion to the mission), most of them changed attitude and became acting in a friendly manner"; "Initially, there is a stage of learning, but if you win the trust, the coalition partners are cooperative, helpful and responsive".

Furthermore, the analysis of the data gives an opportunity to identify some factors that can help improve mutual understanding and cooperation in multinational military coalitions. On the first place the interviewees focus on the role of military professionalism in building trust and integrity with coalition partners. Interviewees argue that "Mutual respect and trust are best achieved by demonstrating professionalism, accuracy, integrity and readiness for mutual assistance in interacting with joint tasks"; "Relationship with coalition partners from X nation was great, professional, because we all spoke the same military language. We were equal partners"; "Relationships were great and very friendly, made out of professional relations and mutual respect". Additionally, the previous experience or working in the framework of NATO/EU operations is of key importance. Some typical statements are: "Working with other NATO-countries went generally well"; "Work with them was easy, because most of their troops had come from the Nordic Battlegroup's rotation training so we knew them from before"; "The relations with other armed forces the relationship of mutual trust was based a lot on personal knowledge. It would, therefore, be appropriate to create in the phase of pre-deployment and of amalgam also a relationship with the staff of other services that is intended to cooperate with us"; Thirdly, the role of the military culture which appears to be very close despite national difference is also important according to the interviewees: "Military mind-set is always similar"; "In general, the military personnel around the world share a common language". Last but not least, an important factor for the success in the coalition operations is the well-organised process of information sharing. There are some classic examples of proper information-sharing behaviour: "We share information with the police. We also do joint planning pertaining to common security concerns"; "The police, army and local government have intelligence and information sharing. We also provide each other operation support". In order to improve information sharing within the coalition forces, the interviewees indicate the need for a strategy for changing people's minds and attitudes of "reluctance to share information." The close military culture, specific military ethos and expertise are obviously among the factors that enable better cooperation and teamwork in multinational coalitions.

Finally, the "process of social networking" and the development of "informal networks" is a key factor for successful task accomplishment. For example, some respondents argue that "The ability to be able to establish networks is even more important than the language skills" and that "If social relationships are good, men and women respect each other and understand one another things can be taken care of". In this regard, they suggest the organization of "ad hoc meetings in open environments within multicultural settings", "sports", "mixed joint Staff meetings", as well as to "create the opportunity for people to talk to each other informally" through ice-breakers/social events, etc.

2.2.2 Negative Experiences and Impediments of Operational Effectiveness in Multinational Coalition Environment

Along with the predominantly positive evaluations of the relationships among the coalition partners, the analysis of the data identified also some negative tendencies that deserve attention.

The most frequently discussed issues in coalition context are related to the role of cultural differences among national contingents and their influence on operational effectiveness and the process of formation of unique organizational culture within coalitions.

A particular example are differences in the organizational cultures and organisational processes which are strongly prejudiced by different national cultures. The examples provided by the respondents cover these issues: "The X nation in principle, are very standardized. We, (as nation), have regiments that work each in its own way"; "I have observed that X nation are more bureaucratic and doctrinal then us"; "The X nation I've seen them less careful in applying the rules"; "At first we had a little of complications in relationships, because they have another vision of the mission compared to ours. They have very strict procedures that apply slavishly regardless of the situation, without assessing the human factor, etc. The way we approach the population is completely different because of different culture"; "Sometimes each went his own way, according to their own cultural approach to problem-solving."

In addition, the study identified existing different mental models of coping with uncertainty in the decision-making process which is related to culturally based biases in the need for information to make a decision. This process might affect the unwillingness to make a decision if the person needs more information or the fear of making an incorrect decision, both of which could undermine operational effectiveness.

Another issue, resulting also from different national cultures which asks for attention, is task orientation versus the need to spend time building and maintaining relationships.

Last but not least, the study identified the problem with the effect of different leadership styles (for example: direct vs. indirect) which could lead to misunderstandings or misperceptions of the intention of the leader.

A positive fact is that many of the respondents recognise the role of cultural awareness as a factor to prevent tensions and misunderstandings. For example, some of them share opinion that: "Central here is cultural awareness. The X nation's Special Forces seem not to be very aware. The X nation forces do what you tell them to do. The X nation use a lot of force most of the time, and that is a problem. I mean, two operations with different purposes and different doctrines in the same area"; "It is important to understand cultural diversity. With the X nation there is a blind loyalty, they have a task and execute it"; "The challenge is in respecting and understanding that there are different ways to do things".

A very small group of the respondents say that at some point the relationship with the coalition partners has been strained. This is mostly related to the perception of attempts at domination, disrespectful attitude, perceptions of double standards, etc.

Few people believe that there is an element of dominance among the leading nations in the coalition relationship. The arguments that they give are: "All issues (SIPRINET, NIPRINET, CENTRIX) were resolved between the ABCA countries – the A nation, the B nation, C nation and X nation. All operational issues were discussed and decided in a narrower circle between the above-mentioned nations. Two nations X and Z solved things between them, and the rest of the staff at the headquarters were performing their technical duties"; "The most striking impression of tense relations is created with the X nation coalition partners in Iraq, where our contingent has placed tasks disproportionate to the composition, arms and national restrictions of the (national) contingent"; "The X nation personnel applied a little bit double standards"; "In certain cases tension arose because the coalition command did not take into consideration national caveats and contingent's capabilities and charged the company with more tasks that it could accomplish".

The analysis of the data gives an opportunity to formulate at least two conclusions in the form of possible "remedies" to mitigate potential negative effects of cultural diversity in multinational coalitions.

The first conclusion is related to the role of the leadership in multinational military operations as a factor that shapes the organizational culture in the coalition, and thus, influences effectiveness of the operations. The role of the leader and specific leadership competencies in a multinational environment are critical factors regarding the establishment of shared vision and shared awareness with respect to goals and tasks.

The second conclusion is linked to the process of building and developing cross cultural competency as a key to better international cooperation in multinational missions and operations. Therefore, building cross-cultural competency should be incorporated as an essential part of the professional military education and the pre-deployment training. The most important components of the cultural awareness training are related to the coalition partners' national and organisational culture; understanding different leadership styles; mission area local population culture and history; adversary culture, etc. Briefly, the cultural adaptability education and training should become a necessary pre-requisite to take an international assignment.

2.3   Interoperability Issues in Multinational Coalition Forces

One of the central issues in this study is the respondent's assessment as regards the level of interoperability with Allies and Partners. Interoperability in multinational military operations is a broad concept, including areas, such as organizational structures and processes, concepts, doctrines, tactics, equipment, armaments, command and control systems, information sharing, logistics, language barriers and many others. Interoperability is extremely important for the effectiveness of multinational forces in the mission area [7]. For that reason, it is necessary to identify problem areas that the military contingents encounter during missions. Considering this, the study identifies three main areas that demand consideration: first, interoperability in concepts, doctrines, tactics and procedures; second, interoperability in the area of military equipment and armaments; and third, human interoperability.

2.3.1   Interoperability in Strategies, Doctrines, Tactics and Procedures

The analysis of the results from the study shows that the majority of the respondents did not encounter serious problems with respect to interoperability in the area of military strategies and doctrines, except the issue with the so called "national caveats". Some respondents argue that "The limits to interoperability are tied to some national caveats. There was still an evolution inside NATO towards a greater interoperability". This fact certainly needs attention because the nation-centric politics, related to imposing restrictive caveats to employ the troops during the operation have negative influence on coalition operation's effectiveness. The problem is that the troops are forced to work around these political barriers, which may increase the immediate risk to the people on the ground and undermine the trust among the coalition partners.

Single respondents say that some coalition partners were imposing their doctrinal documents within the coalition. This creates to some extent difficulties. Some of them maintain that "In the first mission in Afghanistan there were minor problems with the discrepancy between X country national documents and NATO documents but there were no big problems". There are also single interviewees who say that they had initial problems because they were not sufficiently familiar with NATO documents: "We need to catch up with doctrinal comprehension with our allies."

The interviewees report for more problems at tactical level which are related to the implementation of the Standard Operating Procedures (SOPs), coordination among different coalition contingents and services, different understanding and application of procedures, etc.

Few of them believe that there was mutual misunderstanding in the organization and execution of the tasks on the field, or that there were some discrepancies in perceptions about the implementation of the SOPs, which have subsequently been cleared in the course of the work. Some of the examples are the following: "Different understanding of problem-solving among high-ranking X nation vs. Y nation officers; The X nation and the Y nation procedures are very alike, but there are differences. We are well coordinated thanks to NATO; Not only technically but also our procedures"; "It's not about the radios, but rather about the different ways we in which understand the different orders. Even if we are all NATO, the way officers give 'orders' are different. For instance, it's very different how detailed orders are, and so how much is left for the soldier to decide himself. As far as I know, there are 4 different understandings of the order attack"; "The problem was that the planning was not combined. Often happened that our requests for air support were not fulfilled, because the aircraft had finished his period of support, or was running out of fuel or other".

2.3.2 Interoperability in the Area of Military Equipment and Armaments

The problem of technical interoperability with allies and partners appears to be among the most serious because it is an important condition for the successful implementation of the joint tasks in the mission.

After the analysis, two categories of technical interoperability problems are highlighted:

First, interoperability in armaments and equipment, as well as the organisation of logistics: "Our vehicles were not interoperable with these of the coalition partners"; "It usually takes one to two months before the spare parts, particularly for the radio, to arrive".

Second, interoperability in communication and information systems (CIS): "There were mainly problems provoked by other nations' command and control systems"; "On both NATO missions, i.e. in Bosnia and in Afghanistan we were challenged with the different communication systems within NATO. We were also challenged to bring our own spare parts from X nation as no other countries have them".

In conclusion, this study confirmed the fact that the capabilities and technological gaps among the coalition partners, as well as the lack of adequate resources allocated to implement the mission are traditional barriers to the effectiveness of coalition operations. Among many other important challenges, the lack of technological interoperability in national CIS hamper information sharing and creates difficulties for cooperation among the different troop-contributing nations in the coalition.

2.3.3 Human Interoperability

An equally important issue for the effective cooperation in multinational coalitions is the topic of human interoperability, with the main focus on cultural interoperability. Recent studies show that "cultural interoperability is distinct due to its inclusivity. Whilst divergences in equipment and technology can hinder interoperability, human factors are applicable to all nations" [8]. Other authors use the term "cultural adaptability" which is defined as "the ability to understand one's own and other's cognitive biases and to adapt as necessary, to ensure successful team performance" [9].

The analysis of data revealed two groups of interoperability problems in this respect: first, lack of cultural awareness training of personnel, participating in multinational operations and the problem with the quality of English language communication; second, different national systems for PME and training.

With respect to the first problem, most often respondents identify the language barrier or inadequate language training as a major interoperability issue. They say that they have had problems with understanding coalition partners: "The challenge is that sometimes there are misunderstanding due to language problems"; "There were difficulties in communication and language differences in concept with other actors"; "Problems derivative from the lack of language skills".

The problem with the quality of English language communication is certainly multifaceted. On the one hand, non-native English speakers often did not comprehend the meaning or context of English speech. On the other hand, native English speakers also had difficulties with non-native speakers and therefore, sometimes assumed incompetence on the part of non-native English speakers.

Regarding the second problem—differences in national education and training systems, most often respondents emphasized issues like: "the lack of joint and combined pre-deployment training", as well as "differences in training level with some other actors in the field". The problem with different level of PME and training is that it hampers the mutual understanding in the field. These are some typical experiences: "We had mainly interoperability issues in Lebanon, as they are not NATO forces, and come from very different cultures. That creates issues of operational understanding, sometimes due to not standardized procedure or other cultural reasons"; "There are national differences; The X nation pilots, for example, have a different risk acceptance and also intervene in situations objectively difficult. There are also differences between the helicopter pilots and the aircraft pilots".

The process of standardization of PME and training in NATO, for example, is the right avenue to mitigate the negative effect of national differences in military education systems on interoperability in multinational coalitions. Some respondents say that "Obviously, things are more complicated in missions with allied armies outside the NATO area."

2.4 Interactions of Coalition Forces with Local Militaries

The majority of surveyed people indicate that they had working relationships with the local armed forces in the mission area. Many of them define these relationships as "collegiate", "very good", "honest", "cooperative", "constructive" and "professional". In most of the cases, the representatives of the local armed forces were cooperative and respectful. For example, the respondents say that: "During joint patrols, especially at night, the Afghanis were not afraid, they just lacked experience, and they embraced tasks with bravery"; The Afghani servicemen as soldiers were very dedicated, with strong motivation; "The relation with the local armed forces was very close and leaded by the principles of mutual cooperation, camaraderie and respect";

"I had daily relations with the Army and the Police in counselling, coordination and combat. In general, it was good with mutual respect although in some cases cultural differences in military issues were notorious"; "The Afghan soldiers appeared at the end well-motivated, despite logistical shortfalls and equipment."

Along with these positive assessments about the relationships between the militaries from the various coalitions and the local armed forces, some negative experiences are presented that deserve attention.

The first identified problem is related to the lack of individual, organizational and national trust, particularly in a situation of information leaking. Here are some examples: "In some scenarios these people leaked information to the insurgency and other criminal groups"; "The relations were basically good. However, both parts were a bit suspicious, which prevented the relation from being totally frank and open"; "Insurgents were hiding between the security forces and civilians. This was a problem in building relations and trust"; "Needed to be done also attention to the dissemination of confidential information: when you communicated an information of this type to the police, then it was often known by the local population, including insurgents"; "The reliability of locals is relative and we must stand with eyes open because sometimes it occurred episodes of blue on green"; "The relation was good. Despite that, it's necessary to be alert for possible insiders"; "We made joint operations with the ANA of course, their reliability is low and wide corruption".

The second problem is related to some concerns with regard to the level of professionalism and reliability of local security forces. Some of the arguments provided by the respondents are: "The confidence level was low, corruption was widespread, people went on leave and did not came back"; "I had no confidence in Iraqi Armed Forces. Their esprit de corps was broken. Their morale was gone"; "The Iraqis as soldiers make the following impression: they are mentally weak, timid and one cannot rely on them. They can be bought easily"; "Afghan National Army (ANA) and Afghani police do not follow the ROE"; "You cannot count on them. They are not well educated. We acted less tactically offensive in our mutual units. We did not trust them as much as we did our X nation colleagues"; "The reliability of the Afghans, as for the adherence to orders promptly and so on decreased as you went down in the hierarchical level"; "Their scarce technical skills have also created problems: on one occasion we were under fire from mortars of 120 mm by a close Afghani unit, due to incorrect shooting calculations"; "With local forces I have worked as a mentor to an Afghan company. Their desire to work, commitment, patriotism among Afghan soldiers were very low. There have also been some problems with the drugs, widely used by them".

The third problem is related to interoperability troubles, both in technological and human domains, as well as coordination between the two sides. There are some examples: "I cooperated with Afghani forces. Under the professional point of view certainly there was a big gap. They must make a long way"; "With Afghan forces was a bit more difficult because there were the police, there was the Afghan army, there was the Afghan border police. All of them had different ways of working. So, you had to try to have a different behaviour with all these three types of units"; "There was a problem in doctrinal field between the U.S. instructors and the Afghani trainees. It was mainly about expectations of the Americans for the trainees to follow standards and the perceptions of the Afghans that they could do it their own way"; "We cooperate but their lifestyle and the way they view our presence complicate things"; "There was difficulty in dealing with the ANA because a completely different world view and language difficulties".

To summarize, most tensions between coalition partners and local armed forces have arisen as a result of the different mentality of the soldiers, some doubts about their credibility, especially after incidents, level of professionalism, attempts to leverage co-operation, style of work, and lifestyle. In addition, the relations with the local armed forces depend much on the different national units involved, management and leadership skills of commanders, the ethnic and religious groups, etc.

3   Lessons Learned and Suggestions for Improving Operational Effectiveness in Multinational Military Coalitions

A number of implications for practice regarding planning and execution of multinational operations can be drawn from this study. The conclusions and recommendations are not ordered strictly in accordance with their importance. And finally, the results of this survey should be viewed, on one hand, as an opportunity for enhancement of the enablers, and, on the other hand, as a possibility for mitigating the effect of the negative implications.

One of the most important recommendation is related to the political-military decision-making when multinational operations are planned and executed. First of all, clear and stable goals and tasks, as well as comprehensive approach to doctrines and concepts are essential in order to ensure common understanding of mission end-state among coalition partners. In addition, the effectiveness of coalition operations strongly depends on reducing the capability and technology gaps amongst the coalition partners and enhancing the technological interoperability in national systems to improve information sharing and cooperation among different troop-contributing nations in the coalition. Last but not least, the decision-makers should minimize the restrictive national caveats in the employment of the troops during the operation. This is an important issue that directly influences the level of trust among the coalition partners. All of these factors could be considered also as preconditions leading to the creation of an environment which stimulates co-operation and teamwork which has been already proved to be one of the most powerful enablers of operational effectiveness.

Next are the suggestions regarding PME and training for multinational operations and missions. Having in mind the nature of current military operations, one can identify joint, multinational and interagency education of the military leaders to create cohesion and a common understanding as a key factor for coalition operations effectiveness. Some recent studies proved the strategic effect of joint and combined PME and training to develop homogeneous culture, shared vision and mutual understanding in multinational environment [10]. Joint efforts and shared experiences create the power.Besides, it would be useful for the officers to receive education in broader scale that develops their social competencies and builds new skills corresponding to the new tasks performed in these operations. This includes knowledge and skills how to interact with civilian agencies; how to work with local population and local authorities in the host country; how to react in hostage situations; how to restore public order; how to handle media, etc. It is very important to promote understanding among the military professionals and to help them identify many actors (diplomatic, military, NGOs, media, etc.) They should be prepared to assist the work of the civilian organizations and to understand the way these organizations work. Briefly, the cultural adaptability education and training should become a necessary pre-requisite to take an international assignment. Finally, particular attention should be focused on further improvement of language skills of the military to work in multinational environment. The language training should focus not only on the language issues themselves like difficulties in comprehension as a result of fast speaking on behalf of native English speakers, using slang, abbreviations, etc., but also on the culturally based cognition biases and perceptions. Only after overcoming the above-mentioned shortfalls a common understanding will be assured, which we believe is fundamental for the successful integration in multinational teamwork.

The third recommendation concerns development of specific leadership knowledge, attitudes and behaviours, particularly for participation in multinational operations. The good leadership is critical for operational effectiveness. There is a need for a strong leader who would listen to people, who can make decisions quickly, and who can make the best of a bad situation. The leader in multinational operations must be adaptable to change, i.e. to develop the ability to learn from mistakes and quickly adjust to the situation.

The fourth group of suggestions is focused on the ways to enhance the individual, organizational and national trust among coalition partners. One of the statements used most frequently by the respondents in this survey is that professionalism and responsibility lead to respect on behalf of the colleagues from other nations. In addition, they think that it is important for everyone to communicate with respect, regardless of the size of the national contingent, the person's rank and previous experience in international missions. Moreover, honesty and openness in relations with foreign colleagues contribute to increase mutual trust. Likewise, mutual understanding and support among the colleagues from different nationalities will be achieved by stimulating social networking and the development of informal networks. These are some of the key factors for improving teamwork in multinational setting and successful task accomplishment.

4   Conclusions

First of all, analysis of data from this international study shows that there are many different assessments of the relationships among the coalition partners, some of which are completely controversial. Probably, this variety of assessments is the result of the different personal experiences of the surveyed people, their different preconditions for work in a multinational environment, their attitudes towards the different nations and cultures, their specific situation, the personality of the different individuals, the nature of the missions, etc.

In addition, analysis of data found out that the multicultural environment of international military operations is definitely encouraging better mutual understanding and deeper cooperation, but at the same time, it can lead to some points of tension that need to be considered and further explored. The organizational culture of a multinational coalition, as a mixture of different national, military and service cultures, undoubtedly affects the success of the multinational operations. The biggest question which embraces both scientific and practical dimensions is how to build an inclusive culture and common identity in the coalition.

Finally, when cultural differences are discussed as a barrier for effective collaboration in multinational coalitions, most often the tensions appear at personal level, and a few—at organizational level. As far as this was just a qualitative survey, we cannot generalize this conclusion. Therefore, a broader and interdisciplinary research is needed to analyse the role of organizational, cultural and individual-focused issues as barriers to effective human performance in multinational environment. In addition, the survey's results confirmed the important role of cultural adaptability and interoperability in a multinational setting. Besides, it recognized the lack of trust among coalition partners (including local armed forces) as a problem that deserves particular attention because it is related to information sharing and the coalition operations' effectiveness as a whole. There is an urgent need for a focused international comparative study on the issue of trust to identify different dimensions of trustworthiness and factors to establish trust in coalitions.

References

1. Moskos C, Williams J, Segal DR (eds) (2000) The post-modern military: armed forces after the Cold War. Oxford University Press, New York
2. Soeters J, Szvircsev T (2010) Towards cultural integration in multinational peace operations. Def Stud 10(1):272–287; Soeters J, Manigart P (eds) (2008) Military cooperation in multinational peace operations. Routledge; Febbraro A, McKee B, Riedel SL (2008) Multinational military operations and intercultural factors. Neuilly-sur-Seine, pp 3–7
3. Klein P, Haltiner K (2005) Multinationality as a challenge for armed forces. In: Military missions and their applications reconsidered: the aftermath of September 11th, 2005

4. Sutton J, Pierce L (2003) A framework for understanding cultural diversity in cognition and teamwork. In: Proceedings of the 8th international command and control research and technology symposium, Washington; Sutton J, Pierce L, Shawn Burke C, Salas E (2006) Understanding adaptability: a prerequisite for effective performance within complex environments. In: Advances in human performance and cognitive engineering research, vol 6, pp 143–173

5. Abbe A (2008) Building cultural capability for full-spectrum operations. ARI study report 2008-04. US Army Research Institute for the Behavioral and Social Sciences, Arlington; Yanakiev Y, Horton J (eds) (2012) Improving the organizational effectiveness of coalition operations. NATO Science and Technology Organization; Cops C, Tresch S (eds) (2007) Cultural challenges in military operations. Occasional paper. NATO Defense College, Rome; Soeters J, Szvircsev T (2010) Towards cultural integration in multinational peace operations. Def Stud 10:1; Resteigne D, Soeters J (2009) Managing militarily. Armed Forces Soc 35(2):307–332

6. Yanakiev Y, Horton J (eds) (2012) Improving the organizational effectiveness of coalition operations. NATO Science and Technology Organization

7. Stewart K et al (2004) Non-technical interoperability in multinational forces, 21 Apr 2004. https://www.dodccrp.org/events/2004/ICCRTS_Denmark/abstracts/130.pdf

8. Paget S (2016) RUSI J 161(4):42–50

9. Sutton J, Pierce LG, Shawn Burke C, Salas E (2006) Understanding adaptability: a prerequisite for effective performance within complex environments. In: Advances in human performance and cognitive engineering research, vol 6, pp 143–173

10. Atkinson C (2014) Military soft power: public diplomacy through military educational exchanges. Rowman and Littlefield, Lanham; Valaker S, Lofquist E, Yanakiev Y, Kost D (2016) The influence of predeployment training on coordination in multinational headquarters: the moderating role of organizational obstacles to information sharing. Mil Psychol. https://doi.org/10.1037/mil0000123

Captain (BGR-N) (ret.) Yantsislav Yanakiev is a full professor in sociology at the Bulgarian Defence Institute "Prof. Tsvetan Lazarov". He graduated from the Naval Academy in Varna, Bulgaria in 1982. After serving as a commissioned officer at Naval Base Varna, the Navy Headquarters and the Ministry of Defence, he applied for a doctoral study degree in 1988 at the Institute of Sociology, Bulgarian Academy of Sciences in Sofia, Bulgaria and received his Ph.D. in 1995. In addition, he acquired the degree of Doctor of Science in sociology from the same institute in 2009. Prof. Yanakiev specialized as an International Research Fellow at the NATO Defense College in Rome, Italy in 1999 and at Cologne University, Germany in 2001 and 2007. He was a Fulbright Visiting Research Professor at the Defense Equal Opportunity Management Institute (DEOMI), Patrick Air Force Base, FL from October 2012 to March 2013. While at DEOMI his research was related to diversity management and cross-cultural competence in defence organizations. He has been a principal national representative to the NATO Science and Technology Organization Human Factors and Medicine Panel since 2005 and received Individual Scientific Achievement Award of NATO Science and Technology Organization for 2018. Prof. Yanakiev has published more than 200 monographs, articles and research papers in the field of the sociology of the military, human factors in defence organisations, different aspects of civil-military relations, interethnic relations in Bulgaria, in Bulgarian, English and Russian languages.

The Rules of Engagement. An Essential Tool in Need of Improvements

Rafael Martínez

Abstract The rules of engagement (ROE) are designed for maximum protection of the local population and the final success of the mission; however, in high-risk situations and other rare cases they provoke a deep sense of vulnerability. Because of ROE's necessity in international asymmetric warfare missions and of their controversial nature amongst those who have to act following them, this work will try to find out what is the reason for ROE to exist in these operations and the perceptions about ROE from militaries who have been involved in asymmetric warfare missions. This chapter, through in-depth semi-structured interviews with more than 700 military personnel from twelve countries, also intends to check the extent to which ROE are followed by the military and what irregularities the military sees in their practice. Among the respondents the causes of inadequate valuation include: unexplained, restrictive, nonspecific, helplessness, lack training, inapplicable and refused by soldiers.

1 Introduction

The key documents in place to ensure that international missions are properly executed include, among others: (i) the Status of Forces Agreement (SOFA), which governs the status of personnel in international forces such as NATO, and (ii) the Rules of Engagement (ROE). The SOFA is a legal instrument which provides the legal framework for the troops on the ground ([2]: 200). It regulates various issues, including (i) criminal and disciplinary actions (ii) administrative issues (mostly

---

[1] Recently, environmental protection has prominently featured when planning the use of force, and therefore, within ROE.

This study uses the same theoretical and conceptual basis as the one published in [1]. It forms part of the Asymmetric Warfare Project by ERGOMAS' Working Group 'The Military Profession'.

R. Martínez (✉)
University of Barcelona, Barcelona, Spain
e-mail: rafa.martinez@ub.edu

© Springer Nature Switzerland AG 2021
M. Nuciari and E. Olivetta (eds.), *Leaders for Tomorrow: Challenges for Military Leadership in the Age of Asymmetric Warfare*, Advanced Sciences and Technologies for Security Applications, https://doi.org/10.1007/978-3-030-71714-8_7

117

related to finance, funding and aid administration), and (iii) privileges and exemptions enjoyed by multinational forces.

The ROE ensure that reasonable force is used in extreme situations, and only as a last resource. The ROE are important because (i) they are a predetermined tool to help reach operational objectives, and (ii) they provide a legal framework for operations [3]. 'They are a resource (...) in the form of directives or instructions that define the circumstances, conditions, extent and procedures to be followed for the use of force, including lethal force, in the course of military operations' ([4]: 47). These Rules are based on the three main principles of the Law of Armed Conflict: necessity, proportionality and avoiding collateral damage.[1] This is why they tend to be linked to concepts such as 'Transfer of Authority' (TOA) and 'Escalation of Force' (EOF). TOA refers to the limitations imposed by troop-contributing countries for the units of the international organisations that head a mission, whereas EOF relates to the use of resources and force deemed necessary to repel different hostile acts and intents ([4]: 50–51). While the armed forces are subject to these constraints, military companies and private security companies are only subject to the Rules on the Use of Force (RUF) established in their contracts. 'Unlike military personnel, who are guided by rules of engagement that derive from the Law of Armed Conflict, contractor personnel are civilians who are not subject to the military or legal norms reflected in the Geneva Conventions of 1929 and 1949 or the Hague Conventions of 1899 and 1907, in that they are not combatants under the law of war. The Rules on the Use of Force (RUF) for contractor personnel are those set forth in the contracts themselves and in directives issued by each combatant commander' ([5]: 665).[2]

In general terms, the ROE are a tool that leaves little room for improvisation. They are intended to help achieve an effective mission without excesses. In fact, the ROE for ordinary combat action are highly mechanical and group-focused; they do not leave space for the use of individual initiative. 'The relatively straightforward rules of engagement for war fighting are based on highly trained collective skills and drills performed by cohesive groups' ([6]: 713). It should therefore be clear that ROE are not exclusive to peace-keeping operations. The terms 'warlike', 'peacemaking' and 'peacekeeping' operations have specific definitions as regards the rules of engage-ment' ([7]: 223). But it is in the field of peace operations where criticism of the ROE appears in the literature, as they are seen as hindering the normal course of these missions.

As clearly stated by Azari et al. 'Specifically in peace support operations, roles and rules of engagement ambiguity can lead to increased feelings of frustration and helplessness' ([8]: 589). 'When deployed, servicemen face moral issues on a day-to-day basis. They are confronted with moral questions and dilemmas such as the use of weapons, cooperation with other (civil) parties, or unclear and ambiguous rules of engagement in humanitarian missions' ([9]: 619). Mandel opposed this view by arguing that, in these types of operations, it is never easy to identify who the

---

[2]However, the US Deputy Secretary of Defence's memorandum of September 2007 required that RUF be reviewed periodically and changed as necessary in order to minimise the risk of innocent civilian casualties.

opponents are and, therefore, a measured use of force must be reached through robust rules of engagement and by following the commanders' judgement. But he later returned to the inherent ambiguity of ROE: 'We may relax the rules of engagement in order to enhance mission accomplishment or force protection through increased freedom in the application of firepower, but this potentially decreases the safety of noncombatants. Conversely, when we increase the safety of noncombatants through restrictions on the use of firepower, our troops become potentially more vulnerable and their mission more difficult to achieve' ([10]: 520). Vogelaar and Kramer [11] also noted that the ROE can be a hindrance to peace support operations and claimed that military personnel may not be the most suitable to address the complexity of these missions. [12] further discussed the kinds of mental health problems that have been identified among troops involved in peacekeeping operations where the ROE have prevented them from responding in a natural manner. Campbell and Campbell highlighted a major cause for concern caused by the ROE in this type of scenario. 'The relatively straightforward rules of engagement for war-fighting give way to the relatively convoluted rules of engagement for peacekeeping or nation-building. Automatic decisions and instinctive reactions based on combat training give way to considered judgments and measured reactions based on cultural understandings' ([13]: 341–342). After analysing operations carried out in Africa and the usual ROE restrictions, Blocq expressed doubts as to whether Western officers are trained to protect civilians when their rights were violated, and further stated: 'While the rule does not reflect an obligation to use force, the authorization in combination with the mandates does certainly indicate a quest for action in the face of physical human rights violations' ([14]: 293). Van der Meulen and Soeters recalled that a Dutch sergeant was court-martialled for killing an Iraqi civilian who engaged in looting. The sergeant was suspected of not having followed the rules of engagement correctly. The dominant public sentiment was that, if soldiers run the risk of being court-martialled when they have to make vital decisions in split seconds, their safety is in real jeopardy. 'To the degree that the soldiers are being looked upon as enemies instead of friends, the mission runs the risk of losing its feasibility as well as its legitimacy. In such a scenario, the political and public acceptance of any further casualties would dwindle rapidly, not because of their number per se (though that might play a role), but rather because the fragile balance between mission accomplishment and force protection would be seen as unsustainable' ([15]: 550).

To a large extent, for international missions to be accomplished they depend on public opinion being favourable to, and legitimising them [16]; but, at the same time, the views of military leaders in support of military action increase the social legitimacy of the mission ([17]: 17).[3] If this is achieved, and the mission is carried

---

[3]The study indicates the actual danger of blackmail that this support from military leaders may involve. 'Our results suggest that there is an incentive for political leaders to get public endorsements from senior military leaders, which necessarily increases the bargaining power of senior military leaders vis-à-vis their elected civilian leaders. Military commanders might be able to threaten—or even simply insinuate—that they would withhold their support for, or voice skepticism about, a particular military mission unless civilian leaders promised to give in on demands related to troop levels, scope or duration of the mission, restrictions on the rules of engagement, or autonomy in

through to completion, social ethics will be an integral—limiting—part of what is required of the military in their activity [18]. This is what has come to be called post-heroic behaviour [19, 20].[4]

Certainly, as pointed out by [21] when analysing paragraph 0614 of the Norwegian Armed Forces Joint Operational Doctrine: 'Today's complex operations can never be fully covered by manuals and rules of engagement. Our ability to fulfill our tasks depends rather on individuals whose judgment is well developed and mature'; or, as Ruffa showed, each country interprets the ROE according to what happened in the theatre of operations: 'the armies with a better experience (…) are keener on framing their discourse around the rules of engagement and the UN resolution. In contrast, contingents with worse (…) or less (…) experience tend to refer with greater trust to the national chain of command and national reference doctrines' [22]: 215).

In spite of the deserved criticism of the ROE, it is undeniable that they provide guidance and direction for the mission's purpose to be successfully fulfilled. They also seek to protect both the military contingent involved and the civilian population caught in the middle of the conflict. The ROE must prevent the troops in international missions from becoming part of the conflict, and therefore, from generating unnecessary damages. Since they impose restrictions on the armed forces as to when, how and against whom force can be used, the ROE may seem limiting; but ultimately, they strengthen and legitimise a State's foreign military action. When they allow the use of violence, it is because it is essential for self-defence and to avoid greater evils.

This dual role of the ROE, whereby they are both a guarantee and a limitation, has made them controversial. This conflict was already analysed elsewhere in connection with soldiers and non-commissioned officers who had participated in asymmetric warfare [1]. In that study, sponsored by ISA Research Committee no. 1 and ERGOMAS' Working Group 'The Military Profession', was conducted in nine countries: Bulgaria, Denmark, Italy, the Philippines, Slovenia, South Africa, South Korea, Spain and Turkey. It used data collected from semi-structured interviews with 541 military personnel who had taken part in missions in asymmetric warfare environments, with the aim of obtaining information on their experiences.[5] As a

---

carrying out the task. If senior officers were to engage in this type of behavior, they could exert significant policy influence that would undermine the legitimate ability of elected political leaders to make policy decisions' ([17]: 17).

[4]Kober explained the ethical impact that the Intifada has had on the Israeli army. 'As a result of the Intifadas, issues of just war, discriminate use of force, proportionality, and civil liberties have penetrated into Israeli military thought (…). Israel's strong commitment to fight morally has been expressed inter alia by (…) rules of engagement and methods of dispersing demonstrations that tried to ensure that loss of life or serious bodily injury was minimized' ([19]: 111). But this post-heroic behaviour by the Israeli military is justified by the fact that the low-intensity conflicts it has had to face have never threatened the very existence of Israel. 'This type of conflict has never posed any existential threat to Israel and has therefore warranted neither high number of casualties nor negative international opinion as a result of the unintended killing of innocent enemy civilians' ([19]: 115).

[5]We were fully aware of how nebulous and elusive the concept of 'asymmetric war' still is, and this was often discussed while the project was in the design stage. We were also aware that concepts such as the US Army's 'New Wars' [23] and 'MOOTW' (Military Operations Other Than War)

continuation of that study, the ERGOMAS' Working Group 'The Military Profession' carried out the 'Officer and Commander in Asymmetric Warfare Operations' project. This also used semi-structured interviews conducted with officers from seven countries with specific command experiences at every level: platoon, company, and battalion or equivalent. Four of the participants' countries of origin were the same as in the previous study (Bulgaria, Denmark, Italy, Philippines and Spain), and three were new (Cameroon, Finland and Lithuania). They were asked about their experience of the ROE, in particular, their views about these Rules; whether they caused them problems; and, if so, how they had been solved.

2 What Are the ROE?

When we use the term *engagement* we think about fighting and combat, but also, about commitment, duty and obligation. In Mandel's words: 'traditional military weapons require commanders to make difficult "trade off" decisions regarding the proper balance between mission accomplishment, force protection, and the safety of noncombatants' ([10]: 520). Therefore, the Rules of Engagement are commanders' rules for the use of force. According to NATO, they define the circumstances, conditions, degree and manner in which—sometimes even lethal—force, or actions which could be construed as provocative may be applied by armed forces during a military operation.[6] The ROE implement strategic policy decisions. 'ROE are the means by which the NAC [North Atlantic Council] provides political direction for the conduct of military operations, including authorizations for or limitations on the threat or use of force or actions that might be construed as provocative. The purpose of ROE is to ensure that the application of force is controlled by directing the degree of constraint or freedom permitted when conducting an assigned mission' ([33]: 258). As a result, ROE must be concise, brief, clear and understandable by officers of all ranks so as to

---

are more widely accepted. But the international team believed that asymmetry was the concept that best described the type of mission that was sought to be analysed, as it was understood as a conflict between actors with different strengths, values and tactics. It is, at times, an unconventional fight between unequal belligerents. This implies a great disproportion of forces, of unequal status, with unequal numbers, different forms of combat, different methods, procedures, all with dissimilar resources, motivations and different alliances, geographic factors that involve a different familiarity with the terrain, and unequal strategies and technology. The term 'asymmetry' should not be confused with that of dissymmetry, which indicates the mere disproportion of force or quality between two actors, but never in terms of different levels of resources and way of acting [24–32]. The concept of asymmetric warfare reappeared after the 11 September attacks and, although most of the analyses carried out since then have focused exclusively on studying conflicts such as those in Iraq and Afghanistan, asymmetric wars can be grouped into a broad typology that encompasses a multitude of conflicts. It could even be said that the vast majority of contemporary conflicts are asymmetric. However, this study is confined to those cases in which the State has participated; that is, when the armed forces have participated.

[6]See MC362/1 'NATO Rules of engagement' document approved by the North Atlantic Council (NAC) on 30 June, 2003.

avoid contradictions, ambiguity or confusion. ROE should be a flexible instrument designed to best support the mission through various operational phases and should reflect changes in the level of threat.

ROE limit the use of force without undermining the military legitimate right to self-defence. Therefore, military action under ROE can result in either under-reacting or over-reacting to a situation. 'ROE are designed to ensure that the activities of military personnel remain within the law and are consistent with Government policy; they are not a comprehensive statement of either the law or policy, although they take account of both. ROE define the constraints placed upon military activity, as well as the freedoms permitted, and they reflect the operational context in which it is envisaged that force may be used. An enduring accompaniment to ROE is the inherent and inalienable legal right to act in self-defence, where such activity is both reasonable and necessary' [34, Chap. 1:16].

The statements above show that legal, operational and political issues are taken into account in the design of ROE. Concepts such as necessity and proportionality are always borne in mind in order to keep collateral damage to a minimum and, obviously, to maximise efficiency. ROE are a civilian control system on the armed forces and allow political leadership to prioritise political and strategical objectives over military procedures which advocate the use of force in the host country and when facing threats. However, the military still have a predominant role, and a commander will be appointed for each operationally hierarchical level in charge of decision-making and execution. ROE may limit military decision-making capacity, but they will never release the military from their responsibilities. Still, since Multinational and International Military Missions are different from war situations, ROE are far more restrictive when it comes to determining the amount of force to be employed. Similarly, ROE must be fully compliant with the law: they can never justify illegal actions and cannot have rules that contradict either National or International Law [35]. In fact, if multilateral operations were in conflict with the law of any of the participating States, there could be room for caveats and the rule in question could be invalidated.

Two basic procedures are normally followed when devising ROE. They can be developed from scratch for each operation or, alternatively, some key aspects of the previously approved SROE (Standing Rules Of Engagement)[7] can be selected with the supervision of the UN, the EU or NATO. The SROE are a collection of possible responses regarding the use of force and the amount of force to be employed in hypo-thetical situations. They also provide the global objectives and outcomes expected by each organisation involved in the operations.[8] Decisions about which applicable

---

[7]The SROE of UN, EU and NATO are MC 362/1 'NATO Rules of Engagement', 30 June, 2003; EUMC Mtg. Doc. 67/1/05 REV1, February 20, 2006 and UN MD/FGS/0220.0001(2000) 'UNDPKO, Guidelines for the Development of Rules of Engagement for Peace Keeping Operations'. They are also valid for making instruments such as the Rules of Engagement Handbook by the International Institute of Humanitarian Law.

[8]The UN applies restrictive criteria in this regard: 'In the volatile and potentially dangerous environments into which contemporary peacekeeping operations are often deployed, these ROE should be sufficiently robust to ensure that a United Nations peacekeeping operation retains its credibility and

SROE measures are to be incorporated into a mission's OPLAN (Operation Plan) and become ROE will only be made after analysing the mission's specific scenario.

ROE can therefore limit the use of force depending on the type of mission, its political goals and the legislation at hand, but they can never contradict the basic RAMP principle: (R: Return Fire with Aimed Fire. A: Anticipate Attack. M: Measure the amount of Force. P: Protect with deadly force only human life and Property designated by the Commander).[9] This principle ensures self-defence while, at the same time, complying with the requirement of necessity and proportionality to be used when acting in self-defence. *Necessity* requires a necessary use of force only as a last resort, and always to ensure self-defence: 'The necessity principle permits armed forces to engage only those forces committing hostile acts or clearly demonstrating hostile intent. Definitions of hostile act and hostile intent complete the meaning of necessity. A hostile act is an attack or other use of force. Hostile intent is the threat of imminent use of force' [38, Chap. 8:5].

The request for *proportionality* in the use of force allows for the use of the minimum amount of force to ensure self-defence: 'The principle of proportionality requires that the force used be reasonable in intensity, duration, and magnitude, based on all facts known to the commander at the time, to decisively counter the hostile act or hostile intent and to ensure the continued safety of armed forces' [38, Chap. 8:6]).

To sum up, [39] advised that unless ROE are understood and military personnel are trained in them, they can have a disastrous effect on the execution of a mission. In other words, 'training and dissemination of ROE shall be a part of the general training and the mission specific training of the troops. The dissemination of ROE is evidently limited due to classification reasons, but the Knowledge of Standing ROE, the planning, interpretation and structural logic of the ROE is evidently a necessary subject of the general trainings' ([33]: 261–262). The same could be argued about familiarity with RAMP when it comes to self-defence.

---

freedom of action to implement its mandate. The mission leadership should ensure that these ROE are well understood by all relevant personnel in the mission and are being applied uniformly' (UN [36] and EU shows a lot concern for human rights: 'Human rights elements should be incorporated into the full range of planning documents for ESDP (European Security and Defence Policy) missions, including CONOPS (Concept of Operations), OPLAN (Operation Plan) and rules of engagement. These documents should incorporate elements related to both respect for human rights by ESDP missions and the way in which the mission should promote respect for human rights in the mission area' (EU [37: 11]).

[9]*Return Fire with Aimed Fire:* Return force with force. You always have the right to repel hostile acts with necessary force. *Anticipate Attack:* Use force if, but only if, you see clear indicators of hostile intent. *Measure the amount of Force* that you use, if time and circumstances permit. Use only the amount of force necessary to protect lives and accomplish the mission. *Protect with deadly force only human life, and property designated by your commander.* Stop short of deadly force when protecting other property [38, Chap. 8:15].

3   Views on ROE Given by Officers with Asymmetric Warfare Experience

As mentioned earlier, the literature shows that some criticism has been made about ROE in these types of missions. Similarly, the data gathered from soldiers and NCOs seem to suggest that military personnel have been critical of whether ROE are suitable for their role.

According to Table 1, almost a third of the respondents simply stated that, as soldiers, they must follow ROE because of the obedience due; such straightforward answers seem to hide a negative opinion on the rules which determine the use of force in international missions. Only 28.6% said that they consider ROE adequate, and a fifth of the interviewees did not answer. In other words, there seems to be a problem either in how ROE are designed or in how military personnel are trained in them.

Two fifths of those who answered the question (28.7% of all interviewees) considered the ROE used in the missions in which they had participated as inadequate for the conditions found on the ground. They argued that the ROE they were restrictive and seemingly went against military intrinsic nature. Respondents from some countries argued that ROE caused helplessness. Another reason why ROE were seen to be inadequate, in the respondents' views, was that they were not clear and specific enough to the mission in hand, and did not allow for changing circumstances. These reasons deserve different consideration. Perceptions on the restrictive nature of ROE should be obvious and not controversial, since constraint is at the root of the ROE; but when this perception becomes a complaint, it reveals a problem related to military training.

When helplessness was argued as a reason for the inadequacy of ROE, this should be of concern if following ROE had caused loss of life; but only two respondents gave this as a reason. The rest of the interviewees hinted at a feeling, a subjective judgement that should become stronger when one's ability to use force is powerful enough to eliminate a potential threat, or to repel enemy fire with no further consequences. However, it should not be forgotten that one of the *raisons d'être* for ROE (and for their restricting the use of force) is to prevent international troops from becoming further involved in the conflict. The use of force is only permitted when the troops' lives are perceived to be at risk, which did not seem to be the case for the interviewees.

Contrarily, lack of flexibility and specificity are different issues altogether. The data obtained from the interviews seemed to point to the fact that the same ROE were used for different missions, were not appropriate for the mission at hand, were too vague or were rapidly outdated by the changing pace of events. People who devise ROE should do a thorough job: an exhaustive analysis needs to be carried out about the host country and about what to do; agreements need to be made on specific and purposeful ROE, avoiding the existence of conflicting ROE between intervening nations; and ROE should be flexible enough to change as conditions also change. If these aspects are neglected, the commitment contained in the ROE to use limited force (necessary to achieve the political and strategic aims ensured by ROE) will be

Table 1 Soldiers' and NCOs' opinions about the ROE

	Bulgaria		Denmark		Italy		Philippines		Slovenia		South Africa		South Korea		Spain		Turkey		Total	
	%	(n)	%	(n)	%	(n)	%	(n)	%	(n)	%	(n)	%	(n)	%	(n)	%	(n)	%	(n)
Doesn't know/Doesn't answer + Classified Report	6.8	(4)	13.5	(5)	26.5	(22)	0	(0)	0	(0)	21.3	(20)	94	(47)	6.5	(6)	23.5	(8)	20.7	(112)
Answered the question	93.2	(55)	86.5	(32)	73.5	(61)	100	(41)	100	(50)	78.7	(74)	6	(3)	93.5	(87)	76.5	(26)	79.3	(429)
Total	100	(59)	100	(37)	100	(83)	100	(41)	100	(50)	100	(94)	100	(50)	100	(93)	100	(34)	100	(541)
a/No problems	80 (44)[1]	(1)	25	(8)	11.5	(7)	53.7	(22)	32	(16)	45.9	(34)	33.3	(1)	20.7	(18)	23	(6)	29.9	(112)
b/Adequate			28.1	(9)	70.5	(43)	4.9	(2)	20	(10)	13.5	(10)	–	–	34.5	(30)	11.5	(3)	28.6	(107)
c/Inadequate	20	(11)	46.9	(15)	18	(11)	41.5	(17)	48	(24)	40.5	(30)	66.6	(2)	44.8	(39)	65.4	(17)	41.4 (155)[2]	(2)
	100	(55)	100	(32)	100	(61)	100.1	(41)	100	(50)	99.9	(74)	99.9	(3)	100	(87)	99.9	(26)	99.9	(374)
(i) Unexplained	36.4	(4)	–		–		5.9	(1)	8.3	(2)	–		–		15.4	(6)	–		7.8	(13)
(ii) Restrictive	45.5	(5)	73.3	(11)	54.5	(6)	35.3	(6)	20.8	(5)	36.7	(11)	–		46.2	(18)	23.5	(4)	39.8	(66)
(iii) Non-specific	18.2	(2)	6.7	(1)	45.5	(5)	11.8	(2)	62.5	(15)	23.3	(7)	100	(2)	25.6	(10)	70.6	(12)	33.7 (56)[3]	(56)
(iv) Helplessness	–		20	(3)	–		35.3	(6)	8.3	(2)	33.3	(10)	–		12.8	(5)	–		15.7	(26)
(v) Lack of training	–		–		–		11.8	(2)	–		6.7	(2)	–		–		5.9	(1)	3	(5)

(continued)

Table 1 (continued)

	Bulgaria		Denmark		Italy		Philippines		Slovenia		South Africa		South Korea		Spain		Turkey		Total	
	%	(n)	%	(n)	%	(n)	%	(n)	%	(n)	%	(n)	%	(n)	%	(n)	%	(n)	%	(n)
Total	100.1	(11)	100	(15)	99.9	(11)	100.1	(17)	99.9	(24)	100	(30)	100	(2)	100	(39)	100	(17)	100	(166)(4)

(1) In Bulgaria the question was rephrased. The answers of all those who admitted to not having problems with ROE have been included here

(2) Bulgarian results have not been included, since it was not possible to make a difference between those who thought of ROE as adequate and those who simply followed them

(3) In Turkey, an example to illustrate the answer was explicitly elicited and this change meant that many interviewees did not answer about ROE, but about whether these could change depending on the allies, on the mission or on ongoing changes during the mission

(4) The 11 cases in which Bulgarian military personnel did not think of ROE as inadequate have been included here

seen as a pure formality, criticism of ROE will also increase, and to make matters worse, they may not be followed.

To summarise, devising good ROE is paramount if the political aims behind international missions are to be achieved. Suitable ROE requires working at all stages: preliminary tasks will help adjust the predicted use of force to the real conditions that the troops will encounter. This is the time to for clear information about the mission's goals to the public to be provided and for comprehensive, appropriate troop training to be delivered. During the operation, the objective will be to ensure transparency when informing the public about the mission. They must be told what the troops are doing within the ROE framework so as to prevent negative public opinion. It is also during deployment that ROE efficiency and efficacy must be tested. At a later stage, relevant changes should be made to the regulations on the use of force, according to the changing scenario and needs. Lack of information, training and flexibility will only make ROE unpopular among the military and contribute to render operations illegitimate in the public eye.

Both officers and commanders were interviewed in this subsequent phase of the study on asymmetric warfare. The questions were identical in six of the seven countries in which the study was carried out, namely:

(i)   Did you have the opportunity to apply the ROE at any time?
(ii) If so, what were your views on them?
(iii) Did you encounter any problems in applying them?

The questions were slightly more detailed for Spanish respondents:

(i)   Did you ever have to apply the ROE?

    a.   *(If they answered in the affirmative)* How often?
    b.   What were your views on the ROE?
    c.   Did the ROE ever cause you any problems?
        i.   *(If the answer is in the affirmative)* Can you describe the situation, please?
    d.   Did any subordinates complain to you about the ROE?
        i.   *(If the answer was in the affirmative)* What were their complaints?
        ii. Can you explain them?
        iii. What was your response to your subordinates' complaints?

The tabulated responses of the officers from the seven countries involved provide comparable data with which to analyse the important differences and similarities found in their responses (Table 2). The officers were clear about what Rules of Engagement are and should be: baseline, unquestionable rules. 'The ROE are the army's creed. They have to be followed every time as guiding principles' (PHC7). 'ROE are the most essential things for every member of the mission, including civilians' (LTC3). Therefore, obeying the ROE has little merit. 'Law enforcement accomplishment is not a military accomplishment' (PHC16). It can be complicated for officers to manage the ROE if they are asked to apply them when they are not on the ground; but the Rules should help to resolve a conflict without making it worse.

Table 2 Officers' and commanders' opinions about the ROE

	Bulgaria		Cameroon		Denmark		Finland		Italy		Lithuania		Philippines		Spain		Total	
	%	(n)	%	(n)	%	(n)	%	(n)	%	(n)	%	(n)	%	(n)	%	(n)	%	(n)
Not applied	51.6	(31)	18.2	(6)	4.2	(1)	8	(2)	30.2	(13)	0	(0)	0	(0)	25.9	(7)	24.5	(60)
Applied	45	(27)	81.8	(27)	95.8	(23)	92	(23)	67.4	(29)	100	(4)	100	(29)	74.1	(20)	74.3	(182)
No answer	3.3	(2)	0	(0)	0	(0)	0	(0)	2.3	(1)	0	(0)	0	(0)	0	(0)	1.2	(3)
Total	99.9	(60)	100	(33)	100	(24)	100	(25)	99.9	(43)	100	(4)	100	(29)	100	(27)	100	(245)
a/No problems	74.1	(20)	77.8	(21)	13.1	(3)	52.2	(12)	51.7	(15)	25	(1)	72.4	(21)	35	(7)	55	(100)
b/Problems	25.9	(7)	22.2	(6)	87	(20)	47.8	(11)	48.3	(14)	75	(3)	27.5	(8)	65	(13)	45.1	(82)
	100	(27)	100	(27)	100.1	(23)	100	(23)	100	(29)	100	(4)	99.9	(29)	100	(20)	100.1	(182)
(i) Restrictive	14.3	(1)	33.3	(2)	55	(11)	18.2	(2)	57.1	(8)	33.3	(1)	12.5	(1)	46.2	(6)	39	(32)
(ii) Non-specific	57.2	(4)	0	(0)	20	(4)	63.6	(7)	14.3	(2)	33.3	(1)	0	(0)	7.7	(1)	23.2	(19)
(iii) Inapplicable	28.6	(2)	50	(3)	15	(3)	18.2	(2)	28.6	(4)	0	(0)	37.5	(3)	30.8	(4)	25.6	(21)
(iv) Refused by soldiers	0	(0)	0	(0)	10	(2)	0	(0)	0	(0)	33.3	(1)	50	(4)	15.4	(2)	11	(9)
Not specified	0	(0)	16.7	(1)	0	(0)	0	(0)	0	(0)	0	(0)	0	(0)	0	(0)	1.2	(1)
Total	100.1	(7)	100	(6)	100	(20)	100	(11)	100	(14)	99.9	(3)	100	(8)	100.1	(13)	100	(82)

'The hardest part of using ROE is when you're not involved in the accident, but you have to coordinate everything via radio' (LTC3). 'After a while, I realised that it's much more practical to settle their conflicts by peaceful means (...). We must be fair' (PHC24). Over time they have been improved and perfected. The experience in the Balkans was a significant determining factor in not allowing atrocities to happen again. 'I actually think the Balkans were worse than Afghanistan in the beginning, as we didn't really realise there was this (asymmetry), so we could be "played" by the enemy... We learned from that and used it during the Afghanistan mission. We didn't observe atrocities being carried out without intervening, as we did in Bosnia' (DKC21). However, ROE are certainly not so easy to apply in counterinsurgency (COIN) scenarios. 'ROE are "a must", but a huge challenge when operating in a COIN environment' (DKC16). Even so, they are essential when insurgents are mixed with civilians. 'I feel it's clear that ROE are needed. It is a necessary evil when facing irregular opponents who are mixed with the local population' (DKC13).

The first major finding of interest was that, while 20% of soldiers and NCOs refused to answer questions about ROE, only 1.2% of officers refused to do so. This reveals that the reserved nature of ROE has become much more integrated and normalised among senior officers. In some countries, their exact content cannot be revealed, but this does not prevent them from being assessed without any problems.

A quarter of the respondents had never used ROE, usually because the type of duties they carried out did not entail their use. Therefore they were unable to assess the application of the ROE. In Bulgaria more than half of the sample fell into this category. From the other three quarters of all respondents, 55% of those who answered said that they had not had problems with ROE. 'We did not have any problems with ROE because all the personnel knew when and how they could use weapons, and they were ready for it before the mission' (LTC4). The rest had experienced difficulties regarding their implementation. Of those, 1% did not specify what these difficulties were; but all the others did. This complex issue has been dealt with under four categories applied to ROE: (i) Restrictive, (ii) Non-specific, (iii) Inapplicable and (iv) Refused by soldiers.

'Restrictive' refers to opinions to the effect that ROE were insufficient and caused them frustration. 'Another situation was that the British were engaged and a soldier was shot. We saw a flash which might have been from a sniper—a monocular or perhaps a shot? We were 99% sure that it was the sniper. So, we called in that we had him observed, and that we were 2000 metres away. The British soldiers were still engaged and took another hit. I was told not to engage. I must admit that I started to shout in the tower then. (...) So, it was really frustrating to sit and watch, without being used to help in the fighting' (DKC1). They felt that being compelled to follow the ROE was inefficient and even awkward. 'They cause me problems because sometimes the ROE don't allow me to take action' (SPC3). Therefore, some of the respondents thought that the ROE prevented them from acting accordingly to their military condition. Respondents who had to ignore their military status and constrain themselves admitted to feeling frustrated. Some 39% singled out frustration as the main reason for them to feel that ROE were inadequate (46% among Spanish, 55% among Danish, and 57% among Italian).

    In general, the complaint that ROE were restrictive alluded to the lack of room for
manoeuvre which, ultimately, delegitimised their command position. 'The language
in the ROE is not practical, and they tend to be too restrictive. They fail to take into
account that very frequently it is the OSC (On Scene Commander) who must make
decisions, since they are on the ground' (SPC13). 'In general, the ROE regarding
threat are a bit 'limiting and do not give the right space to commanders' (ITB2).
Many think that the ROE come from an office. 'Restrictions, however, were not
that well thought through. For instance, only a major could give the order to fire,
but the officer in command of our squadron was a captain, and so he was forced to
ask every time he wanted to open fire…' (DKC7). Rules therefore did not relate to
the conditions found on the ground. 'I have no criticism to make on a theoretical
level. In practical terms, we often shouldn't have done what we did…' (ITB9). The
commanding officers on the field stated that their commanders did not trust them and
their troops enough, and they held it against them that they were far removed from
the fighting fields. 'ROE make good sense from a distance, but they make it much
more difficult to fulfil the mission. They hinder us from doing the mission' (DKC9).
'It was as if they did not really trust the lieutenants who were facing the fighting. So,
I couldn't decide… And they were in a secure room. Actually, I think they should
try to get out there too; perhaps then, they would trust the man out there' (DKC10).
They complained that having to distinguish between hostile act and hostile intent,
while clear on paper, was often difficult in the midst of conflict. 'They are sometimes
restrictive; we played on the definition of hostile act and hostile intent to take timely
action' (ITB10). 'In most cases, the ROE favoured hostile acts, since the enemy knew
our limitations and used them against us (the enemy could shoot the unit, hide away
and leave their weapon, and then you couldn't engage in fire)' (SPC11). 'There was
a discrepancy between our ROE and those of the Americans, who could afford to be
much more aggressive. They give a much broader interpretation to "hostile intent"
(ITC25). 'But when I was working with the Americans, there was a diversity of rules
of engagement: their rules were more permissive than ours' (ITC31).
    The most controversial complaints about the restrictive character of the ROE were
those with undesirably restrictive—and even perverse—effects, given their limiting
nature. Some complaints were recorded about: (i) the loss of ability to open fire.
'They were related to the conflict occasionally created between the application of
ROE and the security of the Force' (SPC27); 'I translated the meaning of both 421
and 429 alpha. I said if you are in doubt, then you are not in doubt '(DKC18); (ii)
the loss of the surprise factor. 'There might be situations when I will not apply the
ROE. We are fighting REBELS and they played us up treacherously. There might be
some aspects that don't need to be applied. For example, if we conduct an ambush,
we can't attract attention to ourselves, or else we lose the surprise element and they
will usually try to fire at us first' (PHC13); (iii) excessive self-control of the troops,
which can lead to orders being disobeyed. 'ROE are more restrictive, but they're not
a solution: Then, the fear of making mistakes is greater than the fear of waging wars'
(DKC23). 'Our ROE are quite strict, people are afraid to break them, afraid to take
responsibility for shooting. (…) Even after the command to shoot is given, action
itself often gets delayed for fear of the possible consequences of killing a person;

psychologically it's not easy. Specific training is needed' (LTC1); (iv) putting your subordinates at risk. 'We saw a lot of them who were armed in the area, but it was still a community, so I just asked for back-up and we waited' (PHC19). 'Later deployments/teams had problems, as the use of violence became more restricted. We had to get their trust, so no killings. This is a problem when you want to protect your 130 soldiers (DKC2); they were prepared to defend themselves and it is a mistake when the ROE prevent this. 'ROE were very strict during UN missions (...). We still had to observe proportionality in our interventions, and this could be frustrating for our soldiers' (DKC21). 'I think it would be dangerous if the ROE were too tight. It could be life-threatening if permission was given too late... well... you know, a soldier should always be allowed to defend himself, that's described on his soldier's card' (DKC25); (v) giving the initiative to your rivals, who take full advantage of your ROE. 'If it hadn't been for the ROE, perhaps I would have wished for more chances to have different levels of force there. They were very limited. (...) The problem is that the locals know the ROE much better than the soldiers themselves' (FINC3). 'In Afghanistan, the ROE in general were not in our favour. They demanded courageous restrain. The idea of 'if possible, don't fire back' was passed down as being a victory for us, but it wasn't. The Taliban didn't perceive us as strong fighters when we didn't shoot back' (DKC6). 'The Taliban shot and ran in nine out of ten times, so I couldn't pursue them. The Taliban knew our ROE. You quickly lose the legal right to shoot because you need sufficient and continuous evidence that they're enemies. You cannot be pre-emptive, only reactive' (DKC13).

All those statements that alluded to the impossibility of following the ROE every time or following them 100% have been collected under the heading 'Inapplicable'. According to these statements, the ROE are a set of principles that can be perfectly replaced by common sense (26% of all respondents, 31% in Spain and 38% in the Philippines). The great majority used different arguments to say that ROE are removed from reality. This distancing may have resulted from the fact that the ROE had been created by a bureaucrat who was not aware of what was happening on the ground. 'The rules of engagement used to be established by bureaucrats who know nothing about the field; but it should be noted that these ROE usually make the task at hand difficult, but guide us to act according to the law' (CMRC30). 'Whoever writes the ROE does not take into account the situation on the ground' (ITC1). In addition, they reported that in theory, the ROE were excellent; but when applying them this was not so obvious. 'One might write down something legal, but (ROE) are sometimes very difficult to follow in an operative situation' (DKC8). 'ROE are easy to explain but difficult to apply. Control of access to areas occupied by different ethnic groups ensures freedom of movement, distribution of humanitarian aid to opposing parties...The complaints are always related to excessive or scarce use of force, bias, and spurious interests' (SPC26). 'The rule: "if you see an enemy you call to him first and say "stop or I'll fire"... I just find this rule hard to apply' (PHC7). 'Supposedly, before we increase the strength of any joint operation, there is a Memorandum of Agreement (MOA) or a mother MOA for coverage; if the worst comes to the worst, that is, if there is a problem' (PHC16). 'You can physically see somebody who you think is a bad guy, but if you don't see any weapon, you can't shoot him. This is what is at the back of your mind. It was the same in Iraq but less often. In Afghanistan situations built up all the time, so you just wondered: when do I shoot? (…) But the rules are unclear sometimes' (DKC15). Or simply because it is impossible to meet the goals set if the instructions provided in ROE are followed. 'They are not easy to follow because almost everyone has guns. It is hard to imagine. If we make an arrest, we may annoy someone. What we do is talk to them if there is conflict, so that we don't turn small issues into big conflicts. If it could be done peacefully, we tried to do it like that' (PHC24). 'But until the mission obtained the right to implement Article VII of the UN charter, fulfilling the mission of protecting civilians wasn't easy' (CMRC34).

This difficulty in applying the ROE is sometimes overcome by arguing that they are not a set of rules to be rigorously enforced, but merely an inspirational principle. 'It is hard to apply the ROE literally: you have to decide in just a few seconds' (ITC20). Some respondents also maintained that, given the difficulty in interpreting the ROE, they cannot even be used as an inspirational principle. 'The various situations that can arise sometimes make it hard to interpret the rules' (FINC9). And some other times it was argued that each country that uses the ROE interprets them differently. 'It often happens that the forces involved are multinational, and then we have to apply the ROE of different countries and reconcile them all' (ITC5). Some respondents also said that applying them could still be worse. 'Applying ROE correctly requires being savvy at all levels, from the individual soldier to the commander. If we had applied the ROE rigidly in an actual operation we would have killed a lot of innocent people. (…) I don't think that you can change the ROE; they can't take all possible scenarios into account' (ITC9). This happened practically on a daily basis in the first missions. 'It's important not to go back to the time of the first UN-led missions, when the ROE were illogical and the forces were rendered impotent' (SPC10). 'It is important not to go back to the illogical ROE of the first United Nations missions where the military forces were powerless' (SPC22).

Some used grotesque arguments to refer to their inapplicability: 'We always use them … No problems applying them … but I have the impression that international organisations (UN) are supporting terrorism' (DKC2). Another resource used was irony. Whereas ROE were portrayed as being crucial, at the same time it was stated that they were not met. Taking the argument to the extreme, the ROE were assessed only as an interpretive tool, since their fulfilment would lead to failure: 'The same ROE can be implemented in a mission in Afghanistan or in another one in Lebanon. It all depends on a selective and gradual implementation based on the knowledge of the environment and the actors. Based on this, the key factors are: (a) a thorough study of the content and the spirit of the ROE, as well as the constant training and analysis of situations where they would be used; (b) based on the above, the development of intuition and initiative; (c) common sense' (SPC25).

The 'Non-specific' heading included answers which saw ROE as being unclear or not specific, too vague or not fit for purpose (23% of all respondents, 57% in Bulgaria and 64% in Finland). ROE were perceived as a constraint which did not fit the different and often fast-changing circumstances of the mission at hand. In short, they were not precise enough to meet the expectations of military personnel. 'Our soldiers are very afraid of killing non-combatants because it's a grey area... So they often call in and ask if they are allowed to kill this man, and if they get a 'yes'... we may have to pay 'blood money' afterwards, but what can we do? It's a grey area...' (DKC26). 'You had to judge for yourself, and to take individual decisions on how to apply them' (BGC57). 'When you read the ROE they look very clear, but when you're out there to carry them out, they work completely differently (FINC24). 'Let's say that we often found ourselves discussing this. Because it is a thorny issue. Because it is not all black or white: there are many shades of grey and you have to be totally ready, but also be very sensitive' (ITC33). 'In general, the complaints about the ROE arise from the lack of clarity and the reduced flexibility when using them (permission needed from the upper ranks, etc.)' (SPC23).

The complaint made against the 'bureaucrats' who developed the ROE was repeatedly made by respondents. These Rules were described above as being impossible to apply whereas, more condescendingly, these bureaucrats were also accused of having used a 'ROE template' that had been entirely cut and pasted from one international mission to another, without taking into consideration the content, place, and other unique factors. 'Personally I am not competent enough to explain weapon usage rules (ROE), because it is a legal system. People who are responsible for creating these rules understand it better and they are paid for it. However, when it comes to putting this into practice, these rules sometimes work against soldiers' interests. There were several situations when I, as commander of a unit, realised that some rules were too abstract, or sometimes too restrictive. From my own experience in real situations and lessons I learned, I realised that we need to act differently, not according to ROE. (...) It is of course very comfortable to write those rules/papers when you sitting in an office, but to apply them in practice is really hard' (LTC2). Some respondents were convinced that not even military jurists, who are guarantors of the correct interpretation of the ROE, are clear about what they mean. 'Yes, the biggest problem was the release of deadly force when in danger, but not under direct fire. (...) Outside my camp in the dessert and at night I was called to the tactical operation centre to decide how to react to some Taliban who were most presumably planting an IED. I fired warning shots against them, but it was not allowed according to ROE. I was interrogated by a Danish military legal adviser and I got off the hook by asking him 'would it have been better legally to shoot them?', because I could argue that they were definitively digging and, if so, I was entitled to shoot at them' (DKC16). This lack of clarity is such that asking legal advisors about the correct interpretation of ROE can be a bad decision: 'However, it is a problem to tell the legal advisor from your army how and what we did to take action' (DKC22).

There is a belief that previous experience helps in the development of later ROE; but this is also not one hundred percent true. While there may be a common core, each mission has its own peculiarities that must be addressed differently: 'For Afghanistan the situation was different, more unpredictable, and the commander would often have to make assessments about the local situation' (ITC19). In addition, however hard those involved in devising the ROE try, they cannot cover everything. 'There could be situations in which there was no ready bag of tricks that I could use to act on' (FINC5). Therefore, it is advisable not to generate situations that give rise to areas of uncertainty as far as the ROE are concerned; for example, exposing themselves pointlessly and triggering legitimate defence, and repelling an attack when the ROE intend for them not to intervene so as not to increase the conflict. 'You must avoid situations which can lead you to become a target. You should avoid stopping in crowded areas so as not to become a target for a suicide bomber and, if you have to stop, then you spread out and survey the surroundings' (FINC17).

But the only problem is not that the content of a certain ROE fails to address a specific situation encountered in a mission; there are also ROE from different allied armies which are all applicable on the ground, but each markedly different. 'Danish soldiers were always allowed to react in self-defence, in contrast to UK soldiers. Actually, we had the right to pre-emptive action if threatened' (DKC17). Or as a Finnish officer mentioned about having some doubts about which rule to apply (the ROE or the criminal code): 'So force can be used during the mission, according to the operation's ROE, but every Finnish citizen can use necessary force to defend themselves. If a Finish Company is on patrol and fire is opened on the left, is it acceptable force according to crisis control law or self-defence according to the Finnish criminal code?' (FINC11).

Finally, the category 'Refused by Soldiers' (11% of all respondents, but 50% among interviewees from the Philippines) collected the statements from all the officers who stated that their main problem had been their subordinates not understanding the ROE and rejecting them. 'When the one in command does not know how to control his men, they might violate the rules of engagement. For example, there might be enemies in the area where there also civilians and they asked me to give an order to attack' (PHC25). There were several Filipino officers who told us about the problems caused by the tendency that their men had to looting. In particular, one of them recounted how he had been compelled to take action with his troop, who had stolen, roasted and eaten a goat: 'I have zero tolerance for stealing. I first imposed this rule on my junior officers and then the troops followed' (PHC17).

Differences of opinion between soldiers and military jurists on how to interpret the ROE are not infrequent, as narrated by a Danish officer: 'I had a capable MJUR (military lawyer). She was the image of what soldiers needed, but there seem to be great differences between them. It's not easy to navigate complex combat situations when we're allowed to shoot and when we're not. When you saw the enemy, described the situation over the radio and then got a 'no!' I don't think that that it is appropriate, and I don't think the MJUR always understood the military perspective. My MJUR explained why we could not engage with the target. My men didn't agree, but accepted the argument' (DKC20). But he also acknowledged that trying to comply with the ROE was justified in pursuit of a greater benefit: 'I had to argue for 'courageous restraint'—that we were not allowed to defend ourselves, and that it was not smart to shoot, when we are working on winning hearts and minds, due to the consequences...' (DKC20).

One of the complaints voiced by soldiers and non-commissioned officers (but not by officers) in the first wave of interviews was defencelessness. However, this argument was used by the interviewees as a justification for why the troop rejected the

ROE. 'Sometimes it rendered my unit illogically defenceless. I haven't had any problems with subordinates in this regard, although they have always sought clarification for the correct interpretation of them' (SPC5). 'The ROE were so restrictive that they were almost against the legitimate right to self-defence. For this reason, it was difficult to explain them to your subordinates' (SPC9). Sometimes, soldiers wanted to go beyond what the ROE allowed in terms of the use of firepower. Shooting conferred security due to the higher capabilities this provided; but restricting weapon use made them feel weakened and threatened. 'I noted that sometimes soldiers wanted to use more force than was allowed, but it is the officer's job to control everything and learn from these kind of situations' (LTC3). There were even situations in which the limitation was so frustrating that it was preferable to withdraw the troops than to enforce a ROE that made them nervous. 'Sometimes I feel angry, I want to capture or hurt that person but I can't do anything because I have a very high appreciation of the rules of engagement. If I see my troop becoming very angry about the situation, I simply tell them to go back. I am sometimes afraid that the longer we stay in a village, the less I can control my troops' (PHC13). A Filipino officer told us how difficult it was to ensure that his men abided by the ROE. They had lost a colleague, were very nervous and wanted revenge in the next town they went to: 'The troops appeared angry towards me, but they still followed my orders (…) The troops follow an order despite their anger. They follow because of the instruction given to them' (PHC4).

The interviews with soldiers, non-commissioned officers and commanders showed that around 40% of them had been compelled to apply controversial ROE. Firstly, in the three scales, four out of every ten found the ROE to be restrictive, which was the main complaint among soldiers and non-commissioned officers in six of the nine countries analysed, and in four of the eight where officers were interviewed. In Denmark, Italy and Spain, it was the main concern of all ranks: 73%, 55% and 46%, respectively. Secondly, non-specificity was a complaint in both waves of interviews; as a priority for Slovenian soldiers (63%), Turks (71%) and, to a lesser extent, Italians (46%); as well as for Bulgarian (57%) and Finnish (64%) officers. Thirdly, soldiers complained of helplessness, mainly Filipinos (35%) and South Africans (33%). Instead, commanders noted their inapplicability; the main complaints came from Cameroonian officers (50%), and from more than one third of Filipino and Spanish officers. For the Filipino respondents, however, their main problem with the ROE was that it was rejected by the soldiers (50%).

The answers given in the interviews led to the belief that Danish officers were, by far, the most critical in their responses. This was not seen as a problem for two reasons. First, because it shows that their answers were totally honest and had been freely given (something which, for example, could be questioned in the case of the Bulgarian officers interviewed, who seemed to have given rote answers). And second, because they unanimously stated that, despite the criticism expressed, ROE were overall more beneficial than harmful. The Filipino officers interviewed also recognised that, more than once, the ROE had helped them to save the lives of civilians and also to reprimand a few trigger-happy troops with a certain cultural tendency to war-time looting.

A small group of officers made an interesting comment. They remarked that they had never been forced to apply the ROE in a specific way, although they acknowledged that ROE were permanently present in their routines. In fact, this kind of response made it apparent that there were already a good number of officers for whom ROE were not a protocol on how to use force in exceptional cases, but that they admitted that ROE provided an overall line of action.

It must be stressed that troops are not ordinarily trained in the complexity of these types of missions; they are primarily trained on how to control the use of force to defend both the nation and its national identity. Consequently, it should not be surprising that officers often see ROE as a constraint; and as inefficient and contrary to what they believe to be the logical response from the military in a war setting. An international mission is an asymmetric conflict, it is not an interstate war, and its objectives are not defeating an enemy and re-establishing the status quo. In these complex asymmetric warfare missions, the military are used as a tool which happens to be not too fit for the purpose, but that can still address the needs created by the conflict. For the same reasons, in asymmetric warfare missions, the aim is not to defeat the opposition, but rather what is sought for is the viability of restoring or creating a State in the host country. These are the reasons why ROE restrict and constrain the military. In view of the above, and particularly bearing in mind the training received by officers, the views of military personnel should not come as a surprise, especially if they see their role as institutional rather than occupational. At the same time, the States and International Organisations that engage in international missions should reflect thoroughly on how to best explain the complex nature of these operations (compared to conventional warfare) to both the public and the military. They should emphasise the need of using the armed forces even though they may not be the most adequate tool to carry out such tasks. It must be explained that through following ROE, the military may lose some of their prerogatives about the use of force in order to achieve the ultimate goals set for each mission.

In addition, ROE must be adapted to individual missions. When ROE are identical in different situations, or never change regardless of the mission or of a mission's changing conditions; or when a mission lasts longer than anticipated and there is no room for flexibility, they become problematic. It is to the role of political bodies and authorities to solve these potentially challenging situations, since it is they who— from their offices—devise inflexible ROE which cannot be adapted to the substantial changes that will certainly occur when in action.

4 Conclusions

It has been shown that the Rules of Engagement determine when, where, against whom and which how much force (including lethal force) must be used in a military operation. ROE in MOOTWA (Military Operations Other Than War) become more restrictive because of political and strategic reasons which go beyond the strictly military nature of a mission: this situation is logical and it is reflected in the SROE by the UN, the EU and NATO. The purpose of ROE in asymmetric warfare is to ensure the success of a mission, and to severely delimit the use of force by international troops in order to remain neutral in the conflict and not to increase aggression between the parties. However, this magnificent aspiration is not always achieved, and when it is, it is not always well understood by those who must apply the ROE. This is essentially for three reasons: (i) because the ROE are perceived as being extremely restrictive, excessively limiting the ability to respond to an attack and, therefore, leading military personnel to defencelessness and frustration; (ii) because they are not rules specifically thought out and designed for the conflict in which the armed forces must engage, but rather, they are overly generic rules that arise from a regulatory framework intended to be common to all missions and, therefore, far from the real conditions on the ground; (iii) and lastly, because their strict application may not be possible (in whole or in part); they only cause permanent uncertainty as to how they should be understood and interpreted at each particular moment. Ultimately, they are perceived as recommendations which do not go much beyond common sense and are designed by a 'bureaucrat' oblivious to what the soldiers on the ground will actually face.

In view of the above discussion, it should be of no surprise that there was some criticism of ROE and of mere obedience of them by military personnel. This should be interpreted as a warning about the pressing need for including proper training on what ROE and their aims are, and what they mean. If a mission's ultimate objectives are understood, ROE will be more widely accepted in spite of being seen as a necessary constraint in the use of force.

References

1. Martínez R (2013) Rules of engagement in asymmetric warfare. In: Caforio G (ed) Soldiers without frontiers: The view from the ground. experiences of asymmetric warfare. Acireale-Roma, Bonanno Editore, Gruppo Editoriale s.r.l
2. Jáudenes Lameiro JA (1998) La actuación de la Fuerza: conclusiones Cuadernos de estrategia, n° 94, Instituto Español de Estudios Estratégicos, Ministerio de Defensa, Madrid
3. Fojón Lagoa JE (1998) La actuación de la fuerza: consideraciones sobre el ejercicio de la Fuerza, Cuadernos de estrategia, no 94. Instituto Español de Estudios Estratégicos, Ministerio de Defensa, Madrid
4. Ponce de León RL (2012) Las Reglas de enfrentamiento (ROE) como paradigma del estado de derecho en operaciones militares, Revista Española de Derecho Militar 99, pp 37–220
5. Terry JP (2010) Privatizing defense support operations: the need to improve DoD's oversight and management. Armed Forces Soc 36(4):660–670. https://doi.org/10.1177/0095327x1036 1669
6. Neuteboom P, Soeters J (2016) The military role in filling the security gap after armed conflict: three cases. Armed Forces Soc 43(4):711–733. https://doi.org/10.1177/0095327x16667087
7. Feldman S, Hanlon C (2012) Count us in: The experiences of female war, peacemaking, and peacekeeping veterans. Armed Forces Soc 38(2):205–224. https://doi.org/10.1177/0095327x1 1410859
8. Azari J, Dandeker C, Greenberg N (2010) Cultural stress: how interactions with and among foreign populations affect military personnel. Armed Forces Soc 36

9. Schut M, Graaf MC, Verweij D (2015) Moral emotions during military deployments of dutch forces: a qualitative study on moral emotions in intercultural interactions. Armed Forces Soc 41(4):616–638. https://doi.org/10.1177/0095327x14549594
10. Mandel R (2004) Nonlethal weaponry and post-cold war deterrence. Armed Forces Soc 30
11. Vogelaar, ALW. Kramer E-H (2004) Mission command in dutch peace support missions. Armed Forces Soc 30
12. Britt TW, Adler AB (eds) (2003) The psychology of the peacekeeper: lessons from the field. Praeger, Westport, CT
13. Campbell DJ, Campbell KM (2010) Soldiers as police officers/ police officers as soldiers: role evolution and revolution in the United States. Armed Forces Soc 36
14. Blocq D (2010) Western soldiers and the protection of local civilians in UN peacekeeping operations: is a nationalist orientation in the armed forces hindering our preparedness to fight? Armed Forces Soc 36
15. Van der Meulen J, Soeters J (2005) Dutch courage: The politics of acceptable risks. Armed Forces Soc 31
16. Berndtsson J, Dandeker C, Ydén K (2014) Swedish and British public opinion of the armed forces after a decade of war. Armed Forces Soc 41(2), 307–328. https://doi.org/10.1177/0095327x13516616
17. Golby J, Feaver P, Dropp K (2018) Elite military cues and public opinion about the use of military force. Armed Forces Soc 44(1):1–28. https://doi.org/10.1177/0095327x16687067
18. Kucera T (2014) The strategic significance of ethical imperatives: the case of the german armed forces. Armed Forces Soc 41(4):639–658. https://doi.org/10.1177/0095327x14547806
19. Kober A (2013) 'From heroic to post-heroic warfare: Israel's way of war in asymmetrical conflicts. Armed Forces Soc 41(1):96–122. https://doi.org/10.1177/0095327x13498224
20. Luttwak EN (1995) Toward post-heroic warfare. Foreign Aff 74(3):109–122
21. Sookermany AM (2011) The embodied soldier: towards a new epistemological foundation of soldiering skills in the (Post) modernized norwegian armed forces. Armed Forces Soc 37
22. Ruffa C (2013) What peacekeepers think and do: An exploratory study of French, Ghanaian, Italian, and South Korean Armies in the United Nations Interim Force in Lebanon. Armed Forces Soc 40(2):199–225. https://doi.org/10.1177/0095327x12468856
23. Kaldor M (2003) Global civil society. Cambridge, Polity Press, An Answer to War
24. Bellamy AJ (2004) Protecting non-combatants in war. Int Aff 80(5):829–850
25. Duffield M (2004) Las nuevas guerras en el mundo global. Catarata, Serie Relaciones Internacionales, Madrid
26. Kaldor M (1999) New and old wars. Polity Press, Cambridge
27. Lind William S, Nightengale Keith, Schmitt John F, Sutton Joseph W, Wilson Gary I (1989) The changing face of war: into the fourth generation. Military Rev 69(10):2–11
28. McInnes C (1999) Spectator Sport Warfare. Contemp Secur Policy 20(3):142–165
29. McInnes C (2006) Spectator-sport war: the west and contemporary conflict. Boulder, CO., Lynne Rienner
30. Münkler H (2005) Viejas y nuevas guerras. Asimetría y privatización de la violencia. Siglo XXI, Madrid
31. Shaw M (2004) The state of globalizations: towards a theory of state transformation. In: Sinclair TJ (ed) Global governance. critical concepts in political science. Routledge, London, Tomo I, pp 210–225
32. Nye J (1996) Conflicts after the cold war. Wash Q 19(1):4–24
33. NATO (2010) NATO legal deskbook, (2nd Edn) NATO ed. ACT Staff Element Europe, Belgium
34. Ministry of Defence (2008) Brithish Defence Doctrine; Joint Doctrine Publication 0–01 (3rd Edition)
35. Alía Plana M (2009) 'Las Reglas de Enfrentamiento (ROE)' Cuaderno Práctico de Estudios nº 1 Mayo-Agosto, Escuela Militar de Estudios Jurídicos (Centro de Investigación y Doctrina Legal). Ministerio de Defensa, Madrid
36. United Nations (2008) United Nations peacekeeping operations. Principles and guidelines. United Nations (Department of Peacekeeping Operations & Department of Field Support)

37. European Union (2008) Mainstreaming human rights and gender into European security and defence policy. Belgium, European Communities
38. Headquarters, Department of the Army (2000) FM/27-100.(Army Field Manual) legal support to operation. General Dennis J. Reimer Training and Doctrine Digital Library
39. McClung KJ (2004) Law and land warfare and rules of engagement: a review of army doctrine and training methodologies, USAWC strategy research project. US Army War College, Pennsylvania
40. Jiménez Piernas (2000) 'Comunicación' en Navarrete Moreno et alt. (comp.) *Nuevas misiones de la defensa: un análisis politológico,* (I Encuentro de politólogos españoles para el análisis de las intervenciones armadas por la paz y en defensa de los derechos humanos), Ed. Ilustre Colegio Nacional de Doctores y Licenciados en Ciencias Políticas y Sociología y Maosprint, Ventas de Retamosa
41. Kaldor M (2010) El poder y la fuerza. La seguridad de la población civil en un mundo global. Barcelona, Ensayo Tusquets eds
42. Newman E (2004) The 'new wars' debate: a historical perspective is needed. Secur Dialogue 35(2):173–189. https://doi.org/10.1177/0967010604044975
43. OTAN (1998) Manuel de l'Otan, Bruselas, OTAN Edition du 50eme, anniversaire
44. Pérez Casado R (2000) 'Comunicación' en Navarrete Moreno et alt. (comp.) *Nuevas misiones de la defensa: un análisis politológico,* (I Encuentro de politólogos españoles para el análisis de las intervenciones armadas por la paz y en defensa de los derechos humanos), Ed. Ilustre Colegio Nacional de Doctores y Licenciados en Ciencias Políticas y Sociología y Maosprint, Ventas de Retamosa
45. Reinares F (2000) 'Comunicación' en Navarrete Moreno et alt. (comp.) *Nuevas misiones de la defensa: un análisis politológico,* (I Encuentro de politólogos españoles para el análisis de las intervenciones armadas por la paz y en defensa de los derechos humanos), Ed. Ilustre Colegio Nacional de Doctores y Licenciados en Ciencias Políticas y Sociología y Maosprint, Ventas de Retamosa
46. Sañudo Alonso de Celis V (1998) La actuación de la Fuerza: un nuevo tipo de operaciones Cuadernos de estrategia, n° 94, Instituto Español de Estudios Estratégicos, Ministerio de Defensa, Madrid
47. Study Group on Europe's Security Capabilities (2004) A human security doctrine for Europe, Barcelona September 14th, 2004

Reasons for and Solution to Morale Problems as Seen by Officers from 7 Nations

Henning Sørensen

Abstract 216 officers from seven nations: Bulgaria, Cameroun, Denmark, Finland, Italy, the Philippines, and Spain were asked their perception of the "unit´s morale" during deployment abroad in asymmetric wars. Half of them saw no morale problems. Major national differences appeared here as only 20% of Spanish officers reported morale problems whereas 90% of Danish officers did. The other half of 109 officers did mention 160 reasons for a drop in morale related to either *War, leadership,* or *individual problems.* The 109 officers' views are distributed rather equally on the three categories. Nevertheless, a majority of Danish officers (15 out of 17) reported war factors. In contrast, 10% or less of officers from Spain, Finland, Bulgaria and the Philippines gave the same answer. Over half of the Italian officers saw leadership factors causing morale problems (14 out of 26) while no officer from the Philippines and a few from Spain did so. Almost three out of four officers from the Philippines found that individual problems created morale problems. Only one out of five officers or less from the other nations identified the same cause. Some of the national differences are tentatively explained. Of the 75 solutions suggested, 75% said it was for the military leadership to remedy. The result of the study for the concept of morale and how to handle morale problems in a military unit operating in asymmetric warfare is discussed.

1 Officers Sample

The number of participating officers, their rank and national background is shown in Table 1.

Table 1 shows that 216 officers were interviewed. Most from Bulgaria (56) and fewest from Denmark (21). 59% of the Bulgarian officers come from the upper echelons (Lieutenant Colonel—General), while 81% of the officers from Italy and 72% from Finland and the Philippines come from lower ranks (Lieutenant—Captain).

H. Sørensen (✉)
Borrenosen 13, 2800 Lyngby, Denmark
e-mail: isfdanmark@gmail.com

© Springer Nature Switzerland AG 2021
M. Nuciari and E. Olivetta (eds.), *Leaders for Tomorrow: Challenges for Military Leadership in the Age of Asymmetric Warfare*, Advanced Sciences and Technologies for Security Applications, https://doi.org/10.1007/978-3-030-71714-8_8

Table 1 Profile of the officer sample by nation and rank. %

Rank	Bulgaria	Cameroun	Denmark	Finland	Italy	Philippines	Spain	Total	
								N	%
Lieutenant	–	5	5	6	7	19	10	52	24
Captain	12	6	4	12	14	2	6	56	26
Major	11	9	7	–	1	–	5	33	15
Lt. Colonel	21	3	1	3	2	6	2	38	18
Colonel	9	9	3	4	1	2	2	30	14
General	3	1	1	–	1	–	1	7	3
Total	56	33	21	25	26	29	26	216	100

All persons in the sample are officers as warrant officers from Italy, privates from Bulgaria, and one "no-answer" from Spain are excluded.

The officers have served in three different types of asymmetric wars:

- Only in international wars abroad such as in Bosnia, Iraq, and Afghanistan: Bulgaria, Denmark, Finland, Italy, and Spain
- Both in international and national wars: 23 Cameroun officers were deployed in this country, while 10 officers had served abroad in Sahara, Nigeria, Sudan, Central African Republic, Congo, and China
- Only in national wars: Officers from the Philippines.

The views of officers come from Q 4c of the questionnaire: "Unit´s morale: Trends during mission, influencing factors, cases of defection, and possible cases of PTSD" and Q 5 "Personal Experiences". If an officer tells "no problems" but on the other hand describe frustration, cases of defection, etc. the answer is categorized as a morale problem.

2   Causes of Morale Problems

2.1   No Problems

Half of the 216 officers or 107 persons found no morale problems in their unit whereas the other half or 109 officers did. Officers answering "no morale problems" often accompanied their statement with a reason. This reason belongs to one of three main categories: Physical, organizational and the mood factor and by its presence or absence. Table 2 quotes a few of their answers.

Table 2 shows that the absence of leadership is never mentioned as a reason for "no morale problems". This result can be related to the important study 70 years ago. Then Shields and Janowitz [1] found that the combat motivation and group cohesion in the strongly decimated German Wehrmacht were not harmed by the lack of orders

Table 2 Reasons for no morale problems

Reasons for "no morale problems"	Physical	Organization/Leadership	Mood
Presence	"Unit morale was very high because we had enough food" (CMR 2)[a]	"Troop's morale depends on how the commander manage" (PH 11). "training before and during mission" (DK 9)	"Good atmosphere" (SF 5)
Absence	"As no AWOL, morale high" (Absence Without Official Leave) (PH 4)		"Lack of boredom" (SF 8),

[a]"CMR 2" refers to the officer from Cameroun in the national sample with no 2

and decisions from above. On the contrary, this absence most certainly did help the strong morale of the unit. However, this officer sample nevertheless sees solution to morale problems delivered by the military organization as presented below in Table 8.

National differences exist. Only a minority of Spanish officers (20%) did find "morale problems," at all. In contrast, 90% of Danish soldiers did so. The few morale problems identified by Spanish officers may be due to their deployment experience. The 26 Spanish officers have accumulated served in 100 military operations abroad. One Spanish officer (E 5) alone has been deployed abroad eight times. No other officer corps can match that level. Therefore, Spanish units seem well integrated and experience only few morale problems.

2.2 Problems

Table 3 shows how the 109 officers identified 123 reasons for morale problems related to either

- War: The death of a colleague, fight, enemy, battle fatigue, IED-mines, Taliban, Boko Haram, terror, etc.
- Military Leadership: Poor communication, conflicting or disproval of decisions, prolonged stay, lack of training, material, food, and salaries, dissatisfaction, boredom, tensions in the unit, etc., or
- The individual soldier: Cases of AWOL, PTSD, critic from soldiers, defections, repatriation, psychological challenges, problems in family with wife, children, economy, etc.

Table 3 shows a rather equal representation of the three types of causes of around 20%. Danish officers had a tendency to mention more causes (188) than the other officers, Spanish officers less (96). However, Table 3 also shows national differences.

Table 3 Reasons for morale problems by nation and Type %

Types of morale problems	Bulgaria		Cameroun		Denmark		Finland		Italy		Philippines		Spain		Total	
	N	%	N	%	N	%	N	%	N	%	N	%	N	%	N	%
Officers	56		33		21		25		26		29		27		216	
Total views	61	100	40	100	39	102	28	100	44	100	30	101	25	100	267	99
None	34	56	17	43	4	10	19	68	6	14	7	23	20	**80**	107	40
War, loss of colleague IED, enemy	4	7	12	30	15	**39**	1	4	14	32	2	10	1	4	49	18
National MIL. ORG.	7	11	9 23		12	32	6	22	16	**36**	–	–	2	8	52	19
Individual family	16	26	2	4	8	21	2	7	8	18	21	**68**	2	8	59	22
Views officers	109		121		**181**		108		169		107		96		123	

Relatively more Danish officers (39%) found war factors to cause morale problems in their units than other officers did. Actually, the bulk of Danish officers experiencing morale problems due to war is higher: 17 Danish officers identified morale problems and 4 did not. Of the 17 officers 15 mentioned war factors why the percentage is more correctly 88% or almost 9 out of ten. Italian officers (36%) relatively more often blamed their military organization than other officers did. No Philippian officers said that at all. Instead, 68% of them find the morale problems to arise for individual reasons. At the same time, many Philippian officers understood the situation of their soldiers leading to AWOL.

2.3　War

Table 4 shows what type of war factors the 41 officers did mention the most of the 49 factors, in total. However, national differences exist for all types.

Table 4 tells that Italian and Cameroun officers identified almost all types of war factors as a reason for moral problems. The most selected type causing morale problems was the loss of a colleague, citizens, wounded with 16 views. Danish officers, in particular, did so. The explanation is the high death rate of Danish soldiers in Afghanistan as shown in Table 5.

Table 5 shows that the death rate for Danish soldiers in Afghanistan per one mio. citizens is at least seven times higher than that of the other four nations. Only the US with a death rate of 7.4 and the UK of 6.9 reach this level for their killed soldiers in

Table 4 Types of war factors causing morale problems

Types of war factors	Bulgaria	Cameroun	Denmark	Finland	Italy	Philippines	Spain	Total
Loss of colleague, citizens, wounded	1	1	8	–	5	–	1	16
Fight, PTSD, battle fatigue	3	–	4	1	1	2	–	11
IED. Mortars danger of mission	–	2	3	–	4	–		9
Enemy, Rebels, Taleban	–	3	–	–	4	–	–	7
Lost battle	–	6	–	–	–	–	–	6
Total	4	12	15	1	14	2	1	49

Table 5 Killed soldiers in Afghanistan by nation and per mio. Citizens %

	Bulgaria	Cameroun	Denmark	Finland	Italy	Philippines	Spain
Killed soldiers	7	–	43	2	53	–	35
Citizens mio.	7	–	5.7	5.5	60.6	–	46.6
Killed soldiers pr. mio citizens	1.0	–	7.5	0.36	0.87	–	0.75

Afghanistan. Another factor for morale problems seen by Danish officers is probably the concentrated period in which Danish soldiers died. 81% (35 of the 43) perished within four years, 2007–2010, 87% of the British soldiers (394 of 455) within a six year period 2007–2012, and 82% of the US soldiers (1943 of 2381) in a seven years period 2007–2013. It seems as if Taleban pursued a strategy killing as fast as possible soldiers from the weaker nation first, Denmark, then from the UK and finally from the US. For the Danish soldiers, the IED, snippers, etc. was the most lethal factor. They killed 35 of the 43 Danish soldiers that perished in Afghanistan. A third factor that may have caused morale problems is the "combined strategy" of Danish politicians for soldiers to patrol "light" in order to get faster and more immediate contact with the local population in Gereshk in the Helmand province of Afghanistan [2]. In spite of the fact that the Danish Battalion commander in Afghanistan as early as in 2007 requested heavy vehicles for the protection of his patrolling soldiers such as tanks [3]. The Department of States and the DOD, actually the Danish politicians, ignored his request. Thus, Danish officers had more challenges in keeping up morale in their units on this background.

2.4 Leadership

The officers gave 52 views of how organizational factors caused morale problems. 27 were attached to the organization itself, 20 to the mood or the psychological climate in the unit for which the organization still is responsible, and only 5 to physical factors. Table 6 shows that the main sources for a drop in morale is hierarchy/work intensity and time. In other words. It is for the military organization to solve.

Table 6 shows that absence of physical factors such as food, material, salaries and the presences of organizational factors such as hierarchy, unfair orders together with time at the end of the mission caused morale problems.

Table 6 also shows that in spite of the heavy casualties in the Danish camps, some Danish soldiers wanted "more combat".

Table 7 shows the distribution of leadership factors causing morale problems by nation and type. The two most important factors—however contradictory—are boredom and work intensity. However, they are both for the military organization to handle as discussed below in "How to Handle Morale Problems in Asymmetric Warfare?"

Table 6 Types of organizational factors causing morale problems

"Leadership problems"	Physical 5	Organizational 27	Mood 20
Presence	"Hot climate in Sudan" (CMR 3)	"Problems in hierarchy" (DK 5, SF 3 and 6, I B1 and I B 2, I "problems with orders" (BG 47, I B, SF 25) "Long operations" (Fin, I B9), "prolonged stay" (BG 40 and 51, I C27), "work intensity" (CMR 3 and 5), "morale dropped due to ROE" (DK 16)	"Morale drops over time" (CMR 24, DK 6, 13 and 15, SF 2, I C4, I C30, I B 11, E 18 and 21) "Soldiers (got frustrated when) ordered just to guard" (DK 3), "boredom" (SF 3)
Absence	"Morale drops when troops do not receive field advantages" (CMR 23) or "(likeable) food" (BG9), "Unit morale sometimes low because of salaries" (CMR 15), "Logistics not adequate and prompt" (CMR 4)	"What is the strategy of the whole mission?" (DK 2)	"My men wanted more combat" (DK 12) or "My men wanted to go on patrol but were told to stay (in Camp)" (DK20)

Table 7 Types of leadership factors causing morale problems

Types of leadership factors	Bulgaria	Cameroun	Denmark	Finland	Italy	Philippines	Spain	Total
Boredom, Time, frustration	1	1	7	1	8	–		18
Work intensity, prolonged stay, Others	2	3	4	4	2	–	–	15
Organization, ROE decisions, staff	3	1	2	1	5	–	–	12
Lack of material, food, salaries	1	4	–			–	2	7
Total	7	9	13	6	15	–	2	52

Table 7 reveals that officers from Italy and Denmark, in particular, find the organization to blame. Officers from the Philippines and Spain have none or just two views while officers from Cameroun, Bulgaria and Finland deliver between with 6 to 9 views.

2.5 Individual Factors

59 views on individual factors causing morale problems are registered, cfr. Table 3 above. In particular, officers from the Philippines with 21 views and from Bulgaria with 16 views shared that opinion. Only between 2 to 8 views are registered from the other five nations. It reduces the need for further examination.

3 Solutions to Morale Problems

Instead, it is adequate to see what solutions to the many morale problems the officers have suggested. It is evident that the military organization is seen as the main (f)actor both to cause *and* solve morale problems as 76 of the 100 solutions refer to the organization. Only four views are related to war factors and 15 views to individual factors, cfr. Table 8.

Table 8 displays mayor national differences in the number and types of solutions suggested. Above all, officers from the Philippines (93%) have addressed solutions, then from Italy, while officers from Cameroun, Bulgaria, and Spain have only delivered few views. Finland and Denmark are in between.

Table 9 below shows the types of organization solutions mentioned.

Table 9 illustrates that officers from the Philippines, Italy, and Finland, in particular, have delivered solutions, while officers from Denmark, Bulgaria, Spain, and Cameroun only have delivered between 10 and 3. Relatively most solutions refer to communications, talks, etc. (36). Then officers have defined themselves as the ones to solve morale problems (34).

Table 8 Solutions to morale problems by nation %

Types of solutions	Bulgaria	Cameroun	Denmark	Finland	Italy	Philippines	Spain	Total
Total solutions	11	5	11	17	22	27	7	100
War, IED, Enemy	1	–	–	–	–	–	–	1
Solutions MIL. ORG.	8	3	10	17	17	22	4	81
Individual family	2	2	1	–	5	5	3	18
Solutions Officers	19	15	52	68	85	**93**	26	35

Table 9 Types of organization solutions to morale problems

Types of solutions	Bulgaria	Cameroun	Denmark	Finland	Italy	Philippines	Spain	Total
Communication, talks, briefings	4	2	4	5	7	14		36
Commander, take initiatives, fulfil role, give awards	2	1	2	12	7	6	4	34
Regroup, exclude	2	–	2	–	2	1		7
Training	–	–	2	–	1	1	–	4
Total	8	3	10	17	17	22	4	81

4 Consequences for the Concept of Morale

The concept of morale presupposes values of what is good and right and they define for us how to act accordingly. Morale among soldiers in military units exists a priori. The nation that decided their deployments abroad has equipped them with a morale/legitimacy to kill. Thus, many morale challenges are removed for the soldiers. Still, a dangerous work situation can be so stressful and do cause morale problems for any man. It can lead to defections, PTSD, AWOL, frustration, etc. So can unfair/unjust orders or family problems. Thus, morale goes from being a cause for cohesion and consensus in the unit to a factor vulnerable to the external factors stressing the work situation.

In this study, officers should evaluate the morale of their unit´s soldiers and, at the end of the day, their ability to get or improve morale. Therefore, for officers no morale problems are a win/win situation. They have commanded their soldiers well and demonstrated their capacity as a good officer. For soldiers, no morale problems means that they agree personally with the given orders or either adjust to the situation guided by self-control or by fear of sanctions, i.e. discipline, the external control exercised by the officer. Morale problems appear when neither personal accept, self-control or discipline works. Many Bulgarian officers use the formulation "no morale problems with high morale and discipline". Thus, "morale and discipline" are the same. Others may argue that the "high morale" is present, a priori, and morale obtained positively, where "discipline" is a tool to get morale and is negatively obtained.

No matter how best to define morale, the results of this study reveals that morale is seen both as a cause for no problems and a vulnerable value element affected by external factors such as war, organization or individual issues. Even if some of the morale problems are most understandable due to the dangerous work situation, many more is on the level of normally organizational challenges. Perhaps, the most decisive result is the fact that the military leadership, at the same time, is most aware of its responsibility for causing morale problems, cfr. Table 7 and, for solving them, cfr. Table 9. Accordingly, it seems as if the burden of no morale problems has shifted from individual to organizational responsibility. It does not exclude war factor from affecting morale, cfr. the answers from Danish officers or individual factor from the same, cfr. officers from the Philippines. Here, it is harder for the military officer to cope with the situation. However, their action and attitude can help a lot. In addition, some guidelines—based on their own views—on how to do so are listed below.

5   How to Handle Morale Problems in Asymmetric Warfare

Three types of guidelines are:

- First, the military man as an officer, a staff, a company commander etc. shall serve as an example. Not by words, but by action and attitude. He/she shall define him-/herself as a person rather than a superior. The morale concept now means that the officers must convince his soldiers of the goal of the mission, while he/she still has the right to choose the tools most adequate.
- Second and to some extent, in contrast to the above said, the officers´ right to define tools, orders and decisions shall also be judge by their effect on morale. We know that stress at the work place can cause symptoms of illness or even sickness. This risk will diminish if the employees have influence on their work situation. Therefore, soldiers can bear more stress if they have increased influence on their situation. Officers shall understand that if they increase soldiers´ self-control, it can compensate for a more stress full work situation.
- Third, the military communication can be improved, in general. Officers shall teach to listen, tell, inform, and convince much more than before. In the Cold War period of collective security, many nations in Western Europe saw their existence at stake and therefore took the morale of soldiers for given. Today, we experience selective security, where each nation decide for herself in what conflict or war to engage as no national security issue is at stake for the nations here studied except the Philippines. It means that the political decisions of deployments abroad are well considered and argued for and that those arguments trickle down the military hierarchy to the individual soldier, even if he/she is a volunteer on a contract for a limited period.

However, it presupposes that no officer has any problem of explaining the political strategy. Thus, it is a morale problem when a Danish officer—as quoted in Table 6—asks: "What is the strategy of the whole mission"? And it may cause morale problems when the lethal Danish "combined strategy" has to be pursued sacrificing too many soldiers. Therefore, all soldiers in asymmetric warfare are entitled to ask such questions and entitled to a morale answer. On the bottom line: Military tactics in asymmetric warfare is too important for politicians to decide.

5.1 Conclusion

The study chartered officers' views on their soldiers´ morale and reasons for morale problems. Half of the 216 officers had no morale problems, the other half did. Three types of causes were identified and national differences revealed. The mutual national experiences in the asymmetric wars could explain why officers are so openly aware of their importance of causing and solving morale problems in the military unit. That is probably the most positive fact to conclude from this study.

5.2 Breviations

AWOL, Absent Without Official Leave.
IED, Improvised Explosive Devices, in contrast to landmines, i.e. Manufactured devices.

References

1. Shield EA, Janowitz M (1948) Cohesion and disintegration of the wehrmacht in world war II. Public Opion Q 12:280–315
2. Jyllandsposten (2007) October 19. CLN Kim Kristensen, Chief of the Danish Batallion in Afghanistan: Vi ser meget frem til at vi forhåbentlig snart får kampvogne. De vil øge sikkerheden markant for vore soldater (We very much look forward to hopefully getting tanks soon). They will significantly increase the safety of the soldiers. http://jp.dk/udland/article1135164.ece
3. The Ministry of Foreign Affairs and the Ministry of Defence (2008) Denmark's Engagement in Afghanistan 2008–2012, p 15: The patrols are conducted in open-top vehicles that make it easier to come into contact with the local population… The personal contact with the local population in Gereshk has importance for the entire Danish effort in Helmand Province

Operational Experience

Peter Georgiev Dimitrov

Abstract There were eight countries who participated with a number of interviews in this study. It was obvious that their participation in operations varied according to the type of operation. For instance operations in Afghanistan and Iraq aimed (aim) to recover these two countries after full scale military conflicts that ravaged them and destroyed economic and social fabrics of the state and communities. So that they went through those last phases in the wake of combat operations as stabilization and reconstruction operations. In some other of the researched operations the military personnel participated in peacekeeping missions that had been consequence of civil strife, genocide and national calamities. Whilst the former occurred by using full size military formations from all services in joint operations, the latter happened only after the UN, the EU or other international organizations had decided to deploy missions in order to transform afflicted nations and regions back to normal. Although all of these operations differ in goals and characteristics, after a close look one may say that they have some similarities as well.

1 Introduction

There were eight countries who participated with a number of interviews in this study. It was obvious that their participation in operations varied according to the type of operation. For instance operations in Afghanistan and Iraq aimed (aim) to recover these two countries after full scale military conflicts that ravaged them and destroyed economic and social fabrics of the state and communities. So that they went through those last phases in the wake of combat operations as stabilization and

---

The author works for the Rakovski National Defense College in Sofia, Bulgaria as an associate professor in the field of lessons learned.

P. G. Dimitrov (✉)
Rakovski National Defence College, KV Christo Smirnenski, Bl.80, Fl. 11, apt. 50, 1574 Sofia, Bulgaria
e-mail: pete955d@abv.bg

© Springer Nature Switzerland AG 2021
M. Nuciari and E. Olivetta (eds.), *Leaders for Tomorrow: Challenges for Military Leadership in the Age of Asymmetric Warfare*, Advanced Sciences and Technologies for Security Applications, https://doi.org/10.1007/978-3-030-71714-8_9

reconstruction operations. In some other of the researched operations the military personnel participated in peacekeeping missions that had been consequence of civil strife, genocide and national calamities. Whilst the former occurred by using full size military formations from all services in joint operations, the latter happened only after the UN, the EU or other international organizations had decided to deploy missions in order to transform afflicted nations and regions back to normal. Although all of these operations differ in goals and characteristics, after a close look one may say that they have some similarities as well.

The purpose of the mission itself is another issue one may deem necessary to examine. Is it for the sake of support to international peace and security or is it just for the sake of national goals? Therefore one may find the answer that some operations in Cameroon and these in the Philippines were destined to national goals only, whilst all the rest were under the aegis of an international organization and involved many nations, militaries, international organizations, NGOs and private actors. In order to answer all these questions and have the answer as another determinant of the analysis it is advisable that we have a closer look at all these operations that the surveyed personnel took part in.

It is without a doubt that stabilization and reconstruction of Iraq in the wake of the full-fledged large scale joint multinational operation "Iraqi Freedom" was the largest operation of that type, involved many nations, lots of material and financial resources and took longer than eight years to conclude. The experts consider it as the most complex and challenging stabilization and reconstruction operation undertaken by the coalition led by the United States since the post-World War II occupations of Germany and Japan.

Stabilization of Afghanistan after operation "Enduring Freedom", conducted in the end of 2001 and the beginning of 2002, has also been characterized by many structural, cultural and organizational difficulties. By the time of writing this research the Taliban have recovered and are claiming more and more provinces of the country. Therefore, in order for the operation to be successful in stabilizing the country, a lot of effort and resources shall be expended in future. And what is more, it is not over yet and needs further attention by NATO countries and other international and non-governmental organizations who participate in it.

The operations of the United Nations (Sudan, DR of Congo, Central African Republic, and Lebanon), and EUTMM (EU mission in Georgia) are purely peace-keeping operations and participants in them do not face the same threat and danger as the above mentioned but the results of the interviews show that the peacekeepers faced many challenges there as well.

Cameroonian Defense Forces participated in some of the missions above. Additionally they organized and conducted operations in the northern part of the country against the terrorist organization Boko Haram. The predominance of the interviewees from this country concentrated on this issue.

And the Armed Forces of the Philippines have been conducting operations in the southern islands of the country for the last three decades to neutralize Islamic movements and Maoist militias. Recently the country had been affected severely by

ISIS. All the participants in this research explained in their interviews their experience from these operations.

As one can see the sample of operations that the surveyed personnel took part in is quite broad, so it was possible for the research team to analyze almost full spectrum of land operations. There were no cases of naval operations and a very few cases of air operations that the deployed forces conducted in support to land operations.

The operational experiences of the personnel in this study naturally vary according to some operational, logistic, and national factors:

- First, operational experience was a function of the Theater of deployment, i.e. it depended on the mandate of operation: participation in stabilization and reconstruction operation; peacekeeping operation; operation of military observers; peace enforcement or national operation against radical organizations.
- Second, operational experience depended upon the necessity for the armed contingents to perform a broad variety of operations such as: armed escorts, convoys, patrols, EODs, area defense, and peace enforcement. Humanitarian aid, CIMIC operations, operations of provincial reconstruction teams (PRT), training of local forces and others may also be included as a certain operational experience.
- Third, operational experience had been strongly influenced by the composition of the multinational force, manning, equipping, training and sustaining the force in the field.
- Last but not least, the state of the opposing forces and support of local armed forces and population was of a significant importance to accumulation of experience.

To this end, Kaldor [1] gave the following explanation for this phenomenon, which she has called "new wars": "A typical new phenomenon is armed networks of non-state and state actors. They include: para-military groups organized around a charismatic leader, warlords who control particular areas, terrorist cells, fanatic volunteers like the Mujahedeen, organized criminal groups, units of regular forces or other security services, as well as mercenaries and private military companies."[1]

2 Sample of the Research

There were 246 participants in this survey from 8 countries altogether. The results are shown in Table 1. Most of the countries have followed closely the methodology of the research and filled out semi-structured interviews in the way it was accepted in the beginning of the study.

There were some participants who gave very detailed answers to questions which has helped the analysis to acquire broader information about situation in the mission's areas, battle incidents, contact and joint work with local authorities, armed forces and indigenous population.

---

[1]Kaldor [1]. New & old wars: organized violence in a global era (3rd ed.). Stanford, California: Stanford University Press.

Some of the countries did not follow the research methodology: the interviewees gave very short answers, the description of the events was missing and in the course of the analysis we assumed that the answer (yes or not) corresponds directly to the content of the question.

There were also some cases where the interviewees answered some questions in some other sections of the semi-structured interviews. Therefore it was necessary that the analysis of the operational experience should delve deeply into the whole of the interviews and seek for the information needed in some other sections as well. So that one may not find relevant paragraphs from these countries in the course of this analysis. Otherwise there should be a necessity to repeat the question as a mere quotation confirming it or denying it.

This analysis did not look for a complete breakdown of the interviewees by gender, position, experience or any other discriminant, because there were very few cases of difference. So that it may be assumed that most of the participants were males, commissioned or noncommissioned officers, and the median of their participation in operations approximately equaled to 3.

Questions of the interview.

In order to collect data for the research the author had to investigate answers of the following questions in Sect. 3 of the Questionnaire.

3. f. Operational experiences (baptism of fire and other combat situations; non-combat situations such as participation to local committees, governance experiences with and without civilian leaders and the like, humanitarian support…)?

3. g. Experience of particular problematic situations in the field, solutions and results?

Answers to these questions have been thoroughly researched. However the contents of the answers to these two questions have not provided all the information needed for the analysis so that the author decided to investigate the whole of the interviews, and to find useful information no matter where it was available. Most helpful information was found in the whole of Section III (Field Experience), and some answers in the last part of the questionnaire.

Table 1 Operational deployments by country

Country	Theater	Number of interviews
Finland	Iraq, Afghanistan, Lebanon, Ethiopia, Balkans	25
Cameroon	Cameroon, CAR, Chad, Sudan, DR Congo	34
Lithuania	Iraq, Afghanistan	4
Italy	Iraq, Afghanistan, Balkans	44
Bulgaria	Iraq, Afghanistan, Balkans, Georgia, Ethiopia	57
Spain	Iraq, Afghanistan, Lebanon, Balkans, DR Congo	27
Denmark	Iraq, Afghanistan, Lebanon, Balkans, Sudan	26
Philippines	Philippines	29

3   Operational Experience

In the interest of researching the answers and finding useful information for the anal-ysis there was a need to dissect the questions to separate smaller parts that exemplify certain issues. That is why the following approach was followed. It was accepted that operational experience should be subdivided into series of single categories which embrace the information for the analysis. That is why the question was separated in four principal parts: Baptism of Fire; Combat Situations; Humanitarian Aid; and Experience in a particular problematic situation. There was an alternative left in the end in category called "Any other". Thus the research was concentrated on smaller but more distinct issues.

3.1   Baptism of Fire

First issue of the research was to analyze how the personnel had experienced their baptism of fire. Looking through dictionaries and other literature the author tried to clarify this terminology. For example in the largest on-line dictionary.com it was explained as: "*A severe ordeal or test, especially an initial one, as in this audition would be Robert's baptism of fire. This term transfers the original religious rite of baptism, whereby holiness is imparted, to various kinds of ordeal. At first it signified the death of martyrs at the stake, and in 19th-century in France it was used for a soldier's first experience of combat. Currently it is used more loosely for any difficult first encounter.*" (dictionary.com).

The Military usage of the term is explained well in Wikipedia: „*In the military usage, a baptism by fire refers to a soldier's first time in battle. The Catholic Encyclopedia, and writers such as John Deedy, state that the term in a military sense entered the English language in 1822 as a translation of the French phrase baptême du feu. From military usage the term has extended into many other areas in relation to an initiation into a new role—for example the directorship of an arts festival*" (Wikipedia).

Mary-Jane McKay in her interview with a former marine who recalls his unit's baptism of fire in Vietnam War depicts his words: "*Everybody was excited about going,*" he remembers. "*All this training, all this hard work—everybody and anybody that could make an excuse for being out there was going to go*"......... "*It had a very, very sobering effect on a lot of us young guys, Randol says. Within 24 h, they had become veterans.*"[2]

Taking into considerations all these definitions and experience one may conclude that for a military who takes part in combat operations, stabilization and reconstruction operations, or any other type of peacekeeping operations, this experience could be described as the first, most shocking and sacrosanct experience of a military in a

---

[2]Mary-Jayne McKay, Baptism of Fire, Morley Safer Takes Some Vietnam Veterans Back to 1965, www.cbsnews.com/news/baptism-of-fire/.

war situation that he/she never forgets in his/her life. To say it in play language, it is one's first ordeal in a war situation.

Having in mind that baptism of fire is a "one-time event" and it is connected with the first impression from military operations, it may be searched in some single events. The answers of the interviewees framed some events that were used for single variables to depict baptism of fire. They were encoded as follows:

- Armed encounters (firefights, skirmishes, harassment by fire, ambushes, attacks by opposing forces when executing tasks, self-defense, and any other of similar character);
- Loss of human life;
- Casualties of own troops;
- Activation of IED or VBIED;
- Barbarities and human rights violations (arson, looting, pillaging, rape, and any other of similar character);
- First impressions in theater of operations;
- Frustration (due to cultural differences, lack of communication, misunderstandings, type of leadership, command and control flaws, hardships of different character);
- Road (sea) accidents;
- Contact with locals (local authorities, armed forces, police, elders, population).

Thus, the research from the interviews was organized in a systemic manner and allowed more detailed analysis of participants' experiences. In the interest of the analysis a closer look to all of the above mentioned variables was necessary.

4 Armed Encounters

Answers of the interviewed personnel about their experience with baptism of fire lead to conclusion that the predominance of them ascribe this experience to different type of armed encounters with the opposing forces. Most of the interviewees who took part in stabilization and reconstruction operations in Iraq and Afghanistan pointed out that their baptism of fire had come with some type of armed encounter with the opposing forces. Here are some examples that respondents deem important to their baptism of fire.

DKC06: "*Better screening of personnel.* **Better to have one soldier less** *than to include him as a burden.*" **My greatest challenge was the airborne counter insurgency operation** *we had during nighttime with 50 soldiers deployed by two helicopters behind enemy lines. It was new to us. Such a military operation we had seldom trained as we do not have that capacity. Good training solved the issue*".

DKC15: "*We were in* **close combat** *including the use of mortars, when our major stopped the mortars because of a Mosque—this was not funny, because my men were caught on an open field. ... Another situation was when we were asking for mortars and then the guys in the back didn't do their work and almost* **by accident they shelled** *a house* with a nice family, whom we had just visited, and they were not involved, only taking cover…Other situations are rescuing your soldiers after an IED attack. I have done that—fortunately both soldiers are alive and without injury, today".

ITB02: *"In Iraq I have had several experiences of armed conflicts, in particular the so-called "battle of the bridges.* **It have been strong enough an experience** *because for the first time we were under enemy fire. In the battle of the bridges we were activated one evening and my platoon was in charge of support at the river bank to another platoon in my company who had to pass the bridge. We did not expect a reaction of the fire because there were no precedents. Going by the trucks and taking position we were immediately subjected to enemy fire, obviously directed against us because of the tracers: we responded to the fire. At dawn we could see the attackers who shot at us. They were civilians, and even some policemen who collaborated with us earlier were among the attackers".*

ITC05: *"The baptism of fire has been with a "bersaglieri" company (sharp-shooters), on its first mission in Afghanistan. The men of the company has also responded well because the combat support of already experts paratroopers. The company had fallen into an* **ambush while searching for a weapons cache.** *When our men approached the cache there was a reaction of fire in defense of it. We again had to apply the ROE, avoiding to use all our firepower because the insurgents were firing from inside a village. We therefore reacted only with the individual weapons … and this enabled the insurgents to break away. The firefight lasted about 25 min. …".*

PHC15: *"… I had* my b*aptism of fire in another province where we encountered rebels. That was the first experience. There were no casualties. There were other combat experiences. Whenever there are encounters, the first priority is safety. Even while walking, one is already preparing or looking for covers in case of encounters".*

5   Loss of Human Life

The second determinant that affected most of the personnel and left strong associations with baptism of fire is the loss of human life. Some of the participants, especially company commanders and platoon leaders share that the most harrowing experience in their careers was loss of life of their subordinates. The author selected some examples from the interviews.

CMR13: *"This is my first experience in a war front…but the problem is that I cannot identify my enemy. It is a big challenge. For now no particular experience,* **but I felt bad when I saw dead bodies in the field**….it *becomes too bad when I lose a colleague in the battle ground".*

DKC05: **"Where I did feel uncertain was when I was to send a dead man home.** *In the parade there is 1000 men watching you, the coffin and the 6 carriers. That's command lonely! You have to show emotions to be empathetic and not to just let go and cry as I wanted to. If I did that the personnel would lose confidence in me and the* *situation—isn't he in control any longer? In the situation I got help from the military vicar*".

ITC13: "*In Iraq we have often been the subject of fire and we disengaged according to the ROEs. In Iraq, **our soldier died** because a vehicle of the insurgents rammed his truck knocking it off the road. In Afghanistan, I participated in different activities of humanitarian support both with the French and with the Italians. In mission you always face problems; particularly in Afghanistan in the reconstruction efforts, there was a clear contrast between the Italian administrative rules and the reality of the territory and we had to somehow reconcile the two aspects*".

There are many more examples of intense grief and sorrow expressed by the respondents like DKC05 in his sharing. When one faces the death and if it strikes his subordinates, colleagues and friends in the battlefield, it stays deep in his heart and mind. Therefore it stays for life.

6 Casualties of Own Troops

In this paragraph some citations have been chosen that impacted personnel and contributed to their baptism of fire in cases of mixed casualties (WIA or KIA).

DKC10: "*After combat I was always reflecting/thinking, if I should have done what I did and so… But I'm not getting any wiser, and I can't do anything about what happened anyway. **Especially I reflected when we—or the Brits—had wounded soldiers…**".

DKC12: "*Today **I primarily think of the battle episodes when we had wounded and dead.** We went in and one was killed and another was wounded. I, **today, reflect if I could have done anything differently, and I use it every day in my teaching of the new soldiers**. Also, today, I think that I should have used more time on planning the patrols—the 'what if' part should have been better planned and trained." Yes, it's the same episode I'm thinking of—with the two wounded soldiers. They were to be evacuated by helicopter from a dangerous and difficult place, so I suggested that the wounded were transported to another place. This meant that they lost no time in the helicopter, and got more time—5 min—with the medic. I think this was a good decision…*".

DKC14: "***ISAF 5 is following me**—I don't have any problems, however. I had no dead soldiers, but several deadly wounded that I had to carry away from. I think of the combat situations every day. **It wasn't a tea-party**… so the civilian agenda wasn't put into effect. There was CIMIC there and the means were there as well but it was too difficult, **there was a lot of fear and you didn't know who was a collaborator**… The team 5 experience has defined me as the soldier I am today. I have led my platoon in combat—that's from there my world goes today, now…*".

These shares and numerous other episodes proved that casualties of own troops had left deep imprint in soldiers' hearts and minds. We do not want to miss some incidents with local population where the personnel felt terribly sorry about some casualties given from local population due to misfires or opposing forces attacks. In these cases the multinational forces compensated the bereaved families but they felt and shared that money could not substitute for the losses.

7 Activation of IED or VBIED

BGR04: *"I was firs baptized by fire in Iraq, when I received a report from a patrol on duty that they faced an ambush and were under fire. This was the first time when I smelled the war in earnest, felt agitated and concerned about my people. They escorted a convoy and they bumped into an IED which was laid on the road (3 hand grenades). He alarmed the command and lately they were cleared by the US sappers"*.

BGR24: *"He felt the war for the first time in Afghanistan through* **battle incidents**. *In daily routines on patrols he encountered* **IEDs** *on the way. He and his subordinates were under* **rocket fire** *many times. He thinks that an early warning system against rocket fire should be built. There was a necessity for a double fence to be built in the vulnerable points"*.

DKC05: *"...**The most difficult challenge was the IEDs**. They were developed to be remote controlled. We sent the most time on force protection. In the beginning we didn't have the equipment to jam the signal, so we had to change our pattern of movement and not to use or cross passages where it would be too obvious that we would use that path. We were hit twice and 2 men died"*.

DKC23: *He answered to a question on state of moral:* *"Good, but locally some problems, in particular, the* **IED** *threat. To be fired on, gives you the chance to fire back.* **PTSD**: *Due to many combats and IEDs relatively many wounded. In 2006 in the Helmand province, the war peaked and the Taliban fled from the US Army to our areas"*.

FIN08: *"I personally was not fired upon.* **The closest call was when our vehicle hit a road bomb"**.

8 Barbarities and Human Rights Violations

Those who participated in national operations were mostly struck by human rights violations and cruelty of the insurgents. This phenomenon was typical to all theaters but appeared with greater frequency in Cameroon, Sudan and the CAR.

CMR03: *"I had talks with the villages' chiefs and also some internally displaced persons in order to hear from them, to encourage them so that they don't get discouraged. I went to investigate in a village that has been burnt, what I have seen was really* **a devastating spectacle of men, women, children, domestic animals, all killed**. *I was so frustrated because I felt completely helpless. I could just pray for that barbarity to end"*.

9   First Impressions from Theater of Operations

The personnel that had not encountered firefights or any other live threatening events associate baptism of fire with their first observation of the theater of operations and the feel and smell of war. It is typical to those who participated in stabilization and reconstruction operations for the first time. Here are some examples.

BGR06: *"I first felt that I was in real military environment when we arrived at the base in Kuwait, after seeing the multinational forces, **I felt that I was in a military setting, but the real idea came with the crossing of the Iraqi border when I observed all remnants of recent operations-destroyed combat equipment, burned premises, dilapidated farms, faces of local people …"**.*

BGR08: *"He felt different when they first arrived in the mission area in Iraq. Otherwise he abstained from sharing any other experience from missions concerning real combat situations"*.

BGR50: *"For the first time I felt a twitch from a battle environment in time of leaving Kandahar on the way to the airport, in an open truck, with bulletproof vests, the weapons between our legs and the uncertainty. You could feel the strain in the air"*.

CMR24: *"My main operational experience on the baptism of fire is how to build team spirit and maintain high moral of soldiers even when losing a colleague at the battle front. In the non-combat situations, I reinforce my relation with others especially in meetings or short seminars. My particular problematic situation is the moment I have to identify those soldiers with personal or private problems back home…"*.

PHC08: *When this happens, I should always have presence of mind and think about the position of the enemy. There was a time when there were more than 40 armed rebels inside a house, including women and children, but ROE states that we cannot fire inside a house or in public place and no civilian should be harmed. When we have respect, it's what makes us different from the enemy. **Use not only the brain but also the heart**.*

10   Frustration

Many of the personnel shared that they acquired their baptism by experiencing some kind of frustration most often due to cultural differences, lack of communication, misunderstandings, type of leadership, command and control flaws, and hardships of different character. There were also many cases where discrepancies of local settings and mentality of respondents strongly differed. In all these cases the respondents expressed opinion that they felt irritated, helpless, infuriated, and sad because they could not change or influence the events due to the aforementioned factors. This feelings caused deep frustration which influenced morale and discipline therefore as a consequence it influenced the combat effectiveness as well.

CMR05: "*...My experience was an occasion where I advised my group's site commander not to give an interview to a media, since the Headquarters did not specify it based on the SOP. He **did not listen to me** and went ahead with the press. The result to him was not good...he was transferred to another place*".

DKC19*: "One thing I learned is that **soldiers do strange things when they are scared**. They behave different when they are under pressure. It's hard to tell who will stay stable when it comes to the crunch. This is when it is especially important that you as the commander of the platoon stay calm and show the way. .... Perhaps this: you have to be an example to your soldiers—just do what you want them to do...*".

FIN02: "*.... I noticed it myself too because if you operate for seven months and visit ten villages daily and meet thirty different people and you see how poor the civilians really were. **You see children who do not have clothes in the winter**, dirty. Parents who ask for fuel for warmth. Seeing that for seven months without being able to give any help or quick solutions was hard for me...*".

ITC20: "*...Sometimes the **orders of the operating room did not look close to reality** on the ground and they put me in trouble. A great experience. For the third mission I set myself. I would do it again tomorrow*".

ITC24: "*I worked very well with the Americans, both in Iraq and in Afghanistan, both in joint operations, both* for *logistical support of each other. **Their modus operandi is however different from ours**. In case of activation we generally abandon the position of the attack (killing zone), we go in a more favorable position and there react, they do not. Basically we give priory to maneuver, they—to fire. ....In many cases I found myself in problematic situations as a commander, but yet was always able to react calmly and bring my people out of the danger without losses. It 'was a useful and positive experience professionally, which was growing from one mission to another; I would like to go to a mission again. Even when I was wounded, after a period of care at home, I have just returned to my men as soon as possible*".

11   Road (Sea) Accidents

Road (sea) accidents account for baptism of fire of some of the peacekeepers. When they happened they incurred casualties or injuries. In many cases the local population was also involved in these incidents which in its turn created strain and distrust between the multinational forces and local population. Here are some examples.

BGR26: "*He had a deadly incident that he deems the most important. **A Hammer capsized and two of his subordinates died**. They were securing a convoy. They drove faster to get to the crossroad and secure it. They bumped into a ditch and the vehicle capsized. As a result two personnel were mortally wounded*".

CMR12: "*I have once capsized in a military boat during fight against piracy." Anything expected is not military but it is the unexpected that is military". I managed to survive*".

12   Contacts with Locals

Another important determinant for baptism of fire was the contact with local authorities, armed forces, police, elders of tribes, and local population. As a rule local
populace have been in the center of attention by multinational forces in all operations. Many respondents shared that they were shocked by penury and misery of local
populations. Peacekeepers who participated in operations in the Sudan and Central
Africa expressed opinions that if it were not for the UN peacekeeping forces and
humanitarian aid, many more people, and especially children could have perished
by famine. This sentiment applies to Afghanistan as well. When one observed such
kind of a situation and compared it with the conditions of his native country one
would feel sympathy for the local population. Many respondents realized that it was
impossible to help the locals by providing them with food and other vital items.
Food and water were never enough. They thought that it would be more advisable to
help them step on their own feet and teach them how to take care of themselves. It
has been often shared that stabilization and reconstruction operation in Afghanistan
conducted by multinational forces of ISAF to some extent had a negative effect on
local population in a way that taught them wrong to expect everything for granted
and to drive a hard bargain on everything. It applied not only to local population but
also to local authorities, armed forces and the police. Here are some examples.

BGR17: *During the elections the tension in Afghanistan rose sharply. There
were clashes, demonstrations in front of the base, there were assassinations, car-
bombs near the airfield. The tension escalated. The roads were closed....*

BGR47: *"....The local population is very poor but very proud. **If you respect
them, they respect you**, too. If you treat them well, especially the children, their
respect increases even more".*

CMR18: *"The Bakassi operation is my Baptism of fire and the mission from which
I have acquired all my experience. Through joint and frequent meetings with local
authority and traditional leaders, I have improved on my communication skills".*

CMR20: *"**Combat has always been within the civilian population.** It is difficult
to distinguish between the enemy and the civilian".*

DKC01: *"It didn't affect me the first time (KFOR), **but when I myself got children,
it was hard to see children the same age as my own beg for water and food, poor
children**. But it would be a drop in the ocean".*

DKC13: *"Problems: Combat is combat. The most problematic situations was to
get local armed forces/authorities to get a common goal with us as we return after
6 months. How can I get them to act as wished when they know that I am going back?
Very difficult to maintain the results we got when the next team takes over".*

DKC16: ... *"**In asymmetric warfare, the locals are the center of gravity.** So we
go from fighting an enemy to winning the "hearts and minds" of the locals. You shall
not exercise pure violence but figure out how to win the locals; ...Do not permit your
soldiers degrading language about the enemy, the locals, local security forces, etc.
and do not name yourself "crusader for Christ," etc. Branding must be avoided. Be
aware of being betrayed. I had some local engineer soldiers. They have slept in our*

camp but they unfortunately hit IED placed in there by other locals or someone from their group. Multiple casualties and deaths. I didn't feel a thing because they were not my men...".

All data form the interviews available allowed the author to make some quantitative analysis and see the distribution of baptism of fire by different single factors mentioned above.

The results in Table 2 show that most of the interviewees (58.9%) associate their baptism of fire with armed encounters of different character to include attacks during execution of tasks, harassing fires on FOBs (forward operating bases), OP (observation posts) or HQ, ambushes, and firefights in self-defense. Large group (13%) of the surveyed personnel associate their baptism with their first impression from being in combat situation. Another group of interviewees ascribe the phenomenon to their experience during contacts with local population (10.8%) to include governmental institutions, armed forces, police, local authorities, and tribe (clan) elders. Significant percentage (7.4%) think that improvised explosive devices (IED) or vehicle-borne improvised explosive devices (VBIED) contributed to their baptism of fire. Small percentage of interviewees (3.5%) associate their baptism with loss of life and bereavement of their colleagues and friends, and 1.3%—with casualties of their own troops.

Table 2 Events that caused baptism by fire

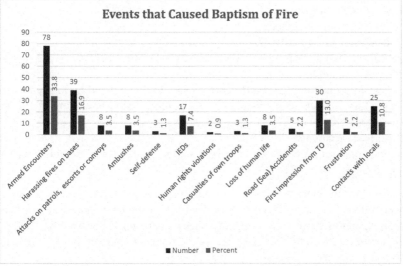

Note 231(94%) out of 246 participants answered the question, so that calculations and graphics are conducted based on these numbers

12.1 Battle Rhythm and Battle Incidents

Another important determinant of field experience for the personnel when in operations of different character turned out to be battle rhythm of operations and battle incidents of various nature that happened during these operations. It was not a surprise that there would be some iteration of events that caused baptism of fire. So that most of the single factors that played significant role in causing baptism of fire appeared in operations as battle incidents as well.

That is why the analysis of battle rhythm was almost a repetition of the above but in bigger details and with addition of some more single events that happened in the field, FOBS, OPs, facilities, or HQs. At this point the analysis concentrated on the following events:

- Armed encounters (firefights, skirmishes, engagements)
- Harassment by fire on FOBs, OPs, HQs or any other coalition facilities;
- Ambushes;
- Attacks from opposing forces on own troops when executing tasks (escorting, convoying, patrolling and any other of similar character);
- Self-defense;
- Separation of warring parties;
- Green on Blue events:
- Loss of human life;
- Casualties of own troops;
- Witness of battle incidents;
- Activation of IED or VBIED;
- Barbarities and human rights violations (arson, looting, pillaging, rape, and any other of similar character);
- Frustration (due to cultural differences, lack of communication, misunderstandings, type of leadership, command and control flaws, hardships of different character);
- Road (sea) accidents;
- Interaction with representatives of Host nation, International organizations, and NGOs.

Many of the interviewees touched on many of these points and gave more than one answer concerning the analyzed factors. That is why the numbers on the graphic do not correspond to the number of the interviewed personnel. Since we have adopted an approach to go through all these events and draw citations from the participants, let us follow the same model for this part as well.

13 Armed Encounters.

Most of the personnel who participated in the study shared their opinion about armed encounters with the opposing forces. It is important to underline that those who participated in Theaters in Iraq and Afghanistan had much more to share. Therefore we may draw a conclusion that acting in the aftermath of combat operations, i.e. in stabilization and reconstruction operations demands from military contingents to be ready to act in different situations such as engagements, skirmishes, firefights or any other action in response of the opposing forces' activities.

Another determinant that defines frequency, span and magnitude of own forces' activities would definitely be the mandate, area, national caveats and specific tasks that a unit performs at designated area of responsibility. The contingents in many circumstances had to perform combat activities they had never expected or practiced before and had to adopt them on the spot.

Last but not least, it is important to note that character of opposing forces' activities differs in different areas of theater depending on their intent and final goals and therefore cause the Multinational force to concentrate efforts on these areas. Example: The most active and ferocious activities of the Taliban were in the southern part of Afghanistan. That is why most of the battle incidents happened there. Some examples through respondents' citations are shown next.

DKC06: "*...My greatest challenge was the **airborne counter insurgency operation** we had during nighttime with 50 soldiers deployed by two helicopters behind enemy lines. It was new to us. Such a military operation we had seldom trained as we do not have that capacity. Good training solved the issue*".

DKC09: "*In Afghanistan: **All of it is essential and I have tried all of it**. Being in actual combat when you experience the extreme situation of killing other people and sustaining casualties. In South Sudan: Killed in action is probably the most defining experience. That is so different from anything else in a long life and taken into consideration Western upbringing, this situation is so much in conflict with what you have learned...The other thing is when you are in a situation of humanitarian disaster and you see problems people suffer from, that will change how you look at the world, forever. In Jan 2012, 8000 men from one tribe in South Sudan marched against a much smaller tribe with the purpose of killing all of them. We as UN-observers tried to get the South Sudan Army and government to intervene. They said no. This **led to a disaster for the smaller tribe** with a lot of people killed and their life stock stolen from them. They dispersed in inaccessible areas where they died from their wound and diseases*".

DKC15: "*We were in close combat including the use of mortars, when our major **stopped the mortars because of a Mosque**—this was not funny, because my men were caught on an open field. I don't know how much you know about mortars, but we use two different types of grenades—one type we use to get close—they smoke. The next type is the real thing... This situation was talked through in my platoon—and it took some time, because here we trusted someone, and then this happened—and we asked ourselves: whom can we trust? Another situation was when we were asking* *for mortars and then the guys in the back don't do their work and the almost by accident shelled a house with a nice family, whom we had just visited, and they were not involved, only taking cover…Other situations are rescuing your soldiers after an IED attack. I have done that—fortunately both soldiers are alive and without injury, today".*

ITC19: "*I experienced several firefights, particularly in the area of Bala Murgab. On one occasion I got the order* **to go out nighttime with the whole company reinforced by a platoon of sappers to go to the rescue of an American unit that was stuck in the mountains with its vehicles bogged down** *when crossing a river and under the fire of the insurgents from the surrounding hills. The Americans tried to intervene with their own helicopter and supply spare parts for the damaged vehicles. It did not work, and what was more the helicopter was shot down by insurgents. We started and, as we went through a village I smelled a threat (absence of people in the streets, lights off) so that I decided for the company to cross the village in platoon formations, one at a time. The platoon's genius has passed without problems, I was with the platoon of head of the company and started crossing; arrived more or less in the center of the village insurgents made me jump on an IED. The vehicle rolled over,* **I was hurt and I did not know how to get out of the vehicle overturned; the other crew members were injured too; the radio operator with broken legs, the interpreter with his head crushed**. *The insurgents have then immediately opened fire; the platoons of the company who had stayed outside the village could open fire on the positions of the insurgents from their position. Once I dragged myself out of the vehicle I could use my individual radio to give orders (that of the vehicle was obviously destroyed); I did not call immediately the medical aid because the enemy fire was intense. I then ordered the platoon of genius which had already gone through the village to go back and clean up the area, but while the platoon was returning its first armored truck jumped on another IED and was in turn blocked.* **The goal of the insurgents was clear: stop the whole column inside the village and then attack it with fire at close range**. *The division of the company in brackets had avoided that this plan had full success. Once the fire of my platoons remained outside the village has neutralized part of the sources of fire of the insurgents, I was able to call the doctor with the medical team for a medical first aid and evacuation of the wounded. The evacuation took place with an American helicopter that was under enemy fire and in the dark has equally landed to load the wounded. The firefight lasted all night. Meanwhile, the American platoon was able to repair the vehicles and had moved toward me, but in the village prior to that I was in its turn made subject to ambush with the same tactic. The next day we were able to clean up the village, to fill the chasms of the explosions, tow destroyed vehicles and return to our camp in the late afternoon. Another significant event occurred in the last month of the mission, when we were giving to Afghans our bases; at this stage it was decided to create a more advanced COP for the ANA and we started work on the entrenchment of a hill in a strategic position. The insurgents, when they saw the work we were doing, started to fire at us, taking cover in trenches dug in the mountains by the Russians several years ago. On that occasion, as there is no danger to involve civilians and cause*

collateral damage, I asked the bombing. So intervened two pairs of F16, a Dutch and
an American, who dropped four bombs on the trench where the insurgents were firing
from, neutralizing them. It was the only time we could use the air bombardment".

14 Harassment by Fire

When reading the interviews one gets the impression that in the operations in Iraq
and Afghanistan the Multinational forces were subject to opposing forces attacks by
small arms, mortars, and rockets in their bases, observation posts, headquarters and
any other facilities they had occupied. Their fire, according to interviews, was not
effective enough but it was disturbing and harassing and made personnel anxious
at all times. It was most typical to Afghanistan. On certain occasions the Taliban
succeeded to combine different types of fire and activation of IEDs to disrupt forces'
daily chores.

BGR12: *"They had experienced **fire attacks on base** by the opposing forces. It*
was done by mortars and small arms. There was a random bullet that went astray
and wounded our soldier. A rumor about that went around the Iraqis and on the
following days the opposing force continued attacks the same way".

BGR37: *"First encounter with fire and combat situations: terrorists blew up a*
fuel truck near the central checkpoint. The base was under rocket fire every day. One
gets used to them".

BGR39: *"During his first mission a **rocket fell in the base** and the container next*
to him was blown up, and it was completely destroyed in the process, he was in his
container and then he had the feeling that he was at war. He thought to himself that
it was a narrow escape. He shared that in Iraq the coalition servicemen were under
fire many times (including him, during movement to military installations, as well as
during flights). He had many cases like this and the setting in Iraq were much more
dangerous and hostile".

ITC08: *"I have not been involved in armed conflicts. We suffered launching of*
rockets on the base in Shimdad, but the alert system is very effective: there are
balloons with cameras and sensors that detect the rockets launched soon and give
the alarm. You have about 10 s from the launch and the impact; each one of us knows
what to do. I do not think they had a great psychological impact on men".

15 Ambushes

Respondents in all theaters shared that they had suffered often ambushes by the
opposing forces. We may consider the ambush an asymmetric tactics of the weak.
According to narratives about ambushes by interviewees, they followed a pattern of
tactics in which the majority of the ambushes happened mostly in inhabited points
where the insurgents mixed with civilian population. They did not wear uniforms so

that it was difficult to distinguish them from the civilian population and neutralize them without casualties of innocent people. Many times insurgents used civilian population as a human shield against multinational forces. Here are some citations:

FIN04: "*The first was probably the one where we were **fired upon far from a village**. It did not even feel like I was fired at. But otherwise the greatest danger was the road mines and the related ambushes*".

FIN17: "*We were going to gather intelligence to find out the security situation of an area and check out some known places. We had prepared the previous day, checked our routes and had been in communication with the local security authorities. We called them that morning and everything was supposed to be OK. However, when we approached a village all the civilians had been evacuated into the yard of a mosque. It was an **ambush in the middle of a village**".*

16 Attacks from Opposing Forces When Executing Tasks

Even though we have mentioned already that there were many armed encounters that the interviewees shared, the author deemed it necessary to scrutinize those encounters. When looking at them in a more precise manner, it was obvious that most of the encounters with the opposing forces happened during execution of daily tasks by multinational units, i.e. when on convoying, patrolling, escorting or any other activity included into SOPs of the contingents.

CMR06: "*During the **confidence building patrols**, at times we were fired by rebels who were against our presence or who did not understand the nature of the operation. The protective force was there to secure, we used to call different fractions for specific meeting but it was not easy at all*".

FIN18: "…**Vehicles got stuck and troops were fired upon**. *Once or twice air support was used. Once there was a **convoy** in the West, which was notoriously dangerous. The road there was called "the shooting range". Grenades were thrown by both sides and a local citizen was slightly injured in the face, but nothing more serious. There were ambushes mostly…*".

FIN20: "…*in the first operation we were in a valley when we were **fired upon**. My first thought was actually that this was just like from one of our training simulations. That this was like the exercise and they were shooting from there. We had practiced a very similar thing and it went well. So that goes to tell how important good and realistic training is…*".

ITB04: "*More or less on a daily basis we got **activations on our advanced base by snipers** cleverly hidden on the mountain; we responded with mortar shots from 60. I do not know if we got them, but I think so because from a certain day forward they no longer fired. Once I was commanded on patrol to meet a **convoy and escort** it to the base; seven kilometers of the base, passing close to a village, we were made to sign a burst of Kalashnikov. We waxed to identify the source and we saw it was in a few houses in the village. We have not responded to avoid civilian casualties, we unhooked and expanded to move away from the fire*".

ITB10: "*…I had a first activation in Afghanistan when I had to make a* **reconnaissance** *reinforced platoon (25 vehicles) quite far from the base. It happened that a truck of genius that preceded the column was embedded in a river, and when we were doing recovery operations the insurgents began to fire upon from all directions with combined fire of RPGs, mortars and small arms. The attack was preceded by an intensive communication activity of the insurgents, who began to turn around with motorcycles, making signals with mirrors, smoke signals etc., clearly to organize the attack. We returned fire with the Browning MG of the armored trucks, anti-tank weapons; besides we required an air support, but that time it was not very timely. We were then able to disengage leaving the vehicle damaged. Then we had to stop and camp out in the desert at night. The next day we returned to the scene to recover the vehicle, which had since been partially dismantled and then burnt. Some insurgents were digging holes to place IEDs around the middle, providing for our return…*".*

ITC11: "*One day we went to make a delivery to a village along with Afghan forces; in the village there was a Shura and the Afghan soldiers who were with us recognized among the participants in the Shura a leading member of the insurgents and decided to capture him. Once taken, and as we left the villagers have accompanied us with a stone-throwing. We then noticed being controlled by a pair of Afghans with a motorcycle, moving sideways to us, at distance. The Afghan soldiers who were with us chased them and captured two insurgents because were discovering that they had put an IED on our way back, in a necessary step. While we were making biometric recognition of the two subjects* **mortar shells began to rain around us**. *We realized that the shots came from the village we had left, but we had no air support to be able to take action on them, nor could we intervene with our mortars firing at random on the village. We then thinned out and called the air force asset, but when it arrived did not see any more, because the insurgents had stopped the action. Faced with this type of action you feel a sense of helplessness. Luckily we had no injuries*".

ITC16: "*During a* **convoy** *from Herat to Bala Murgab, about 200 vehicle, with Italian, Spanish and Afghans, the Afghans were in the lead, the third Italian vehicle took an IED driven by pressure plate, and we had two dead and two wounded. The MEDEVAC operated by the Americans was immediate. …We faced a clear decline in the morale of the men, who despite everything we were able to double check.* **It was an experience that made me grow a lot as a person; yes I would like to come there again**".

17 Self-Defense

Many personnel shared that they had to observe the prescribed ROEs when in self-defense, and in many cases it was frustrating because ROEs were too restrictive if one needed to use force in self-defense. Here are some examples:

DKC20: "*One situation comes to my mind, in which we were involved. We observed a traffic accident. It was a car that crashed into a crowd and seriously wounded several children. Immediately we started to carry out first aid and requested medical* *support. The driver—who was held back—was from a different tribe than the children, and we heard over the radio that rumors were spreading that he carried out an attack on purpose. As a result armed men from the children's tribe were gathering to carry out an attack. In this situation we gathered our weapons and brought both the children and the driver inside our Piranhas for protection. When the shooting started I requested that we did not respond—**even if in self-defense** because we had wounded children and the driver inside the vehicles. But it was not an easy situation… The whole incident has been described in a folder, 'Ethical Leadership in Practice'… (Written in Danish, CK) Here the focus is on the many dilemmas we were in… Another situation was when an IED team observed the enemy burying an IED. I was informed and I requested that artillery or a missile was used against the enemy. My MJUR said that it was my decision, and that it was legal. We had cleared the road for traffic by blocking the road with our military vehicles. The missile took out 2—and 2 were able to run away even if they were wounded. We found the active IED afterwards. The thing is, how could we—how could I know? I had to trust my men, but then in war—sometimes you aim right and sometimes you miss…".*

FIN21: *"….Is it about **finding an IED or avoiding an ambush**? The first time we were **fired upon** was about a few months in. We were entering a village when we were fired upon. Almost all of us were on a road with impassable fields on both sides. It was hard to organize our troops and find safety…".*

PHC16: *"We are mostly on support of law enforcement. There are also Bangsamoro Islamic Freedom Fighters (BIFF) rebels, but before they can act, I would be able to determine where they were and what their intention was, so they wouldn't have the opportunity. It is like a chess game, you occupy space, you show your capability, your preparedness. And if there are atrocities, it would be easy. Engagements are not prolonged and are actually prevented, because the concept of warfare is occupation of space. **Before they can occupy, you have to be in position**. Warfare is different here, you know where they will be coming from and where they will go".*

18 Separation of Warring Parties

It happened in the cited missions described in Table 1 that there was an exigency for the multinational forces to apply peace enforcement, i.e. to enforce cease fire or cease of hostile activities between warring parties. In our case this was most typical to the Armed Forces of the Philippines that had to separate warring Islamic movements and even warring clans.

DKC09: *"…The other thing is when you are in a situation of humanitarian disaster and you see problems people suffer from, that will change how you look at the world, forever." In Jan 2012, **8000 men from one tribe in South Sudan marched against a much smaller tribe** with the purpose of killing all of them. We as UN-observers tried to get the South Sudan Army and government to intervene. They said no. This led to a disaster for the smaller tribe with a lot of people killed and their life stock stolen* *from them. They dispersed in inaccessible areas where they died from their wound and diseases".*

DKC20: *"One situation I remember especially clear was in Iraq where there was a situation in which **we had to stop a shooting between tribes**—it was a conflict going 30 years back. They were estimated to be 150 heavily armed men, and we were 30. So what could we offer to the situation? When we approached the firing zone we didn't fire one shot—also because we actually didn't have much ammo; we were actually out-gunned—but with our vehicles we placed ourselves in between the fighting parties to stop the shooting, because this was the right thing to do, we felt. And the shooting actually stopped. Then we started pushing the fighters back with our vehicles. We also brought in their tribe leaders from 40 km away and started negotiating a peace... I think we made a difference in that situation. I also think that this ascribed meaning to the operation. It was so cool that we succeeded".*

PHC15: *We never had a major engagement or prolonged threat in the area that we had to sustain. There is a peace process with the Muslim separatist rebels (Moro Islamic Liberation Front or MILF). **We are observing a peace mechanism, all actions or whatever operation of the military are coordinated with the MILF**. If you have an activity, for an example and you pass through their area, you must coordinate. Dealing with other armed groups is harder; they are just there in communities with civilians, we cannot easily take action and it is up to the commander to plan on how to isolate them from the civilians.*

PHC20: *During the battle at P. Palma, there was a community with rebels under Umbra Kato (Bangsamoro Islamic Freedom Fighters). Because of the collapse of the Memorandum of Agreement on Ancestral Domain (MOA-AD), they entered the area, all armed. If we wanted war, we could have attacked but instead tried to negotiate with them and asked them to leave, while we took the civilians out. But this did not happen. We had a battle which lasted for three days and two nights. All the village chiefs who were former commanders were really armed; they had high powered arms. I saw this as a threat and I was thinking of the danger if they suddenly turned away from us but we did win them over. **Here clan wars is really a problem, usually between two families and groups**.* Actually we are not involved in this, but there are a lot of displaced people; schools and services that are not working. You have to show the people that you are non-partisan. I have experienced settling a rido (clan wars) and I have eventually won their trust.

19   Green on Blue Events

This event was typical to Afghanistan. It happened many times between ANA and NATO forces in Afghanistan. The interviewees associate it with indiscriminate fire produced by representatives of the ANA against ISAF personnel.

BGR07: *"Afghanistan: 9 June 2013. A bus with 10 unarmed and not equipped military personnel (Slovaks) was moving at KAF, when an Afghani soldier opened*

*fire on them. It was so called "Green on Blue" effect. An Afghani was on a guard
tower and shot them with a machine gun. (7-WIA, 1-KIA)".*

BGR27: *"During the rotation the Bulgarian contingent was **under fire** by an
Afghani soldier".(**Green on Blue**).*

There are probably many more cases of green on blue events but because of the
sensitivity of the issue the personnel abstained from sharing.

20 Loss of Human Life

Loss of life is the most heartbreaking and distressing event in the field. According
to interviewees loss of life and wounded personnel had very deep impact on morale,
cohesion and operational capabilities. In some cases it had negative effects on psychological stability of personnel, in others it played a positive effect on cohesion, willingness to prevent and help colleagues and friends. In many circumstances it happened
that multinational forces had to protect defenseless local population from retaliatory
actions by the opposing forces. Many times it had severe consequences and caused
PTSD. Here are some examples:

DKC07: *"**Dead soldiers took a lot of focus**. I had constantly to evaluate operations—is the purpose of the task in balance with the risk, is my planning ok? What
do I want to risk my soldiers' lives for?".*

DKC11: *"Combat: „What you have trained, works in combat" as you react by
intuition you do not have time to reflect. Non-combat: A **killed** Danish soldier made
one of my soldiers to react **trembling, psychologically in distress,** a situation we were
never trained to do: "the difficult-conversation-training" at home." Problematic
situation: When your unit was very stressed by much combat then **to persuade them
to go on**. In my COY a section had two killed and three wounded and it was headed
by a staff sergeant. Solution: I decided to split the unit to avoid a kind of defection,
but it was not a popular thing to do. Later on though, we realized it was the right
decision. Results: Made the unit go on".*

PHC07: *"There was a time when rebels harassed our detachment. One of my
soldiers was seriously wounded so I requested air transport but the chopper cannot
fly because of bad weather and fog. **My soldier died because we were not able
to evacuate him fast enough**. If only we have capabilities to fly in bad weather
we could have saved more lives. I experienced being on the line of fire on at least
three occasions while deployed in Negros province: March 20, 2009 at Ilog, Negros
province; April 27, 2009; Oct 13, 2009. The most recent was in June 18, 2012 in
which we had an encounter with the communist rebels. The fighting was from 9:45 to
11:30. We launched an offensive strike not knowing that there were 119 rebels and
only 17 of us".*

DKC18: *"…Yes, once I was to protect a 'log train' of 140 vehicles going from
Bastion to Sangin. We were added and used to chase Taliban which is bad usage of
our Piranhas—also we were only 5. The tour was badly planned—we were going too*

*slowly and we were too open for attacks. We had two attacks, with 2 dead soldiers.
So when we arrived the spirit was **anger and irritation**".*

21 Casualties of Own Troops

DKC08: "***I knew that I should be able to look myself in the mirror without regrets
about what I did/did not do.*** *I have the premise that I do act correctly in any situation
but I have always known that the decision-making background could change and so
my opinion, as well. It is a psychological protection mechanism to see things that way
that in a situation my decision was right, but that the situation can change a second
later and then my decision is wrong. But in the moment I decided it, it was correct.
The first time one of my soldiers got wounded. It is a management problem as COY
chief to balance when to evacuate my wounded soldier in the middle of a shooting
situation with Taliban, in particular the question how long my medical team could
keep the wounded soldier "stable". **I had to focus both on my wounded soldier and
on how much danger it will be for my other soldiers** to land a helicopter for the
rescue of my wounded soldier".*

PHC10: *Last August we had a **casualty**. He was hit in the head and was confined
in the hospital. Since his unit have to follow the rules of engagement, he tried to be
certain first before shooting, but they were hit first.*

22 Witness of Battle Incidents

Some interviewees shared their observations of witnessing battle incidents without
being an active part in them. In most of the cases the reason for not participating and
supporting coalition troops was the distance of the incident, and in other cases the
instantaneity of the happening. So those who witnessed but not participated had the
only one thing to do: to be sympathetic and to psychologically support the acting
soldiers.

BGR31: "*On 02. 04. 2011 base Phoenix was attacked by five terrorists with IED
at the main gate, which was guarded by the US military. One terrorist detonated the
IED, the other one was killed, another gunman was killed, and two men ran away.
There were no casualties among the coalition forces but two WIA*".

PHC09: "*One time we had an encounter at a nearby village. There was a harassment from the area that is heavily populated. We had to think of the civilians first,
their safety and we cannot return fire. …. Always assess the area first. If the threat
comes from the area where civilians might be hit, we have to maneuver first. We
were harassed by communist insurgents. They wanted to inflict damage by planting
land mines on the road side. We were in the area, we were going home when the
advance party discovered land mines. They were dismantled and we were saved. In
another occasion, we had to reinforce since the other group was ambushed. The unit*

I was leading arrived at the area while the shooting was still ongoing. I thought how important that was there be on—time rescue, the vehicles are ready for medical evacuation and timely medical attention".

23 Activation of IED or VBIED

Improvised Explosive Devises (IED) proved to be the weapons of the weak. But the weak apply them in an asymmetric manner against multinational forces in the way to purposefully cause death and casualties. Hence, they have been used in stabilization and reconstruction operations and any other peace keeping operations to inflict severe damage and to dissuade forces to pursue their agenda. According to a report by the Homeland Security Market Research in the USA, the number of IEDs used in Afghanistan had increased by 400% since 2007 and the number of troops killed by them by 400%, and those wounded by 700%. It has been reported that IEDs are the number one cause of death among NATO troops in Afghanistan. (Wikipedia). The interviewed personnel that experienced IED activation shared that this was the most treacherous weapon the opposing forces used. The troops hate it because it is hidden, unexpected and inflicts severe physical and psychological damage. In many cases it causes PTSD as well.

BGR04: *"I was firs baptized by fire in Iraq, when I received a report from a patrol on duty that they faced an ambush and were under fire. This was the first time when I smelled the war in earnest, felt agitated and concerned about my people. They escorted a convoy and they **bumped into an IED** which was laid on the road (3 hand grenades). He alarmed the command and lately they were cleared by the US sappers."*

BGR24: *"He felt the war for the first time in Afghanistan through **battle incidents**. In daily routines on patrols he encountered **IEDs** on the way. He and his subordinates were under **rocket fire** many times. He thinks that an early warning system against rocket fire should be built. There was a necessity for a double fence to be built in the vulnerable points".*

DKC05: *"...**The most difficult challenge was the IEDs**. They were developed to be remote controlled. We sent the most time on force protection. In the beginning we didn't have the equipment to jam the signal, so we had to change our pattern of movement and not to use or cross passages where it would be too obvious that we would use that path. We were hit twice and 2 men died".*

DKC13: *"You get an adrenalin rush, confusion, slow motion, excitement, in particular if you are unaware of the direction of shooting. Other combat situation: If all soldiers are unharmed, you get an exhilarating effect and you experience that what was going on as a back bone-reactions was due to received training. **Big difference to be shot at and to be exploded (IED). The latter is a shock, unexpected. It gives a demoralizing effect, as you cannot do anything but see the consequences**. With casualties it is again basic military training that helps you to act (get the soldiers saved, come back to the camp). Back in the camp comes the reaction and reflection* *and as a PL.COMM. You have the burden of keeping up the morale. Then we need to defuse the situation and the frustration and sorrow. Very stressing. Easy to criticize oneself, therefore important to accept that dead/wounded is a factor of war. It happens unavoidably, even if you have done everything right. Non-combat: You must know the local culture norm. A child throwing stones is an "up-bringing" problem not a warrior".*

DKC23: *He answered to a question on state of moral: "Good, but locally some problems, in particular, the **IED** threat. To be fired on, gives you the chance to fire back. **PTSD**: Due to many combats and IEDs relatively many wounded. In 2006 in the Helmand province, the war peaked and the Taliban fled from the US Army to our areas".*

FIN08: *"I personally was not fired upon. **The closest call was when our vehicle hit a road bomb"**.*

24 Barbarities and Human Rights Violations

CMR01: *"My experience was patrols in remote areas of DR of Congo to gather information from the local community chiefs/leaders on matters of security. **There were many armed groups, land conflicts, chieftaincy disputes and human rights violation amongst others.** That is what military observers in UN peace missions do as tasks and that is where my experience lies".*

25 Frustration

One of the main factors that impaired the psychological stability of the personnel in operations and downgraded operational capabilities to some extent was the feeling of frustration caused by different factors. The study of interviews found this factor in many of them. Usually the interviewees associate their frustration with a big chasm in cultures of peacekeeping personnel and local population, and in some cases they mark some differences among different countries of the multinational force. Another cause of frustration appeared to be the lack of communication, not only linguistic one, but also one of basic understandings how things are done. Application of command and control of Multinational forces in an unexpected way in some cases also contributed to frustration. Significant number of personnel touched on the issue of leadership and acknowledged that wrong leadership style may bring a lot of frustration in the units. The environment, everyday hardships, lack of simple but indispensable things were another harbinger of frustration.

DKC04: *"....In battle 'Auftragstaktik' simply works! When you advance in battle—when the first private charges, when the lieutenant in front leads his tanks in a charge... You are in a situation with mine fields, artillery, attack airplanes... and*

the front lieutenant is leading his platoon as if it were a battalion. The only differ-
ence is what we are shooting at and where—There were compounds with women
*and children, and that was **difficult… it's 3 block warfare***! *But it really kicked ass*
down there… Afterwards we had psychological debriefings—this was ordered by the
brigade… so, no we didn't have any problems I think…".

DKC07: "…*My biggest problem was that **the political plan dictated what I should***
***do on the tactical level.** I thought they were crazy. It was about that the patrol baseline*
and how we should plan and patrol there. You can't carry out politics down to that
level. This became, to an extreme extent, decisive for me. The politicians should stay
at policy and strategic level and not issue tactical orders. So this was my biggest
challenge".

DKC21: (After a long pause of thought) *I think my 'baptism' was when I realized*
that it is an illusion that I could understand a situation and what the motives are. You
might think you have an idea as to what is going on—but then you realize that you
are not. There are so many layers and changing motives. Causes and reactions are
*changing rapidly and you have to act as best you can. **The depth you have to think***
in order to understand especially in societies as these where tribes or clans rule,
***is immense.** The indications of something, that you see, might only be one layer. So*
you can only appeal to reason from case to case. This makes you only a tiny little
piece of the big puzzle, and you only have very short time there—and this type of
operations really take a lot of time….

FIN09: ***The Command Centre was not as professional as I would have wanted***
it to have been. If we had a problematic situation, if the patrol was in a situation,
I usually went to follow and sometimes even support it even though officially the
Command Centre should have taken care of it, if the patrol did not get all the infor-
mation it needed. There was a situation or two at night when I had to take leadership
responsibility over the situation, but then it was situational leading at that point.

FIN10: *From the perspective of commandership what I could have done better*
would have been to remind myself that people experience things very differently.
*There I should have had a slightly **more sensitive ear for which way the wind blows***
***from.** For a unit that did not get along that well a hard experience may rise tensions*
whereas in another unit the hard experience might bring the troops closer together.
*I should have been more sensitive. These are **commandership problems**. They can*
be often solved, when I realized that I had been oafish, with bringing the matter up
between the two of you and talking them through. In principle I could have been
smarter, or a bit more sensitive on what the situation is for people.

ITB06: "…*I once had a **conflict with an Afghan officer** about operations manage-*
ment and I had to calm the ardor of that officer and mediate a solution to the problem.
The reason for the dispute was that they felt they were in support of our troops,
whereas the opposite was true. Basically I gave them the support that they don't
have, for instance sending our armored vehicle as the first truck of the column, or
give our contribution from the genius for cleaning the way and so on. But with regard
to the search operations in villages and every other in contact with the population,
that was established which has to be made by them".

ITB10: *"With the ANA, we carried out joint operations and they were quite reliable: they are brave and motivated, but lacked the means, organization and logistics.* **They were often abandoned by their higher command** *(left unpaid, without supplies, etc.)"*.

26 Road (Sea) Accidents

CMR30: *"In securing the "bouée base"; the place where ships encore before their entry to the Douala sea port, it happened one day that one fishing vessel hit our boat and everybody fell in the sea and I had to instruct the soldiers to hold themselves at their arms when sea current was carrying them along. Those who were able to swim were asked to rush for our boats and hastily return to fetch for soldiers who could not swim well. Finally we did not have any human life loss in the darkness and more so in the open sea."*

CMR33: *"During the fight against sea pirates in Bakassi Peninsula because of the bad weather, our vessel sank and we lost two soldiers there"*.

DKC20: *"One situation comes to my mind, in which we were involved. We observed a traffic accident. It was a car that crashed into a crowd and seriously wounded several children. Immediately we started to carry out first aid and requested medical support. The driver—who was held back—was from a different tribe than the children, and we heard over the radio that rumors were spreading that he carried out an attack on purpose. As a result armed men from the children's tribe were gathering to carry out an attack. In this situation we gathered our weapons and brought both the children and the driver inside our Piranhas for protection.* **When the shooting started I requested that we did not respond—even if in self-defense** *because we had wounded children and the driver inside the vehicles. But it was not an easy situation...Another situation was when an IED team observed the enemy burying an IED. I was informed and I requested that artillery or a missile was used against the enemy...We had cleared the road for traffic by blocking the road with our military vehicles. The missile took out 2—and 2 were able to run away even if they were wounded. We found the active IED afterwards..."*.

ITB03: *"...I once received the order to go to recover two logistical vehicles who had a fault and had not been able to follow the convoy to the base. I was with my platoon in QRF and I had in the allotted time (15 min) to schedule the task to be able to safely go on the spot, creating conditions of security during the time technician could repair the damage, find a safe route for the return and the supply of the means to the base. The operation was completed successfully"*.

27 Contacts with Locals

One of the main challenges in stabilization and reconstruction operations and in any other peace keeping operations was the contact with representatives of the host country and local population. Intensity of contacts with locals of military contingents varied depending on their missions. Those who performed pure military missions and had their own area of responsibility or guard perimeters had not had very intense contacts with local population. Example: (Dutch contingent in Afghanistan, Bulgarian contingent in Afghanistan). There were contingents and small units who had to do training (OMLTs, MATs, SATs) of the Afghan National Army (ANA). They had been in constant contacts with representatives of the ANA because they were in charge of their training. Representatives of higher HQs usually had contacts with local authorities and higher HQs of the respectful country. Most intense contacts with local authorities and local population had Provincial Reconstruction Teams (PRT) and CIMIC units that had to deal with local authorities and local population on a daily basis. Military observers and contingents involved in peace keeping operations had no intensive contacts with local population but only when needed. In our case the Armed Forces of the Philippines had to deal with local population (their compatriots) in their country every day. It applies to Cameroonian Armed Forces when they acted in their own territory. Here are some shares from the interviewees:

BGR04: "*He was invited by an Afghani sectarian mullah to visit a celebration by the mosque in connection with their religious holidays. In a sign of a good will he accepted the invitation and headed to the mosque in a convoy of three vehicles. There was a mob in front of the mosque and a child around 8 years of age bumped into their front right tire.* **Everybody around their vehicle bristled**. *He had a goose flesh and jumped out of the vehicle, embraced the boy and made sure that there was nothing wrong with him. The situation calmed down due to his prompt and friendly actions*".

BGR11: "*There was a program for equipping and training new Iraqi Armed Forces. Within the responsibilities of our battalion there was a task to enroll, equip and train an Iraqi Infantry Battalion (401 ICDC). By the time of uprising we had already started training of the battalion. During the fight in Karbala the battalion totally disintegrated and most of the personnel fled away leaving behind arms, equipment, vehicles, premises and anything that belonged to that battalion. So that, our personnel had to gather everything, and put it in order, and later to mobilize again 401 ICDC. It took lots of efforts and time to recuperate the Iraqi infantry battalion once again*".

BGR17: "*…The base was closed and his platoon was stationed in a field camp in tents for three days in order to protect the Observation Point … with an augmentation from snipers. They were in tents and with vehicles defensive positions in sector around the observation point. The intent was that we would be able to protect the OP in any case even in case of blockade of the gates. That was not accepted well by the local population, because their actions were well observed from the new position of the platoon. Immediately a new reason for tension and hostility arose and the locals* *blocked the approaches to the OP with boulders. In this setting, when they were taken out, there was **tension**, caused by the general situation in connection with the increased security measures during the elections".*

DKC03: *"They were very aware of the risk of communicating with us. However, they did not try to avoid us when we met them in the village... Only at a few situations men, i.e. the elderly, did not want to meet us/to communicate with us. Only once, I noticed they were angry with us as we did not help them when they were shot at by the Taliban. In one village, they were afraid of being observed by Taliban if they talked to us. Therefore, they didn't want to do so".*

DKC18: *"...Once we were at the outskirts of a small village, on high ground. I am there with the platoon of next in command when a senior sergeant comes to me and says "There's a local who wants a word with you!" After my radio man had checked him out for bombs and weapons he came to me. He then put this question: "**Why are you here?**" I answered that we knew that Taliban also was here, so it was a show of presence. He then put the question again: "Yes, but why you are here?" And I thought he wanted to know about our government and democracy, so I started telling him, but then he interrupted me: "But why are YOU here?" So I finally realized he wanted to know my personal motives. I knew that a warrior was an estimated person, so I answered that I was a warrior, and that my chief has told me to take the fight here. I live in a place with peace, and I think peace is better—but I am here to fight for you and I will die for your rights if that is what it takes. Then he raised and said "God Bless!" and then he left. He was a teacher".*

FIN04: *"... Probably once I got to know the locals better we were invited for lunch at some point. **That was memorable, to eat local delicacies.** Sometimes they looked odd and sometimes they tasted bad, but you had to eat them if you wanted to be welcomed back again. I cannot think more about the local communities".*

FIN12: *"...In this culture if you are invited you go, you or the Deputy. Or both, but usually one. Ramadan starting and ending also was important, different large events which you have to. I organized a few events myself, such as June Fourth, where I invited the **village elders and local authorities, police chiefs.** We talked and had various rituals. When there were negotiations we checked their ways closely and respected them. There were a few bigger **humanitarian events** in which the locals were for example taught new ways to cultivate the land. I was there too. And they always expected the local forces' Command to be there. There were several and they left a very good picture, and display and respect. I think that is an important part of the Commander's position".*

ITB08: *"We had good cooperation with the Afghan commander. We had not had a lot of confidence in the behavior of Afghan soldiers. For example, when we had to do foot patrols I never set ANA soldiers behind me. How brave fighters they were instead. ...".*

ITB09: *"Afghans are very good fighters, but not always reliable. Their commander said that when his soldiers were returning from leave he did not know what was going through their mind".*

LTC01: *"With a local government relationship was very specific, because governors kept on changing, but generally relationship was good, constructive. A problem was some mutual distrust. They constantly were asking something from us and had high expectation. If we were not able to supply then they started to blame us that we have a lot of resources but we don't give or share. Other difference was cultural: if they promise something, it does not mean they will stick to it, tried to manipulate. They see promises differently. It was difficult for me to fulfil promises made by previous PAT commanders. We came and they say „hey, you promised... "But generally the relationship was constructive; you must earn respect in Afghanistan. They judge you according to how you act, are you afraid or not, are you brave enough to eat their food, are you afraid to get into an unarmoured vehicle, how you react to various provocations like stones, firefight and etc. And that 'show you earn respect. Also I think it depends a lot on the number of incidents happened. Also you are judge by insurgents as well. They have goals and sometimes work together with local administration. Some government institutions had relationships with the Taliban before, and thus during the Shuras a lot of information used to leak out. It was very difficult to figure out how did it leaked, who did it. It was done obviously by some of them, definitely not us. When you see information runs away somehow, then its difficult to keep trust. Anyhow generally relationship was constructive. Afghani administration made a comparison of us and previous PAGs. It was difficult when they say: „listen, previous PAG built a hospital, another one built a bridge, but you only installed new windows at school, and coloured walls.... "We really did not have resources that they asked for. The purpose of soldiers to come and open the gate for engineers that could build, dig, and make the research. As soldiers we did our job—we came and we opened the gate, even, where it was not possible to open them before. We used to come to the villages, to talk about their needs; then we create a safe environment for civil projects. During deployment there was no financing, no projects it was reason why local administration got angrier; so it's not enough just to be there, you should have finance to help. So, the military goals were reached—we even dug some wells, clean up a school, but we were not doctors, engineers and teachers. We did what we were able to do with our medics and engineers, but we were limited. I think the reason of deployment itself was not understood by Joint Headquarters in Afghanistan and Lithuania government, Ministry of foreign affairs and the Parliament".*

LTC03: *"It was very specific mission, very different tasks; it was **different task if to compare with traditional task of infantry battalion**. We really had to put huge efforts to fulfil our tasks; we had to coordinate social development of province we were responsible for. We needed new and specific knowledge and skills. This work gave us a new experience as well. This work demanded higher motivation; the military camp was rather small one, so I was always an example for other soldiers and civilians how to act and behave. **I had to convince myself that I have to concentrate on tasks even if they are not traditional military, because my leadership determined the mood and motivation of entire unit. It forced me to use my inner-recourses and be able to keep it for 6 entire months**".*

LTC04: *"There were some seriously **dangerous situations**, but we managed to overcome them by peacefully negotiating using local police forces or tribe elders. We managed to overcome this even though there was **disturbance and crowd gathered*** *near our camp*. *Only once the patrol group was **fired** at during night in mountains but it was just threatening, so they did not have to fire back"*.

PHC04: *"There is an NGO (Help Panay) that the unit was engaged with (under the previous commander), but I am not really familiar with them; I cannot recall. There's also Gawad Kalinga—they are always with us if we have civil-military operations; they are our partner. Rotary Club also. I think that my boss (the battalion commander) is a member. Right now there are a lot who like us; our image has already changed for the better. Almost all tasks by the government sectors are done by us (**combat, disaster, teacher-soldier**, **ALS** (Alternative Learning System), even TESDA (vocational education) to give locals a chance to change their life). Being a model to the troop on how to socialize with the civilians so that they can help us in doing counter-insurgency. We need the local government to step up because everything is supposed to be their job, especially providing services to the localities. We also need to cooperate with the local government and other agencies that can help"*.

PHC10: *"Mostly in **community development problems**. For example, there is a certain non-governmental organization that wanted to donate supplies. We try to suggest the area where to give the supplies. So far, I'm generally ok and satisfied with our accomplishments. The focus now is to optimize the relationship between the army and other stakeholders especially the local government. It's a matter of time when we can solve the insurgency problem. Of course we want to neutralize the enemy. We have to clear the area one by one"*.

PHC11: *"**Local government services are delayed or lacking**. We also question the sincerity of service by the agencies since they don't want to go to the mountains. But we do encourage them a lot to help. The police is lacking in number. They have no presence in some villages outside of the two proper. If there are activities, we have to augment their troops. We do see that they lack enough people to take care of the remote hamlets so we just help them. Removing problems is always with the local government. We just facilitate"*.

Taking into account all single events that had happened in theaters, it was possible to process information and build a mathematical model of battle incidents that were depicted by the respondents.

Table 3 depicts different cases of operational experience throughout operational deployments of military contingents of participating countries in this research. This graph does not represent real percentage because most of the interviewees gave more than one answer, so that every single item represents a percentage out of the total 100%. It is obvious that Armed Encounters of different type predominate here as well. 44.9% of the interviewees pointed out that they experienced some kind of armed encounter with the opposing forces. What is more, there is much higher frequency of armed encounters in operations for stabilization and reconstruction compared to these of pure peace keeping purposes. More detailed calculations by country had been done and they are available. For the sake of simplicity and getting the right notion about the common picture only the totals are given in this research. Second determinant of armed encounters is harassing fire by opposing forces on multinational

Table 3 Battle incidents by number and participants

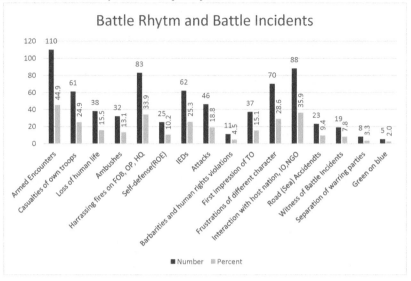

forces garrisons (bases of deployment, observation posts, check points, headquarters, and logistic facilities). The personnel responded that in 33.9% of all cases they experienced some kind of harassing fires(shelling by mortars, rockets strikes, small and medium arms fires). IED and VBIED attacks exploded by the opposing forces in stabilization and reconstruction operations in Iraq and Afghanistan were one of the greatest concerns of the Multinational forces. That is why a significant percentage of the interviewees (25.3%) ascribe their operational experience with facing consequences of an IED activation. 18.8% of the personnel experienced attacks on own force while executing tasks during patrolling, escorting, convoying, reconnoitering or just while en route to different positions. Large amount of personnel has been part, witnessed or experienced closely loss of human life (15.5%) or some kind of casualty of own troops (WIA)—24.9%. Notable amount of personnel (28.6%) associated their operational experience with some kind of frustration caused by discrepancies in operational imperatives, poor leadership, fowled command and control, lack of communication due to either cultural differences or language, and other nonlinearities. And last but not least, very high percentage (35.9%) of the participants regard their operational experience to contacts with representatives of the host country and local population. There are some other factors of operational experience that had been shared as well. See above Table 3.

28   Other Issues of Operational Experience

All operations of the UN, EU, NATO or other international organizations shown on Table 1 had been initiated and conducted as a result of conflicts that ravaged those countries and brought the populace to the brink of extinction. That is why an international intervention was needed to help the innocent and bring them back to something close to normal or at least bearable. Therefore upon explicit decisions and resolutions by the UN Security Council those missions were organized, funded and deployed. On one hand they influenced lives of the peacekeepers that had to train, equip and deploy, thus depart from their countries and families, separate from their beloved, on the other hand they influenced lives of indigenous populations that had to accept, go along with and bare foreign troops on their land. The main goal nevertheless was to provide help for the locals to cope with post conflict situation and benefit from stable and secure environment established by the peacekeepers. In this line of thinking most of the interviewees gave serious credit to aid and support of local communities and suffering populace. They strived to help the population and alleviate their lives to some extent.

However, **humanitarian aid** and **humanitarian support** for local governments, communities and population, according to the predominant part of the interviewees was not the core goal of missions. There were numerous international organizations and NGOs that had the capacity to do that. The military personnel were destined to provide security, stability and stable environment in order for the humanitarian aid to take place and to have positive impact on restoring the normal life or just help the poverty and hunger stricken population. In some cases (Afghanistan) as additional activities to humanitarian support some food programs and agricultural education were organized. This was due to widespread growing of poppy and marihuana in Afghanistan. A substitute of crops was needed to make for local population sustenance. Many interviewees underlined that they were not qualified well in distributing aid among communities but to provide security for the humanitarian convoys and distribution sites. Some respondents stated that aid and support to local communities was not always good to them. One of the officers expressed the following: FIN21: *"Giving something ready to them that does not motivate them to work for their rebuilding does not benefit anything. … You have to help for example the local mayor who takes their own slice and then their subordinates take their own and in the end the ordinary person gets only a little bit. Some organizations try to help with idealistic ideas but they do not really help the individuals"*.

CIMIC projects was another topic of deliberation in the research. In general most of the CIMIC projects are devoted to building some infrastructure for the local communities. Some of the interviewees share that all this projects went fluently and successfully. Depending on the vision, activity, and the ambition of the local authorities those projects achieved different results. If the local governors or mayors acted well, negotiated well and delivered justly, they achieved better results. Some of the personnel shared that in certain occasions local authorities showed very high expectations and impatience in the process of organizing and providing help and

CIMIC projects. This was true for the PRTs. According to some personnel the locals compared work done by different countries (see LTC01 p.22) in charge of PRTs and demanded the same from their followers not taking into account that different countries had different financial resources. Although PRTs ensured security for large scale CIMIC projects they also participated in some aid projects as well. LTC01: "*I gained a lot of experience in commanding an international unit, and to negotiate with locals. Also I participated in local committees, called Shuras, both security and government Shuras. We provided* **humanitarian aid**, *also rice, grain, sheets, and medical supplies; did some things ourselves, handed out things that we used to get from the UN*".

29 Interaction with International and Nongovernmental Organizations

The interviews touched on the issue of collaboration of multinational military forces with international and nongovernmental organizations. Most of the interviewees shared that they had not had contacts with either organizations. Those who were part of platoons, companies and more often battalions did not have to contact representatives of such organizations. Personnel who were directly involved in humanitarian or CIMIC projects had contacts mainly with international organizations like the UN, EU, OSCE or their subsidiaries. They expressed positive opinion about their joint activities. With regards to NGOs most of the personnel who had the chance to do joint projects with some of them thought that NGOs preferred to do things on their own. They had their own lines of supply, procedures and rules and did not want to mix up with the military. LTC02: "*There has been interaction and intensive work with every group that you've mentioned. **Every day's routine involved meetings with the local administration, the press, governmental and non-governmental organizations**, all of which were key parts to restoring the province, as the most of the projects, including roads and supply lines. Hence this was the very specific mission and task, so without those organizations our mission would not be possible. Like I said, it was not a combat mission; it was a mission of restoration of the province. There were some special ISAF projects financed by donor countries, together with NGO. They helped to fulfil projects such as spreading of agriculture, building of roads, etc. It was a civil mission of my battalion....**There was a little bit of everything, and even though it wasn't an ordinary military mission, we did complete a certain amount of military assignments**. I did not get much experience from the military side of things, it was more overall experience development of reconstruction projects, cooperation with local people and military partners, discussions at meetings. Before I've had experience with security issues, military activities, but on this PRT I had to deal with management issues or to work as an adviser. Also my personal life experience was an advantage*".

29.1   Discussion

So far we have analyzed some issues of operational experience with the aid of semi-structured interviews provided by the participating countries in this research. Thanks to the questionnaire the participants touched on very substantial military issues concerning operational experience of military personnel when deployed to stabi-lization and reconstruction operations or any other crisis response operations around the world. Thus we may use their input to discuss all these issues, draw conclusions and formulate lessons how to cope with them in future operations.

Baptism of fire was one of the analyzed subjects. It has become clear that baptism of fire is a one-time event. It happens to the military only once and the thrill of this feeling becomes deeply implanted into one's mind, and unforgettable for the rest of one's life. Most of the personnel proved that armed encounters with the opposing forces contribute predominantly to baptism of fire. The breakdown of data reveals that those countries who mandated and deployed their troops to operational areas that require full-fledged combat operations against deeply indoctrinated, well organized and trained opposing forces, point out armed encounter of different character as the reason of their baptism of fire. In our case the majority of participants of Denmark, Italy, and Spain shared that they owe their baptism of fire to this type of event. It has several reasons. First of all in most cases of these operations (especially in Iraq and Afghanistan) they acted in areas of responsibility with forces from the USA or the UK. Secondly, their mandate allowed them to perform these type of tasks. Last but not least their combat packages enabled them to collaborate and coordinate joint actions with other NATO allies.

Large group of the surveyed personnel associate their baptism with their first impression from being in a war environment (seeing and feeling the atmosphere of war settings). This feeling was typical to personnel who found themselves in a war situation for the first time and their senses were preoccupied with typical signs of war environment, i.e. remnants of destroyed arms and military equipment, ravaged countryside, destroyed infrastructure like buildings, bridges, ports, industrial facilities, the look and attitude of local population (especially children) and many other symptoms of recent war. This phenomenon is typical to the settings in Iraq in the wake operation Iraqi Freedom. Many of the contingents of the Multinational Forces had to march on their own long distances to get to their areas of responsibility. They saw this environment, felt the atmosphere of war, experienced it in practice and took it for granted as their baptism of fire. In our case most of the personnel from the first Bulgarian contingent in Iraq enunciated this feelings.

Activation of IEDs or VBIEDs take a very special place in hearts and minds of peacekeepers. That is why many of the interviewees thought that facing this event influenced their lives in a special way and mainly contributed to their baptism fire. They shared their experience and reactions in cases when IEDs had been exploded. ITC32: "...*I experienced problems especially when we jumped on these IEDs. One always expects to jump on an IED, at least mentally, but is never ready to face the real thing... Luckily we had no injuries. However, it was a critical situation to manage, especially for putting everyone in security (when these things happen you never know what can happen after)..."* Like this Italian soldier said, one always expects it, in almost all situations cannot prevent it, hopes that this does not happen, gives a sigh of relief when everything finishes without it. But if this IED were activated and caused damage one could have only borne the pernicious results from it and do consequence management to clean the area, save wounded and destroyed equipment and go on with tasks execution. Another officer shared that IEDs caused uncertainty and handicapped units to proceed with their duties. A Danish officer had given a heartbreaking statement: DKC04: *"You are slowly being hardened... But we were lucky as the operations started hard and then grew harder by each operation... When you are confronted with 300 dead persons, and there is blood and fuel all over the place it looks like a pig's slaughterhouse—only it's civilian suffering you are confronted with... and there is only so much you can do....tactical medicine won't do it, it's not enough, so with time it grows on you. The only thing you can do is to keep a professional distance—or get another job. When I'm deployed my focus is on: the dessert camp and the fighting. I have to be professional, a leader and also a person—and this weights more than being a father and a husband. However, I estimate the strain I'm taking continuously... when I come home I can feel that I'm still in 'battle mind': last time I didn't walk on grass for more than a year... you know... **I've seen 5 persons get their legs torn off by IEDs**... so it's the accumulated sum of strain that gets to you."*

The research has derived many ostentatious examples that in many cases IED activations had caused serious psychological damages to personnel and the inflicted local population, to include Post Traumatic Stress Disorder (PTSD).

Another determinant that conduced to baptism of fire, according to considerable percentage of surveyed personnel, was the interaction of multinational (peacekeeping) forces with local governments, regional authorities, armed forces, police, and indigenous population. In this group the interaction with the International organizations and NGOs was included as well. Everyday contacts with the aforementioned categories not only caused a lot of positive experience when things went well but also a lot of friction, strain, losses and frustration on both sides—the peacekeepers and the locals. As shown on Table 2, 10.8% of the interviewees associate their baptism of fire with their relations with local population. Most of the personnel connect it with some bad experience like indiscriminate cause of death due to traffic accidents, wrong direction of fire, or other events. In these cases they had to pay to quench the strain and alleviate the situation. Others ascribe it to animosity of some local communities strongly influenced by the opposing forces, or religious considerations. The Philippine interviewees gave high score to their interaction with local communities and thought that they had to work very hard to convince people that their presence there is for the good of local villages, clans, tribes etc.

Last but not least some personnel thought that their baptism of fire came when they saw the eyes of death for the first time in their lives. They associate loss of life and wounded friends as a grief-stricken event imprinted very deep in their memories.

Battle rhythm in missions and battle incidents was the principle question of the research. The inquiry looked for the true incentives of operational experience of the personnel while in stabilization and reconstruction operations or any other crisis response operations. The history of such operations showed that as the concept of operations of multinational forces streamlined and matured. The same applied to opposing forces as well. There were myriad of different qualifications of opposing forces' character of warfare—asymmetric warfare, guerilla warfare, organized resistance, irregular or unconventional warfare, subversive warfare and sabotage, lately we got to know cyber warfare and hybrid warfare. Most of the time opposing forces act illegally in an asymmetric manner. They don't wear uniforms, do not abide by the international laws on warfare, they do not have to follow the universal code of conduct while in war. They proved to be merciless and do not appreciate the sanctity of human life. Most of the times their ideologies come from somewhere outside theater of operations and their political masters and stakeholders follow their own agendas. Their principal aim is to disintegrate social fabric of the communities and whole nations, to disperse uncertainty and instability, and to pursue their agendas. On the other hand most of the fighters of the opposing forces are local citizens who know well culture, habits, topography and every other idiosyncrasy of the theater of operations. Most of the times they hold local population in constant dependency. That is why it is very difficult to organize, conduct and sustain an operation of this character. Nonetheless all these complications that appeared for earnest in the scope of this research the forces succeeded to cope and accomplish their missions and tasks.

Many of the respondents shared that they obtained the largest part of their operational experience from the **armed encounters** with the opposing forces. This research derived most precious information from testimonies of the interviewees who performed their duties in Iraq, Afghanistan, Middle East, and Central Africa. In their narrative they include complex and single events like operations, battles, and skirmishes with the opposing forces that included firefights with small arms, artillery, army aviation and air force. To this determinant of the research the interviewees ascribe also ambushes, attacks by the opposing forces when patrolling, convoying or escorting. There were attacks by opposing forces even when multinational forces were providing for humanitarian aid and donations for the local population. IEDs and VBIEDs were another issue of irritation, casualties and frustration. Another source of frustration was when battle incidents happened in the vicinity of forces with their brothers of arms but they could not intervene and help but witness the incidents. Ambushes in villages, towns, and cities, in different terrains, on columns of friendly forces also happened very often. Harassing attacks on bases and facilities happened persistently and with no remorse. In many circumstances the multinational forces had to stand against warring parties in the middle of crossfire to pacify them and make them cease fire and transit to peace. All these events that the respondents described in their interviews contributed profoundly to their operational experience. They completed their tours of duty, returned home and extended all of the above mentioned to their colleagues and brothers of arms.

Barbarities and human rights violations were significant contributors to operational experience for participants in theaters where these events had appeared. In our case there were 11 events mentioned. All of these events included different cases of arson, looting, pillage, plunder, rape, homicide, and any other of similar character. Most often they happened to helpless noncombatants—old people, women, and children. The respondents shared this information with shock, awe, disgust toward perpetrators and compassion toward victims of this war crimes. It usually happened when peacekeepers found symptoms and evidence of these crimes *post factum* and they had to take care of the consequences. Hence, being in charge of consequence management of this sort of events unquestionably creates enormous frustration and sorry for the innocent victims. It had been a gruesome experience but they faced it and had to overcome it.

We have already discussed the other determinants of operational experience like loss of life, wounded, interaction with representatives of host country and international and nongovernmental organizations. They are all an integral part of the operational experience of the peacekeepers. However there are some nonmaterial determinants that appeared in this research, thanks to the active stance of the respondents.

30   Leadership and Commandership

Leadership appeared to be a decisive part of operational experience. Most of the platoon leaders, company and battalion commanders deemed leadership and command and control as the most important trait of the commander to lead his/her subordinates in every problematic situation. At higher levels of the chain of command, according to many respondents, commanders need to have the right understanding how the things are done down in the troops. For example Danish soldiers put emphasis on training and shared that if training were good the commanders' job could have been easier. DKC03: *"Trust your training and "keep calm. It is as much a question of drawing on your mental training as on your soldier skills. But there will come a post-reaction. Broken or stuck vehicle—Solution: Secure the place, require assistance, extract the vehicle and go back to camp."* In their opinion, good training builds up the right instincts for the commander how to behave in critical situations.

According to many interviewees the commander should know his/her people well. First of all, he/she has to take care of his/her subordinates. Second, he/she gives necessary credit of acknowledgement to the deeds of his/her people. He/she must have precise situational awareness and abilities of deep concentration. A commander never gives up the mission and never lays down his/her people. He/she has to lead people with his/her personal example, must face problems and solve them without hesitance. DKC23: *"…Do not trust your first impression; If the way seems "sunny" (= no problem), you may go into ambush; Have an aim with what you do even if the enemy tries to mislead you. Follow your instinct. Do not react, act instead…"*.

Some respondents believe that a commander needs to know not only how to organize and conduct battles and engagements but also many other nonmilitary stuff in order to cope with stabilization and reconstruction issues and humanitarian assistance of different character. LTC01: *"The commander first of all must learn to listen.*

...Civilians work differently; you must learn how to listen to them. It's easy to say, but difficult to do because in some ways you cannot act like them because they have no limits, they don't wear uniforms, they don't drive military vehicles, they are under different level of threat than you and your soldiers are. So sometimes you have to step over yourself and say what you think, but not threaten. Not everything is possible to be done together, but it is worth trying to reach a compromise. ...I don't believe a commander of these days should have knowledge to fight only".

In time of exigency the commander should think through things, make a decision, announce it, and act. ITC32: *"...At the level of mental process there are very clear guidelines. And so if one has them in mind, even in the moment of crisis, he can put them into practice. And then again you have to stay calm for a moment and look around what happened,* analyze *the situation and apply the solution that seems the most logical, the least dangerous, and the safest. You have to take a moment the pulse of the situation and act."* ITC34: *"In these cases, the first thing is that the commander must have the ability, the lucidity to understand immediately what the situation is. And this is already one of the greatest difficulties. Once this is done, he must try to give the minimum information as possible but the most effective. The important things are to have a few items, but those elements must be clear and those who serve.... **Perhaps there the only way is to set an example, from the company commander, the platoon commander, the squad commander: we need to be the first that do not warm the hearts that much and keeping a low profile".***

National Caveats were another issue of elaboration in the submitted interviews. There were some ideas in the interviews about passing the buck of duties in the multinational forces from one nationality to another. This process is typical to Iraq and Afghanistan. Here, in our case, it was mentioned shortly by some respondents that they had to do tasks which initially had to be done by someone else. It has been a serious problem for NATO in stabilization and reconstruction operations. Some countries vindicated their rejection to do certain tasks because of their mandate endorsed by the national command authorities. This was discussed broadly in NATO and the general opinion was that national caveats significantly diminished ISAF effectiveness and created resentment in other allies and coalition partners who had to bear responsibilities of such tasks. With each following mission this issue shall be solved within the frames of planning conferences, memoranda of agreements, and development of common SOPs.

Perhaps, it is time to start talking and acting again about **nation building**, especially in Afghanistan. So far, there has been an ambivalent policy towards nation building. That is why nation building failed in Iraq. The stabilization and reconstruction operation in Iraq was closed without achieving tangible results in nation building. However there is an opportunity in Afghanistan. Although downsized in the number of troops and with a modified mission it is ongoing nowadays. The efforts to build capacity for governance economic development shall go on. Most importantly efforts to expand and intensify education of the young population and to build adequate infrastructure in the country need to continue. External pernicious influence should be discontinued gradually. It takes a long time for a nation building to succeed. So that a strategic patience, moderate military presence and necessary resources are needed for nation building to succeed. The author believes that there is still a ground in Afghanistan, with the decisive involvement of the UN and the other international and nongovernmental organizations for the stabilization and reconstruction operation to succeed. What is needed there is security and stability, good governance, winning the hearts and minds of the young Afghani population, and keeping the radical destructive organizations out of country.

31 Conclusions

Organization and conduct of this empirical research have helped analyze and discuss operational experience of military personnel in stabilization and reconstruction operations and crisis response operations of different character. Most of the participants in the research submitted very profound and high quality interviews and implied for exceptionally experienced soldiers. The depth and span of sharing was outstanding. Some of the participants touched on many different sensitive features of the operational experience, and what is more, shared openly and honestly their thoughts. It is a pity that the ramifications of the research do not allow us to show more significant part of their sharing. The proposals and sharing of most of the participants are universal and apply to the armed forces of all contributing countries.

The analysis in this research leads to a conclusion that operational experience is a function of multitude of variables which influence it to a different degree. Obviously baptism of fire is a significant part of operational experience. As seen in the analysis above, baptism of fire is the primordial feeling that stays with his/her bearer for life. It is caused by almost the same variables that contribute to follow on operational experience in operations of different character. Armed encounters with the opposing forces, to include battles, engagements, skirmishes, ambushes, harassment by fire, activation of IED, green on blue events, friendly casualties and these of innocent non-combatants and others, contribute to learning necessary lessons and gaining operational experience of the multinational forces for participation in future similar operations.

Analysis of the interviews leads to another conclusion that country training is vital to facing and coping with battle events. However, country training is far away from theater of deployment and real events. Even though it is organized and conducted in the best way possible with fully replicated environment it could not substitute for on the job training. Therefore training in the area of responsibility is indispensable. Recent analyses of the Alliance showed that this applies mostly to staff officers who deploy to joint HQ in a multinational environment.

Leadership and commandership was another issue, which the respondents deemed very important to successful accomplishment of mission's goals and tasks.

Since the purpose of this research was to extract some lessons from all these operations that the interviewees had taken part in, one may try to see for such lessons in the answers of respondents. One will confirm that there are many observations, insights and lessons that he has to hold dear in future deployments. With this said let us try to look for such lessons identified.

Training:

Operational experience is strongly connected with training. Training provides for gaining knowledge and building skills. It helps personnel to develop their inner combat and survival instincts in an operational environment when confronted with opposing forces of different nature. Therefore training is vital to prepare soldiers for the real missions and to get to know how to face and how to react in different battle and humanitarian situations. Pre-deployment training is the major contributor to preparation. However it cannot always supply all knowledge and information for the area of operations. That is why it is prudent that we enrich it with on-line training and induction training on the site. On the other hand NATO practice of joint training centers proved to be an excellent tool for pre-deployment training of multinational formations that will be deployed together and will strive together for the accomplishment of missions and tasks. As we mentioned before this applies to officers who will have to takeover staff positions in multinational headquarters. Following this argument it is reasonable to formulate a lesson: *Continue with improvement of pre-deployment training. If possible sent multinational formations to joint training centers in order to standardize training and concepts, and save resources. Expand and apply accordingly on-line courses, especially for staff officers. Always take and analyze feedback about training.*

Interoperability:

Multinational military operations across virtually the entire spectrum of warfare have played an increasingly prominent role in international security policy since the end of the Cold War. This leads to problems of interoperability between the forces of the various countries of the coalition. Interoperability refers to the ability of different military organizations to conduct joint operations. According to the definition adopted by the North Atlantic Treaty Organization for use by its member nations, interoperability is "The ability of systems, units or forces to provide services to and accept services from other systems, units, or forces and to use the services exchanged to enable them to operate effectively together." (NATO July 2006 Interoperability for joint operations). It is interesting to note that: The term interoperability has evolved over the years. It began primarily focused on equipment-level interoperability, soon was expanded to include inter-service and allied force interoperability, and has now evolved to include a "system of systems" perspective.[3] This was written in 2005. The interviews prove that it is still in effect not only in arms and equipment but also in conceptual approaches and actions. *Therefore we may extract a lesson that there is still a necessity of overcoming interoperability discrepancies and inconsistencies*

[3]Ned H. Criscimagna, "Statistical Assumptions of an Exponential Distribution" Reliability Information Analysis Centre, 2005, through Giuseppe Caforio, Soldiers Without Frontiers: The View From The Ground Experiences of Asymmetric Warfare.

in theaters where many nations deploy forces with organic arms and equipment and a different indoctrination.

Leadership and commandership:

The analysis and discussion have demonstrated that key determinants in how a military formation acts in a combat situation are leadership and the commanders' skills. It applies not only to a certain military formation but to the whole multinational force as well. The higher in hierarchy one goes the more leader's qualities one must have. One who is a leader in high ranks must never forget the skills he had built in the ranks and files. Commandership is typical and indispensable skill (or art) to lead military units. Therefore it is advisable to identify a lesson, based on the shared opinions in the interviews. *Continue to develop competencies to imbue knowledge and wisdom, and build skills to lead and command military units in combat situations and humanitarian crises. Raise commanders capable of resolving quickly and effectively all issues of moral and ethical nature that arise in the course of critical situations, as well as those related to the cohesion of formations and multinational forces. Create commanders who are capable of taking bold, timely and adequate decisions, and are able to influence subordinates through their personal deeds.*

Language proficiency:

The interviewees shared that in some circumstances they had difficulties understanding each other when in multinational environment. Nations who had good knowledge and proficiency in English did better not only in operations and humanitarian activities but also in everyday life. So far English language is adopted as a *lingua franca* so that every nation shall speak it when in missions. *This necessitates permanent improvement of knowledge and skills how to speak and comprehend English.* General understanding of host nation's language is a plus.

National caveats:

Another thorny issue that appeared in the analysis was "national caveats". Many interviewees shared that there was interference in operational chain of command by the national command authorities. This hampered commanders and caused confusion and ambivalence. On the other hand there was a tendency that some nations imposed national caveats in order to avoid casualties and loss of materiel and equipment. The commanders and HQs of multinational forces had been strongly influenced and incapacitated to pursue their tasks with less forces available for missions and tasks accomplishment. It was broadly discussed in NATO and was repudiated by most troop contributing nations who took the brunt of the most dangerous missions. *Therefore we may identify a lesson that national caveats should be avoided by any means. All operational issues shall be discussed, distributed and put to effect in planning conferences in pre-deployment period, and agreements should be signed, and in this way each contributing nation shall be well informed about chain of command, responsibilities and procedures in the area of operations.*

Appropriate code of conduct:

In operations in Central Africa, and in some occasions in other theaters it has happened many times that barbarities and human rights violations had been done by the opposing forces. It was mentioned however in some interviews that it happened in some cases with some forces we have analyzed. Therefore it is never needless to turn our look to international legislation that treats this issues. *There is a permanent need to remind the peacekeepers the appropriate code of conduct stated in UN Charter, Geneva and the Hague Conventions. It is important for the commanders to know well and implement SOFA (Status of forces agreement) with the host country, as well as the stemmed ROE.*

Lessons learned dissemination:

As a result of this research it is important for all readers to perceive the importance of lessons learned sharing and application in military practice. This said, *it is important to establish continuity and implement traditions in sharing lessons among the multinational forces in theater and among troop contributing countries. Lessons learned sharing improves the efficiency of multinational forces, saves system errors and assists commanders in successfully accomplishing tasks.*

As a conclusion of this analysis it is important to underline that all respondents shared their conviction that they did good job in contributing to international peace and security in respected theaters. This applies to the Armed Forces of the Philippines for their national security.

There were two distinct groups of respondents. The first one was the group of countries that participated in various theaters (see Table 1). The second one was represented from the Armed Forces of the Philippines who fought against intransigence in their own territory. Nevertheless these differences all interviews contributed greatly to the analysis. It is obvious that all personnel accumulated operational experience. It was shown in the analysis (see Table 3). In most cases it differed because of different theater settings; opposing forces' ideology, constitution and tactics; national caveats, and different arms and equipment.

Although there were some differences all of the respondents proved their operational experience valuable and necessary for their future service to their countries. They took pride of their performance and contribution to peace and security around the world.

References

1. Kaldor M (2012) New and old wars: organized violence in a global era, 3rd edn. Stanford University Press, Stanford, California
2. Alesina Alberto, Igier Bocconi, Bryony Reich (2015). Nation-building, Harvard University, https://scholar.harvard.edu/files/alesina/files/nation_building_feb_2015_0.pdf
3. Boot Max, (2017). Back to Nation-Building in Afghanistan. Good. New York Times, Aug. 22, 2017;

4. Caforio Giuseppe (2013). Soldiers Without Frontiers: The View from the Ground Experiences of Asymmetric Warfare, 2013—Gruppo Editoriale s.r.l. ACIREALE—ROMA;
5. Dimitrov P (2017) Some Lessons Learned from Participation in Stabilization and Reconstruction Operations, International Journal of Advanced Research. Int. J. Adv. Res. 5(2):2146–2158
6. Alan D (2003) Thirteen Years: The Causes and Consequences of the War in Iraq. Parameters, Autumn, p 2003
7. Ignatieff Michael (2003). Why Are We in Iraq? (And Liberia? And Afghanistan?), New York Times, September 7, 2003;
8. International Crisis Group (2016). Cameroon: Confronting Boko Haram, Africa Report N°241 l 16 November 2016 . https://d2071andvip0wj.cloudfront.net/241-cameroon-confronting-boko-haram_1.pdf
9. Jennings Salvatore (2003). The Road Ahead. Lessons in Nation Building from Japan, Germany, and Afghanistan for Postwar Iraq, United States Institute for Peace, April 2003, www.usip.org;
10. Katzman Kenneth (2003). Iraq: U.S. Regime Change Efforts and Post—War Governance, Congressional Research Service Report for Congress, Order Code R31339, October 10, 2003, www.usembassy.at/en/download/pdf/iraq_change.pdf
11. Pennekamp Matthew, (2016). The Philippines' Own War on Terror, The National Interest, April 25, 2016, https://nationalinterest.org/feature/the-philippines-own-war-terror-15903;
12. Richard W. Stewart (2003). Operation Enduring Freedom, CMH Pub 70-83-1, October 2001-March 2003;
13. Thomas RB (2006) The Fiasco: The Military Adventure in Iraq. Penguin, New York, p 2006
14. Thomson Reuters News (2014). Philippines—Mindanao conflict BRI, https://news.trust.org/spotlight/Philippines-Mindanao-conflict/?tab=briefing
15. Yanakiev D, Petkov I (2016) The Lessons from Participation in Operations to Support of International Peace And Security. Military Press, Sofia

Logistic Mission Processing

Plamen Petkov

Abstract In the 20 of century NATO followed the principle that logistics was a national responsibility. Accordingly, its only focus at that time was the establishment of and compliance with overall logistics requirements. By January 1996, NATO logisticians recognized the new challenges facing the Alliance. In particular, the downsizing of military resources underscored the necessity of increased cooperation and multinationality in logistic support. Viewed from the life cycle perspective, logistics is the bridge between the deployed forces and the industrial base that produces the weapons and materiel that the forces need to accomplish their mission. It is important to recognise that the various logistic and logistic-related functions come together to form the totality of logistics support. This chapter is based on analysis of the experiences which is accumulated in multinational missions and operations. This experiences are presented and analysed to identify common issues related in logistic support that deserve attention. Operations are quite different, as well as the national experiences, that why it is difficult formulate criteria for comparative cross-country analysis. When it is possible, commonalities and differences among the national cases are also commented. The following key issues are discussed in the chapter:

- Provision of individual equipment
- Military equipment and armament;
- Accommodations;
- Medical service;

In conclusion some implications for practice regarding planning and execution of multinational military operations, as well as lesson learned and best practice implementation in training of the participants in such operations are summarized.

The author serves in Rakovski National Defense College in Sofia, Bulgaria as an assistant in the field of lessons learned.

P. Petkov (✉)
G. S. Rakovski National Defense College, 82 Evlogi & Hristo Georgievi Blvd, 1504 Sofia, Bulgaria
e-mail: papetkov@armf.bg

Logistics, occasionally referred to as "combat service support", must address highly uncertain conditions. While perfect forecasts are rarely possible, forecast models can reduce uncertainty about what supplies or services will be needed, where and when they will be needed, or the best way to provide them.

Ultimately, responsible officials must make judgments on these matters, sometimes using intuition and scientifically weighing alternatives as the situation requires and permits. Their judgments must be based not only upon professional knowledge of the numerous aspects of logistics itself but also upon an understanding of the interplay of closely related military considerations such as strategy, tactics, intelligence, training, personnel, and finance.

However, case studies have shown that more quantitative, statistical analysis are often a significant improvement on human judgment.

In addition, different national and organisational structures and decision-making processes, concepts of tactics and mission planning, different disciplinary codes, different command and control systems, equipment and armament, and payment differences can be viewed as challenges to the coalitions' effectiveness [1].

The research team may devote its attention to another major research task, namely the assessment of military service logistics in missions. The issues examined are related to:

- the individual equipment of the soldiers;
- armament and equipment of contingents;
- accommodations;
- medical service.

The results of the interviews show that logistics is a key factor for the successful implementation of the tasks. At the same time, the interviewed servicemen outlined approaches and methods to improve the service support of contingents and the acquisition of capabilities to independently ensure our participation in operations upholding international peace and security.

The process of internationalization of the military, participating in coalition operations and multinational formations is among the most important distinctiveness of the post-modern defence organisations [2].

1 Provision of Individual Equipment

In accordance with the survey methodology in this section, interviewees shared their opinions on the individual equipment assigned to each soldier who subsequently performs the tasks on site in the mission area. The specific items include the quality, the ergonomics of clothing and the individual equipment: kevlar helmets, backpacks, ballistic protection, tactical goggles, tactical vests, gloves and other equipment. In the interviews, the soldiers include in this category also the individual weapons.

About a quarter of the respondents (26.73%) estimates the procurement of individual equipment as high-grade and completes (Fig. 1). Their view is that the acquisition in this group was at a high level and was in accordance with the tasks performed
in the mission area. The majority of the respondents appreciate the improvement
in supply. The point out that commanders and headquarters (responsible for military formations, fitting, and training of contingents) respond more adequately to the
needs because of the increased participation in missions abroad and gaining experience. Every contingent departed with equipment better than the one of the prede-
cessor. Interviewees noted that the contingents had received everything available by
the moment of departure. Figure 1 is a graphical representation of the servicemen
assessment of the equipment used in the three categories. The first category reflects
the assessments of the quality of the individual equipment as completely satisfying
the conditions, the second category shows the opinions that the individual equipment
as not completely satisfactory and the third category focuses on the negative ratings
of the servicemen characterizing the poor quality equipment.

Part of the respondents expressed the view that there were lapses in the supply
of individual equipment. In this sense, the soldiers specified several key areas where
attention is needed:

- Improving the quality of clothing and footwear;
- Updating the individual equipment according to the immediate needs;
- Fitting out with advanced individual equipment—ballistic protection, night-vision
  goggles and other personal protective gear.

There are ratings that also record the poor quality of the equipment, *"The Eagles
were old and broken, but not in critical situations … Also, the equipment we had,
wore too fast."*

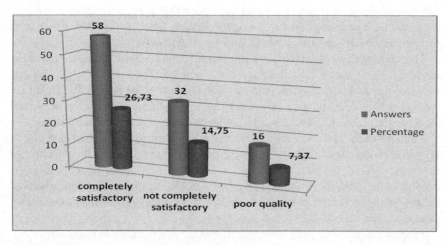

Fig. 1 Evaluation of individual equipment (in%), broken down by categories (completely
satisfactory, not completely satisfactory and poor quality)

**The quality of clothing and shoes is deemed problematic during the partici-
pation of Bulgarian and Philippine contingents.**

In this respect, a large proportion of the findings above are also valid in the specific case of the supply of clothing and footwear for missions. The analysis of the data from this study shows that much work is needed to improve the individual mission equipment. The interviewees from the above-mentioned contingents mentioned as a rule the low quality of the shoes, unfit for the severe environment and with an extremely short life-cycle. In other cases, it is stated that the shoes of poor quality. *"Enlisted personnel receive uniform issue only every 3 years so we need to invest [purchase at own expense first, then be reimbursed] if the uniform is not good as well as the shoes"*. *"However there were different types of shoes that created problems. For example they had some Turkish shoes that were very low quality"*.

There are similar findings in the study of the Bulgarian and Philippine contingents. A number of interviewees say they have bought field shoes with their own money from military stores to be able to perform their tasks.

First, half of the interviewed Bulgarian soldiers express dissatisfaction with the quality of the clothing. In a few missions (Afghanistan), staff was given poor quality clothing, which, according to soldiers, literally disintegrated till the end of the mission. In some cases, they did not receive everything they needed. Difficulties were also encountered in finding a suitable clothing size. In part of the interviews, it is emphasized that the state of the uniform affects the self-confidence of the soldiers among the coalition partners.

Second, many soldiers emphasize the need of adequate outfit and equipment to perform tasks in line with modern requirements. For example, Danish soldiers say they did not have MINEHOUND VMR3 minesweepers as their British counterparts, and after raising the issue several times they received ones. Others believe it is necessary to upgrade the bulletproof vests. Italian soldiers commented, *"The bullet-proof vest gave difficulty in pointing the rifle"*, and their Philippine colleagues considered their absence a serious problem. *"I was the platoon leader, a lot of my troops died because we do not have enough bulletproof vests and helmets"*.

The same applies to surveillance equipment and tactical eyeglasses. Lithuanian soldiers pointed out as a disadvantage the procurement of night-vision equipment and observation devices, which in the next missions were delivered. The Bulgarian soldiers had the opportunity to use American armor plates instead of the heavy and inconvenient *Pancerflex*, but it was forbidden because of the insurance clauses.

From all of the above-mentioned it can be summarized that at the beginning of the participation of most military contingents in operations to maintain international peace and security, the individual logistics of military servicemen does not meet the conditions in which they performed the tasks. Some improvement can be observed because of the increased intensity of missions and the lessons learned from our own experience and that of allies or partners.

Problems with outfit and equipment arise primarily in the following cases:

- the environmental conditions in the mission area differ sharply from those in the countries sending a contingent (Africa, Lebanon, Guinea, Philippines, Afghanistan, etc.);
- Increase in the strength of contingents when the resources do not match the ones available for the mission.

2 Military Equipment and Armament

During the interviews the research team paid attention to the provision of contingents with armament, military vehicles and machinery and their suitability for mission tasks. Nearly half of the respondents, who commented on the armament and equipments (47% of the cases), gave a positive assessment and considered that they met the mission challenges (Fig. 2). The majority of military personnel consider that regular armament (individual and collective) have good tactical and technical characteristics and fulfill the requirements of modern operations. Interviewees say the weapons are completely in line with the tasks and have not encountered problems. For example an Italian soldier, when on a mission in Lebanon, said, "*I did not encounter unexpected problems*" and Filipino soldiers give a positive feedback on the organization of the armament service, "*No problem with guns because there is personnel in-house who can fix them*". The Bulgarian soldiers praised their personal weapons, "*The AK-47 is the best weapon, the PK machine gun too. Our weapon is better than the American one.*"

The assessments of the combat and automotive equipment do not stand out as an exception. The servicemen say that in most cases the equipment meets the task

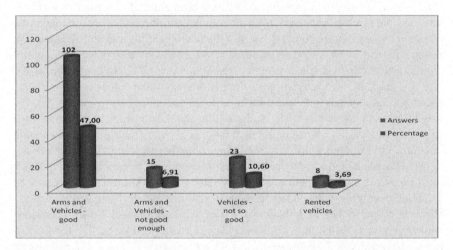

Fig. 2 Armament and equipment assessment (%), broken down by respondents' answers

requirements. In missions in Afghanistan, some of the tasks were carried with equipment of coalition partners, which, according to the interviewees, also met the requirements of the tasks assigned. A positive example was set by the EU missions in Bosnia and Georgia, where good practice was established to hire cars for lighter tasks (transport, unarmed patrol, etc.). The opinion of the soldiers is that in these cases that was the most appropriate way to provide equipment.

In spite of that there are few cases in which respondents admitted that armament and equipment corresponded only to a certain degree to the mission requirements. According to them, tasks can be performed with the regular armament and equipment, but with some reservations. In this case, the armament ratings are rather positive. On the other hand, the ratings for the equipment are mixed. Some respondents are of the opinion that, although with some reservations, it corresponded to the mission tasks. Many of the Bulgarian interviewees say that in the first missions (Cambodia, Bosnia, Kosovo, Iraq) we performed the tasks with the regular equipment (UAZ-469, ZIL-131, GAZ-66) and in spite of the compromise the equipment was fulfilling its purpose. The Finnish and Philippine soldiers expressed dissatisfaction with the insufficient number of military equipment they had. It is reported that the equipment used in Lebanon was very often out of order as a result of the high temperatures [3].

About 7% of respondents consider the armament and equipment not match the mission requirements. Some soldiers emphasize that the above-mentioned specimens are hopelessly obsolete and difficult to fulfill the tasks. Bulgarian, Italian, Spanish, and Danish servicemen are of the opinion that part of the equipment did not meet the environmental conditions of the area of operation. Some of the machines were too heavy, difficult to move, with limited visibility for the driver, and this created considerable precondition for accidents, especially in cities where soldiers performed some of the tasks. Mission participants in Bosnia and Kosovo say that the maintenance of old gasoline equipment was labor and time consuming. For repairs of machine parts and units it was necessary to make a request to the National Command and to deliver them from the country that sent the contingent. In Iraq and Afghanistan, all the cars and other combat equipment of the coalition were powered by diesel engines, and fueling vehicles with gasoline engines proved a serious challenge.

It was noted that the automotive equipment was not suitable for combat missions due to the lack of any ballistic protection for mounted troops given the particularly hostile and dangerous environment in Iraq and Afghanistan. Extreme environmental conditions contributed to frequent failures of part of the equipment in certain locations. For example, *Dardo* armored truck is inefficient at high temperatures.

From the point of view of the use of combat equipments to perform tasks (patrols, convoys, escorts, search operations) it was found that heavy armored vehicles were not suitable for urban tasks due to the reduced visibility and the limited firing sectors. The military personnel think that the *M1117 Guardian* is unsuitable for operations in town or a city; furthermore, it is even dangerous because of the limited field of vision. The said,"...*and it is crowded in Kabul, children scamper and because of the limited fields of vision Guardian and MRAP are extremely unsuitable*". These machines proved much more reliable when operating in open areas.

The servicemen rank positively *HAMMER* (HMMV) military specimens. They say that, despite the insignificant ballistic protection, the necessity to install a machine gun and the frequent failure, these vehicles fulfilled their original purpose of patrolling and moving in urban areas.

The assessment of the interviewees for the *M1117 Guardian* Armored Security Vehicle (*ASV*) is that it is not suitable for combat operations in mountainous woodlands, rough terrain and in populated areas: *"It's unstable, and in urban conditions, because of limited visibility, the driver is at risk of causing unintended road accidents, especially in a city like Kabul, where traffic rules do not exist."* Servicemen who have used the machine also say *"Browning's onboard machine gun is extremely capricious, has a difficult operation, and often detects."* Similar are the assessments of the use of the *MRAP7 machine* in urban environments. The interviewees said that the repair of the equipment exploited by the coalition partners was organized very well and did not have any difficulty.

Concerning the provision of contingents with the necessary equipment, two opposing opinions are outlined. The first is to provide the contingents with light armored and manoeuvrable equipment for execution of tasks in populated areas as well as with heavy armored equipment for performing combat tasks in open areas. Other soldiers are of the opinion that the contingents are overwhelmed with much and unnecessary equipment which, when closing missions, is a major problem for re-transport.

3   Accommodations

In the context of the quality of logistical support, some of the troops commented on accommodation, food and communal services.

The analysis of the results shows that this is one of the areas where a very high degree of approval is expressed (Fig. 3). In 76.04% of the cases, the interviewees value this type of support. As a rule, in missions in Iraq and Afghanistan, issues of accommodations are provided centrally within the coalition or under the terms of a bilateral agreement with the leading country (US), or with the lead in the accommodation facility (with the Italian contingent at Camp Invicta, for the first missions in Afghanistan, with the German contingent in the Warehouse base, subsequently with the US), with the Dutch contingent—in Kosovo, etc.). Accommodations are traditionally provided by civilian contractors (*Supreme, KBR*, etc.) hired by the leading coalition partner. Typical answers in this area are, *"Accommodation, food and communal household service were excellent. Everything was excellent, there were no shortages and shortcomings. Very good conditions, air-conditioned premises, use of the Internet. In Lebanon we had an organization pitched enough."*

In about 26% of the interviews, the respondents are of the opinion that there were shortcomings in the organization of accommodations. An additional analysis makes it possible to identify the missions in which logistics was inadequately organized.

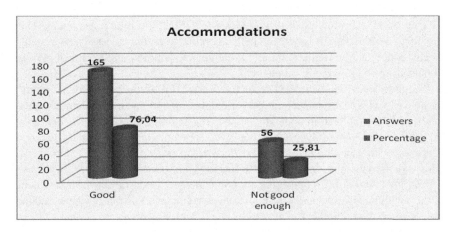

Fig. 3 Assessment of accommodation (in%), broken down by the number of respondents

The deficiencies are mostly related to the first missions in Afghanistan (ISAF), Iraq (SFIR), and Cameroon (Opps Delta).

In Afghanistan, Bulgarian soldiers relate difficulties with accommodation and community service. Initially, the contingent was accommodated in *Pirin* tents, unsuitable for the big temperature amplitudes in the country and the staff was experiencing great privations and difficulty, as well as lack of normal rest after the completion of their tasks. The contingent is not provided with walk-in sanitary facilities and the issue is solved on the spot with the help of the German partners. *"Because of the harsh weather conditions during the winter and the bad living conditions in the Bulgarian tents, we were accommodated in the Warehouse headquarters."*

In Iraq (Karbala) there were a number of gaps and shortcomings in the organization of accommodations. The servicemen say that the accommodation conditions were bad—too many servicemen shared a room; lack of air-conditioning in the premises in extreme heat and impossibility for rest after duty. The access to water for sanitary purposes was difficult and it happened very often. The situation did not differ sharply with the Lebanese and the Cameroon missions where they faced shortage of drinking water. Typical answers to these questions sound like, *"Inconvenience of housing certainly, but due to the situation, climate and so on especially in Iraq. In the second one logistic challenges were water supply, which did not necessarily work all the time, food provided challenges through the supplier."*

4 Medical Service

The interviews with the servicemen also provide data concerning the quality of medical support during missions.

Interviewees regard the medical service in the missions as good and adequate to their needs of specialized medical care (Fig. 4). About 29% of respondents say that much attention was paid to this issue and they had highly-trained medical teams, which, according to their capabilities, provided medical assistance Role I in the missions. In all missions where our contingents were involved, specialized medical assistance Role II was administered in field hospitals or in stationary hospitals. For all emergency medical cases requiring highly qualified medical assistance within the coalition, centralized transport (air or car) was organized for medical evacuation. Highly specialized medical assistance for the contingents was also provided at the Military Hospital in Landstuhl, Germany, where the Bulgarian servicemen received medical treatment.

The interviews from Bulgaria, the Philippines, Cameroon and Denmark for medical assistance include answers such as, *"The medical provision during the mission is of good quality, the medical teams are from people with professional experience. When we conduct the MEDCAP, there were vehicles provided to us apart from the military vehicles. We have air support here for medical evacuation. We had an experience with medical evacuation by air and it was done efficiently."*

In five of the interviews, servicemen say that medical service was not fully in line with mission requirements. Attention is drawn to the medical evacuation by air. A serviceman from the Philippines is convinced that, *"If only we have capabilities to fly in bad weather we could have saved more lives. I requested air transport but the chopper cannot fly because of bad weather and fog. My soldier died because we were not able to evacuate him fast enough."* Certain interviewees point to weakness in

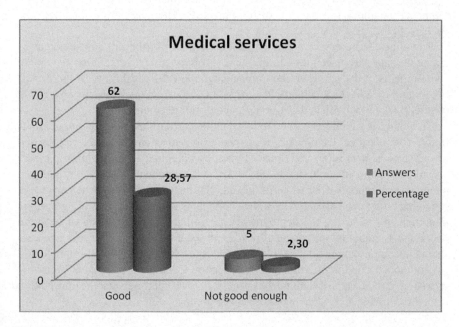

Fig. 4 Assessment of medical services (in %), broken down by number of respondents' answers

insufficient medical drags and obsolete medical equipment. Others (Ethiopia, Eritrea) point out that the mandatory immunizations that needed to be given in advance were not complete and that they had to be further administered on the spot.

5   Suggestions

- Acquisition of quality clothing and footwear appropriate to the environmental conditions in the mission area;
- Acquisition of appropriate equipment that meets the requirements of the task and the theater of the operation;
- Unification of the clothing of the servicemen for use on the territory of the country as well as abroad. This will eliminate the need to purchase and assemble clothing for contingents before departure for missions;
- Perform control of the state of the military equipment and monitor its proper operation.

6   Conclusions on Logistics

It is necessary to perfect and diversify the provision of soldiers with individual equipment that meets the requirements for the fulfillment of the tasks and the environmental conditions of the area of responsibility. The interviewees highlight the quality of clothing and shoes.

Providing the necessary armament and equipment for the missions emerges as one of the fatal flaws according to the survey. It is essential to take into account the commitments of the parties to the implementation of the capabilities of the Armed Forces and the NATO Readiness Plan, it will obviously require serious changes in this field, which will affect the overall image of future contingents.

The analysis of military interviews shows recurrent flaws in accommodations in the first missions. Contingent troops were on a mission inadequately prepared in this aspect. It is often necessary to seek co-operation from coalition partners and to send extra material assets to the national command. That is why national planning and support need to be improved. National logistics must be capable of providing comprehensive support of the contingents in missions. This is particularly important in organizing the deployment of contingents to participate in coalition operations to maintain international peace and security. National logistics agencies should take into account all the initial parameters of deployment of the contingent—environmental conditions, possibility for accommodation in permanent premises, provision of food, etc. In planning, it is necessary to take into account the information from the conferences and the reconnaissance groups.

Medical service during missions was in line with the requirements. It is necessary to raise the attention of the medical authorities in the provision of the contingents with medical drugs and in carrying out the compulsory immunizations for the missions.

The shared views of the interviewed and the analysis lead to the conclusion that the future involvement of military units in operations to support international peace and security requires **improvement in the planning and the delivery** of logistical support in missions.

References

1. Klein P, Haltiner K (2005) Multinationality as a challenge for armed forces. In: Military missions and their applications reconsidered: the aftermath of September 11th, 2005
2. Moskos Ch, Williams J, Segal DR (Eds.) The post-modern military: armed forces after the cold war (New York: Oxford University Press, 2000)
3. Yanakiev Y, Dimitrov P, Petkov P, Ivanov Z (2016) The lessons from participation in operations to support of International Peace and Security, Sofia, Military Press, ISBN 978954-9348-74-3

Engaging Locals: Operational Experiences of Military Officers in Overseas Non-combat Missions

Rosalie Arcala Hall and Duvince Zhalimar Dumpit

Abstract Commanders perform a variety non-combat tasks for which they engage civilian actors. These dyad engagements are contingent on the nature of the military units and stratified according to rank. The commanders' relationship with civilians appear pragmatic and un-institutionalised given language difficulties and short deployment horizons. Commanders understand local politics and employ strategies towards building social capital with formal and informal civilian leaders alike. Their relationship with local authorities is nuanced by interdependency in resources, communications and rules. They have limited engagement with humanitarian actors and media.

1 Introduction

In recent years, there has been tremendous expansion in the ancillary tasks assigned to militaries. Apart from its core function of defense, militaries have been deployed overseas for a variety of peacekeeping, humanitarian assistance/disaster response (HADR), peace building and stabilisation missions. In Bosnia, Kosovo, Afghanistan and Iraq, the military has taken on policing tasks and become directly involved in direct humanitarian provisioning. In these missions, they also had to work with a more diverse set of co-located civilian actors—UN civilian administrators, humanitarian NGOs, private military corporations, local authorities, and local population. In places with continuing internal security challenges like the Philippines, state security forces are deployed within the territory and similarly undertaking tasks which bring them in collaborative, competitive or contested relations with local civilian actors.

These developments pose challenges to the traditional construction of civil-military relations (CMR), which is premised on distinct functional remits between the duly constituted civilian authorities, and the military's in expertise in the use of

R. A. Hall (✉) · D. Z. Dumpit
Division of Social Sciences, University of the Philippines Visayas, Miagao, Iloilo 5023, Philippines
e-mail: rbarcalahall@up.edu.ph

© Springer Nature Switzerland AG 2021
M. Nuciari and E. Olivetta (eds.), *Leaders for Tomorrow: Challenges for Military Leadership in the Age of Asymmetric Warfare*, Advanced Sciences and Technologies for Security Applications, https://doi.org/10.1007/978-3-030-71714-8_11

violent force. In overseas missions, the military is the instrument of state's foreign policy and is given mission objectives that do not necessarily dovetail neatly with this presumed expertise in combat. Where the military goes out of its assumed CMR domain, its effectiveness is put to question and its relationship with civilians more tenuous. Wide differences in goals, philosophies, organizational culture and decision making styles between the military and civilian outfits affect interactions [1–3]. Disparities in time horizons-short-term rotation for military personnel versus long-term project commitment of humanitarian organizations and UN agencies- also make cooperation difficult [4].

This paper describes civil-military interactions among tactical commanders, from platoon to battalion level in seven (7) countries. Two hundred forty-four (244) interviews were conducted amongst male and female officers of ground forces in Bulgaria, Cameroon, Denmark, Finland, Italy, Philippines and Spain from 2015 to 2016, using a common instrument.[1] The participants commanded units at the platoon, company and battalion levels in overseas and internal security missions. The interview questions probed their rank, service and speciality, years and months of service in the ground forces and operational experiences. Their training, including language, in-theatre field experiences, hierarchical relationship, inter-operability problems as well as the conditions of their commanded unit (personnel training, equipment, morale) were examined. The first part provides conceptual anchors on the nature, dynamics and challenges of engagements between officers and the local population and co-located international humanitarian actors. The leadership requirements for these type of engagements are also mapped. The succeeding sections present findings of the study pertaining to the officers' relationships with local leaders, community members, security forces, international government agents, non-government organisations NGO personnel, and media. A section on problems encountered is also provided, followed by a concluding section pointing to thematic trends and implications for leadership.

2   Civil-Military Relations on the Ground

Unlike traditional CMR which is constructed at the strategic level and anchored at oversight mechanisms by national policymaking apparatus (e.g. civilian defense ministry, legislative control over budget and promotions), CMR in missions abroad place equal premium to operational and tactical levels [5]. Wide media coverage of military activities in these far-flung areas can create political consequences in their home country, particularly where they involve misconduct of troops [6]. There are profound reputational costs of norm breaches to the military institution and to their home government writ large.

---

[1]Thematic attributions were made to respondents, which are indicated according to the following formula: country (BGR for Bulgaria, FIN for Finland, ITC for Italian Constabulary, ITB for Italian army, PHC for Philippine army, CMRC for Cameroon Army, DKC for Denmark army) and respondent number (01 onwards). Some quotes also indicated their rank, e.g. Colonel, Captain, Major, Lieutenant, etc.

Militaries deployed abroad also have to build social capital with local civilian actors in order get the latter's cooperation in accomplishing their non-combat tasks. Whether engaging mayors, warlord or community leaders, some knowledge and embeddedness into the local and language and culture are necessary to get things done. The military's business of winning-hearts-and-minds becomes more complicated, and goes beyond simply attaining actionable intelligence.

Civil-military coordination depends on mission type (peacekeeping, peace building, stabilisation operations, HADR) and actor type (whether public/government or private) [7]. Within mission types, the military's role, e.g. assisting civilians, also inform coordination. Like UN agents and local authorities, the deployed military is public in that they are authorised service providers by their home governments and are held accountable. Private military contractors and humanitarian NGOs, on the other hand, are answerable to their employers and donors. Within this private/public configuration are also nuances in organisational culture and decision making processes.

The high number of actors on the ground increases coordination cost, which can be reduced through institutions [2]. NATO has a CIMIC doctrine in place which provides guidance to the military on how to interface with civilian actors.[2] It emphasises the use of liaisons between military and civilian actors in the same area operations, with the goal of providing assistance to the civilian government and to support the force [3]. There had been differences in the ground applications of the CIMIC doctrine. In Afghanistan, humanitarian agencies were invited in the Joint Task Force that oversaw the nation-building efforts; the Provincial Reconstruction Teams had integrated military and civilian personnel. As noted in the Dutch experience, a synchronised engagement plan centered on identified key local leaders provided a solid framework for civil-military interface [4]. However, in the same theatre, the military task force groups were involved directly with community projects, rather than outsourcing these services to private contractors. These different dynamics made the local population suspicious towards humanitarian NGOs working in the same theatre as the military. Humanitarian organizations argued that the humanitarian space has been compromised as a consequence [3]. Egnell [2] cautions that CIMIC requirements for integration work only at the strategic level; that a separation of political actors (military, development agency and diplomats) from humanitarian actors is necessary. Synchronization between political actors is attained through vertical cooperation, with each actor maintaining its core competency. Most authors forward the formula that the military should confine itself to providing security, lift and other logistics capacity to support humanitarian organizations [2, 3].

The application of CIMIC doctrine at the tactical level in various peace support operations varied across theatres [8]. In Bosnia, Civil-Military (CM) liaison officers initiated, executed or outsourced small reconstruction projects to win the approval of the local population and support the military commander in attaining the military

---

[2]CIMIC is different from Civil Affairs which provides guidance in dealing between the military and the civilian population. Civil Affairs is focused on military needs, and its intent is to gain support from civilians towards mission completion [3].

mission (which was to separate the warring parties). By the late 1990s in Kosovo, there was a shift towards supporting civilian goal of establishing interim government and police. However, the Dutch CIMIC officers took on governance functions within their area of responsibility (AOR), taking over civilian administration and policing themselves. In Afghanistan and Iraq, the military was doing more counterinsurgency operations rather than peace support operations. Rietjens et al. [4] observed that in the case of Uruzgan province in Afghanistan, the shift towards a Task Force framework and a reconstruction/rehabilitation goal came with infusion of civilian personnel, thus allowing for more structured engagements with local actors. Key local actors were identified and engagement strategies were jointly formulated, chosen, carried out and evaluated. However, even within this set-up, there were acknowledged differences between civilian and military mandates, resources and perspectives that animated their interactions with local leaders. Angstrom [9] noted a similar institutionalised interaction between civilian and military personnel in the Swedish PRT from goal setting to goal-attainment. Yet, there remained serious gaps in coordination because of differences in their fundamental norms and lack of government directive on how coordination should occur.

At the core of civil-military relations are debates over the appropriate domains and acceptable remits of actions of military and civilian actors. It also raises the issue of the military's identity- whether it should maintain its war-fighting expertise as institution or adopt new skill sets in line with the increasing array of non-combat tasks it is asked to perform. Civil-military coordination is important in-theatre, but these are themselves contingent upon the interdependencies (shared resources, communications and rules) [4], with varying intensities depending upon the nature of the area of operations. An examination of CMR must necessarily take into account context-specific tactical level dyad-engagements between co-located military units and specific civilian actor types, with an emphasis on the local authorities and groups whose support are deemed crucial in achieving mission goals. For instance, in-theatre relationships between the military and international humanitarian organizations are informed by differences in their respective organisational cultures [10]. While the military values formalisation and hierarchy, humanitarian organisations emphasise team work and consensus. A mutual dependency exists where by the military depends on local knowledge the humanitarian organisations, while the latter cooperates for intelligence and access to government funds that the military has. Joint projects and regular task force meetings provided for these relationships to take root. In the end, however, the extensive informal relationships formed by relatively long-term presence of each actor in the area were eroded with new rotations [10].

3   Leadership and Civil-Military Relations

In many operations either in remote conflict areas within the territory or abroad, the expansion of military tasks beyond combat provides opportunities to bolster the institution's prestige at home. With media coverage, the degree of autonomy or independence exercised by the deployed unit magnifies the importance of military leadership at the ground level [6]. The competence and appropriateness of behaviour by lower level commanders carries risks, given exposure to conventional and social media. Wong [5] notes that direct leadership from battalion level below in deployment or combat context tend to be more collective-focused and unit-performance based. Leadership thus would be more oriented toward troop safety and mission accomplishment.

In overseas deployed settings, there is premium on networking and building linkages with civilian actors. For tactical commanders, this is more than tick box in a checklist, as investing on relations with local groups in the area deployment enables accomplishment of tasks, whether getting a project done or ensuring that unit members are not harassed or made targets of. Awareness of larger issues in host community and unit responsiveness to these civilian stakeholders are key [11]. Whereas preparatory training for civil-military interface has become standard in many deployed militaries for peacekeeping and peace support operations, gaps in terms of organizational culture, values and time-horizons create serious challenges for coordination. Moreover, with rules for civil-military interface not having been sufficiently institutionalized and where deployed units exercise some degree of autonomy, there are more nuances expected in the way civil-military interaction takes place.

Increasingly, there is also emphasis for commanders to be culturally intelligent and sensitive [12]. This requires understanding of the cultural anchors, the ability to communicate and diplomatic skills. Under the military's counterinsurgency doctrine, commanders are assigned new tasks (e.g. establishment or reinforcement of political institutions, infrastructure project management, negotiating with local leaders) for which the aforementioned skill sets are greatly needed. The smallest unit (platoon) has to have a good grasp of the social norms in the area, identify authority figures or influential persons, and communicate with them to convey their mission [12]. Emotional control and the ability to decode communication signals (where shared history and perspectives are lacking) are important ingredients to developing and improving the quality of relationships with locals. Negotiation skills are a premium for junior officers vis-a-vis local civilians across concerns like security, infrastructure projects and civil affairs. They employ strategies like offering incentives, and striking a balance between the threat of use of force and demonstration of respect [13]. The ability to effectively discern whether local civilians are negotiating based on cultural-based technique or because of selfish motives are important skills to have.

The relationship between NGOs and CIMIC units is fraught with contestation and negotiation over their respective organizational ethos. As [14] observed, there are role overlaps at the operational level. Military support to NGOs (by way of protecting relief supplies and providing security to relief personnel) and the military providing direct humanitarian assistance have introduced new nuances in civil-military relationship. In Kosovo, civil-military relationships were strained because of several factors: military attempts at coordinating numerous and diverse NGOs are seen as hegemonic; mutual lack of familiarity and knowledge of the other institution's practices; and differences in organisational culture [14]. These cultural rift is pronounced because NGOs do not want to be labelled as add-ons to military power or are unwilling to share sensitive information. The establishment of Civil-Military Cooperation Centers and assigned liaison officers to NGOs in the field are steps towards institutionalising better civil-military cooperation and coordination [14]. In Afghanistan where NGOs are smaller in number but are critical in service delivery, NGOs and the military compete for resources (from the host or home governments) and legitimacy [15]. The adoption of COIN doctrine and the military's subsequent shift towards more soft rather than hard power eroded boundaries between them as a coercive apparatus and the NGOs, as indicated by the creation of human terrain teams (HTTs) and the growing similarity in language used. For instance, the creation of a Civil-Military Mission in Helmand province saw the shift in the military's mission from kinetic to stabilisation support, bringing them into relationships with NGOs who are then seen as extensions of foreign military power and a sign of the securitisation of the humanitarian space [12]. There had been attempts to create a platform whereby NGOs can raise concerns to and resolve issues with the military, but these were not sustained.

4 Relationship with Local Security Forces

One of the key mission areas for units deployed abroad involve training of local security forces, which include the police, military, and intelligence agency personnel. The Bulgarian and Finnish contingents in particular were advisers to General Headquarters for the training of the Afghan National Army (ANA) or provided the training themselves. The relationships between commanders and the local police and military were framed by activities such as strategic planning for the development of local security forces (BGR 52), their education or training (BGR 05, BGR 10, BGR 12, BGR 15, BGR 23, FIN 12, FIN 13) and drafting of doctrines (BGR 39). There were other reported activities: joint patrols and checkpoint operations (FIN05, FIN09, FIN 10, ITC 15, PHC 12), co-sponsor for CMO activities (PHC 14), exchange of intel and logistics support for CIMIC activity (CMRC01, BGR 58, ITB 05). There was an English-speaking ANA personnel assigned to the Finns who undertook the training (FIN24). As some of the commander-respondents have gone on multiple missions (e.g. Italians), the quality of their contacts with local security forces improved with succeeding missions.

Qualitative assessments of the local security forces are mixed. Negative assessments point to trainees and active-duty local security forces as having no confidence and low morale (BGR 03), low endurance (DKC 11, DKC 14, DKC 16), very low desire to work and patriotism (ITB 02), unreliable (BGR 29, FIN 08), not to be trusted (DKC02, FIN08), having poor hygiene and lazy (BGR 59). Positive assessments include local security forces having good communication and confidence (BGR 02, BGR 40), prepared and disciplined (BGR 04, BGR 07), congenial and cooperative (BGR 13, BGR 14, BGR 15), reliable (ITB 05), dedicated and strongly motivated (BGR 19), responsible and brave (BGR 26), and providing assistance to solving illegal traffic of fuel and lumber (BGR 33, BGR 46). Assessments also differ between police, army and border police forces. The local army are seen as less corrupt, more reliable and can be trusted with information compared to the police (DKC17, ITB 05, FIN 08, ITC 01, ITC 12).

The commanders understand that dealing with local security forces is difficult given the paucity of even basic training amongst them (DKC 14, DKC 16) and their distinct cultural moorings (DKC 06). One commander-respondent said he even had to explain how to keep clean, i.e. brushing (ITC 19). They were not interested in planning; rather they worked around rules (FIN 12). The local security forces have a different way of doing things, a different world view and different motivations, which foreign troops need to take into account (FIN 05, FIN 20, ITC 03). They do not understand Rules of Engagement (ROE), applying them only when suitable to their desired end (ITC 05). The local culture has an inherent distrust of outsiders and put premium on moving around with protection (FIN 22). Despite long training, local troops remind tribal in orientation, putting strong family relations first (including their family safety against Taliban threats) before their military duty (ITC 16, ITC 19). Defection rate was high particularly among enlistees (ITC 18).The Italian commander-respondents had considerably improved assessments of the local army in their succeeding missions. They note that the local troops have become more motivated, their professionalism improved, more pronounced adherence to orders, adopted more caring attitude towards their men (ITB 03, ITB 04, ITB 06, ITB 09, ITB 25). Some commanders recognise the need to build more long-term relationship with the local army by way of mentoring and exchanges of lessons learned (DKC 23, BGR 42) for gains to be more concrete.

5 Relationship with Local Authorities

Local authorities are important players in communities where troops are deployed. In Afghanistan, Iraq, Bosnia, Kosovo and Bangsamoro area (Philippines), both formal and informal power-holders are recognised by commanders. The village chiefs, sheiks, elders, spiritual or religious leaders, and tribe leaders are equally important as mayors and provincial governors, given the low salience of the central government apparatus in these contested spaces. The authorities also include bureaucrats/administrators whose role as gatekeepers are critical particularly for getting projects started or completed. Contact with local leaders is important for confidence-building (CMRC05) and good will (BGR 39). Symbolic recognition of their authority and respectful attitude towards them are also required (ITC 31).

Contacts with local authority figures are also task-based (likely for CIMIC, CMO or PRT units) and contingent on rank. Thirty one (31) respondents, all Lieutenants and Captains reported not having any contact with local authorities as this was not their unit's task or that it was the task of their unit commander or head, or the assigned Liaison Officer. Ninety (90) respondents reported contact with various types of local leaders for a range of activities. For small infrastructure projects (e.g. schools), the commanders met with village chiefs, local officials and administrators whose cooperation are necessary from planning to implementation (FIN 10, FIN 11, FIN 13,PHC 14). The commanders also attended meetings (BGR 039, ITC 19), made courtesy call or visits (PHC 14, PHC 02, Fin 19) and attended sessions of the local council (PHC 12, PHC 28, PHC 26). Some Italian respondents reported attending shura (religious ceremony) (ITB 03, DKC 08, DKC 11). An officer in the Finnish contingent (liaison officer) was assigned the task of maintaining relations with the religious leaders (FIN 09). Some reported contacts were more informal in character, such as dialogues with village chiefs about problems that were brought to the commander's attention (PHC 28, ITC 32), joining the celebration of important religious holidays (BRG 11), or chatting outside of work context (FIN01). The commanders are aware of the local power dynamics and potential consequences of their networking activities. For instance, two commanders said that it was important to unite the local tribal leaders in Taliban-influenced territories because the provincial governor wanted to remove them (DKC 16, DKC 20). In another case, the commander knows that the village chief is also a rebel commander (PHC 18), or influenced by the enemy (PHC 05), or that there is bad politics between local leaders (PHC 09). The unit commander's role as local power-broker is also acknowledged (DKC 04).

Creating a more solid relationship with local leaders, however, is more difficult given the fast rotation of provincial governors, particularly in Afghanistan (ITC 27). Elected local government leaders also vary in terms of performance. Where the mayors are good, i.e. open to talk regarding problems and doing projects together, the commanders are able to do more activities such as post-disaster rehabilitation and CMO activities (PHC 06, PHC 09). Mayors who are also keen on improving security provide material support to military operations within their jurisdiction, and give the military representation within the Peace and Order Councils (POC) (PHC 15, PHC 18). Where there is no Peace and Order Council, it becomes the task of the unit commander to pressure the mayor to convene one, and to hold regular POC meetings (PHC 25).

There are acknowledged limits to relationships with local leaders. Some commanders admit that they could only do what local government allows them to do (PHC 16, PHC 17). As such, more than facilitation, the goal is to get the mayor in particular to commit to deliver services in the community (PHC 17).

6   Relationship with Local Host Community

The commanders' relationships with the local communities varied depending on the nature of their tasks and their area of responsibility. Those in CIMIC teams (Bosnia, Kosovo), Provincial Reconstructions Teams (Afghanistan) and Civil-Military Operations SALAAM (Philippines) have more opportunities to interact with the local population than those who are in combat units. Where their units are located far from clustered settlements (e.g. Forward Operating Bases) or in bases/garrisons set apart from surrounding host communities, encounters with locals are intermittent, e.g. doing patrols, or mission-driven such as conducting survey to identify community problems. Local civilians could also be contractors or interpreters who provide services to the team. Less than 20% of the commander-respondent (23), mostly Colonels and Lieutenant Colonels, reported not having any or little contact with locals as such is not in their line of work or field of responsibility.

Of the majority who reported having relationships with locals, premium is placed on building connections with leaders. Among these are village chief and mayor (PHC 04), sheik or elders (DNK 08, DKC 11), village elders and men (Fin08, Fin20). The Finn national contingent has a more institutionalised procedure for local engagement through a community liaison officer and by having a mentor (those already with established connections) when visiting villages. Effort is also made to establish a good rapport with the community by giving small gifts such as books and clothes (BGR 13, BGR26) and food to children (ITB 11). Activities such as MEDCAP are also done in areas around the Forward Operating Base (IT29). The troops provide the community with vital links to the local government and non-governmental organisations with resources they need (PHC 29, PHC 11). There are also independent efforts to go out and meet locals outside of work context, such as in markets (FIN14, DKC 20).

There is diversity in the quality of reported engagements with the local population. Bulgarian respondents generally feel that the local population in Bosnia treated them well given their reputation, the closeness of their language, and their religion (BGR3, BGR 17, BGR 49, BGR 14, BGR 24, BGR 23, BGR 52). But other local populations are not as receptive to foreign troop presence. Finn respondents reported dealing with hostile villagers who spat on the ground as troops drive past or throw stones at them (Fin 19). Italian respondents (ITB 02, ITB 06, ITC 19) note also the difference in treatment from village to village; in hostile ones, stones are thrown at them or even gunfire. Several Philippine respondents also noted difference in local reception, depending on the religion. Muslim villages, more so than Christian villages, they argue are problematic (PHC 1, PHC 29). Several Finn respondents (FIN 07, FIN 09, FIN 16) also reported that Shia villages are suspicious while Christian villages are welcoming. The behaviour of foreign troops previously deployed in the area counts. In general, the respondents feel that locals are receptive as long as there was no prior misconduct among UN troops (FIN 09, FIN 16), or that there were no prior operations that killed locals (BGR 52). More isolated villages fearing Taliban attacks also tend to be more un-cooperative (ITC23).

How the commanders deal with the locals is premised on assumptions about the locals' motives. Locals are aware of the risks involved when seen communicating or being friendly with foreign troops (ITB 06, ITB 10, DKC 03). As they are likely to be targeted by enemy rebels once the foreign troops pull out, locals choose not to cooperate. Or do so only with prospect of gain. Some respondents tend to look at locals as "for rent" (ITC 01), cheats/take advantages of troops (FIN25) opportunistic (ITC 04, ITC 06, ITC10, ITC 13, ITC 16), or who agree on face-value but do not want to commit resources (PHC 10).

Regardless, the commanders' relationship with the locals appear pragmatic-based. Interactions with locals are opportunities to get intel (DKC 20). The relationship is contingent given security issues and related difficulties in getting projects started (ITC 05). It could also be seen as mutual exchange, a quid-pro-quo where the military gets the intel they need and local leaders get prestige from the project completed (ITC 29).

7 Relationship with International Government Organizations, Non-government Organisations and the Media

Commander-respondents exhibit a general awareness of non-government organisations present in the theatre, although only about 40 of them (1/5 of the total respondents) had some direct contact. Of those, engagement with NGOs occurred as part of their tasks (BGR 10) either under a Civil Affairs unit (Fin 13) or as a CIMIC project (FIN 06, ITC 13). The Finnish PRT had an officer assigned to liaise with humanitarian organisations (FIN 12). The nature of the interaction ranged from visits (PHC 20, Fin 19), coordination of activities between military team and NGOS in the same site (BGR 52, CMRC 02, PHC 11) and requests for transportation assistance, protection or additional manpower (PHC 07, PHC 08, PHC 19, ITC 19, ITC 10, ITC 11). Some Philippine respondents offered more sustained and repeat interactions with select NGOs for their MEDCAP activities (PHC 02, PHC 05, PHC 06, PHC 10, PHC 12, PHC 14).

There is a latent mistrust of NGOs among the commander-respondents. Many expressed that NGO Standard Operating Procedures (SOP) include not relating to the military in the theatre (CMRC 22, ITC 01) or that NGO workers are not inclined to work with uniformed personnel given differences in organisational culture and mission (FIN 09, FIN 25, ITC 19, SP01, SP 09). As such, interactions with NGOs where they occur are either necessary (part of checklist) or seen as superficial:

> I met them only about once a week, because we had our own humanitarian worker X (name) who was responsible for these matters. PRT actually turned into a civilian organisation later on, during time it was military-led. We had a political assistant, humanitarian help, juridical help and police personnel, civilian people who attended our meetings. It was natural and needed. Fin 12, Colonel

> Civilian organisations do not want to work with military personnel. They want to be known as civilian actors so we were not in contact with them, except for the minesweeping organisation who let us knew where they were working so we would not be surprised by sudden explosions. But they too are an organisation of their own. FIN 09, Captain.

Fewer commander-respondents (21 or 1/10 of total) reported having engaged representatives of UN agencies, International Red Cross, European Union or government aid agencies, again in the context of work such as election preparation (BGR 37, BGR 45, BGR 52, BGR 60) and force protection (ITC 31). In general, assessments of this international organisations are positive, pointing to good attitudes, friendly and collegiate. There is, however, an understanding that because these are civilian organisations, they have different needs and jurisdiction requirements which must be negotiated with the military:

> We have worked a lot with the UNIAMA to provide protection especially in case of attacks. Even there, it was still all a work of trying to understand what their needs, make them coincide with our needs and also with the limits of jurisdiction. No problem, indeed: you can develop synergies. ITC 31, Lieutenant.

The commander-respondents have dealt with the media in the context of visits to their camps and work settings (for a film documentary, television or newspaper coverage) (DKC 08, DKC 13, DKC 11, ITC 02, ITC 33, SP02) or for interviews (BGR 60, FIN 08, FIN 09). The interactions are mediated; there is an assigned publicist or public relations officer in the team (FIN 24) or the head of the national contingent (FIN 20), and pre-arranged conditions on what can be filmed or photographed. There was also mention about internal rules on what can be posted in social media (FIN 10, FIN 11, FIN 20, FIN 24). Some respondents expressed distrust of media outlets, but understand the need to work with them:

> I do not know how to take a stance on that either. We read the news daily and compiled it and briefings on them. We analysed whether they were for or against the UN. The locals also tried to confuse us through the local and especially social media. FIN 23, 1st Lieutenant

> I had a film crew visiting us to follow our patrolling. However, there is a risk that they do not give the right picture and they may harm more than they inform. Media are not always aware of the responsibility of filming soldiers/interpreters and the risk those people may run being compromised later on. DKC 13, Lieutenant.

In summary, the commanders had little or superficial interactions with humanitarian actors, international government agents and media representatives on the ground. Only those attached to CIMIC or CMO units had dealings with them. The NGOs are generally perceived as not wanting to work with the military, or if they do, only if needing logistical support. There is scant engagement with international government agents, and in the limited context of force protection or election preparation. While more positively viewed, commanders are aware that these agents are "civilians" with different mandates in the theatre of operation. Only designated Press Relations Persons or publicists deal with the media. Interactions with media are guarded with commanders being aware of the dangers of misrepresentation. They are also cognisant of rules about proper behaviour in social media platforms.

8   Problems

Working with local security forces puts premium for interpreters. Some commander-respondents expressed frustration about the dearth of interpreters and language helpers, and their perceived lack of motivation (BGR 23, Fin 14, Fin 23). Incompatibilities between what they perceive as professional standards of conduct and the local forces' way of doing things have led to problems in patrolling, in checkpoint operations and risk from friendly fire (DKC 06, DKC 11, DKC 12, DKC 20, BGR 31, ITB 03). But there is also an understanding that these incompatibilities can be resolved with commanders' initiative. The commander's role is key as mediator; understanding the personality of the local commander goes a long way in preventing these sort of tensions. As narrated by two officers:

> Some difficulty in dealing with the ANA because a completely different world view and language difficulties. In 2009, during an intervention of fire in favor of an Afghan units attacked by insurgents, we ran the risk of hitting the Afghan troops (fire in adherence); as consequence they have turned against us coming to threaten us with their individual weapons. The company commander has been able to mediate and resolve the situation. ITC03, Captain.

> With local forces, the relationship is a bit complex. Because in addition to the problem of language, unfortunately in our area they had small isolated units and a bit in disarray. They were during seven months isolated in that place. So you had to try to get in symbiosis with their commander, trying to figure out what kind of person he was, from that part of Afghanistan he comes (from particular areas or city centers). From day one, it was necessary that they understood that it was their country and it was they who were to conduct operations as the main actors. Then in a relationship of very low trust, however, because you never know what will happen in the end. ITC 34, Captain.

Dealing with local civilian authorities present parallel complications because of the volatile nature power and exigencies in the local setting. Commanders understand the need to work with both formal authorities and informal power holders where they are deployed, but also point to the difficulties in building relationships with them due to frequent rotation, sensitivities regarding their enemy-affiliation (e.g. Taliban, Moro Islamic Liberation Front, communist) and importance given to symbolic displays of power. Navigating these social imperatives is something that commanders find difficult:

> With local authorities, however, the goal was to show that we still recognize their authority as leaders and keep a respectful attitude towards them, that went from the turn-taking in dialogue, talk to one person rather than another, give him the weight that this person was expected to have, etc. ITC 31, lieutenant

> Tribal leaders, representatives from civil authorities, important contact due to the low influence from Kabul. DKC 16, Major.

With the local population, commanders express the need to communicate to them effectively about their mission, and that they do not mean harm. Communicating is difficult often given their limited grasp of local language and culture, but the strategy appears to rely more on "winning hearts and minds" such as providing medical service, food or gifts to children. But even so, commanders are aware that good will is never really earned permanently and so caution is always warranted when dealing with locals. There is a tendency to differentiate local treatment according to religion or tribe, with Muslim, Shia or Taliban settlements expressing more dissident attitude towards the troops.

The relations with the local population depended very much on the area. In principle, they consider the various coalition forces in the same way. In my area I have established good relationships with the inhabitants of the nearby village, always with due diffidence because, as the old local saying goes, " you can rent the Afghan but you can not buy him". ITC 01, Captain.

9   Analysis and Conclusion

Commanders do a lot of non-combat tasks on the ground, which brings them to direct contact with a variety of civilian actors, local and non-local. However, these interactions are contingent on the nature of the unit they're in. Those in CIMIC, CMO, Public Affairs and PRT units are more likely to have direct contact with local authorities and communities. There are also units whose missions involved working with or training local security forces. These engagements tend to be stratified, with more junior commanders or assigned liaison officers dealing with lower-hierarchy civilian officials (e.g. village chief, mayor, local administrators) while more senior commanders deal with governors and officials at the national level. Tactical level dyad-interactions are also nuanced depending on the type of civilian actor and with local security forces.

Relationships between commanders and local authorities appear un-institutionalized. Except for the Fins which had a more institutionalised basis for relating with civilian actors (appointed liaison officers for religious elders, public relations officer, etc.), there are no indications of regular platforms in which sustained engagements are possible. The troops' lack of facility for the local language and the dearth of interpreters make such endeavours difficult. The short deployment horizons is an acknowledged limitation, but there are also insights of gains in social capital from iterative missions, especially when it comes to training of local security forces.

Commanders exhibit a keen understanding of the exigencies of politics at the local level. They are aware of local power dynamics of tribal and religion-distinct communities, tenuous relationships between national leaders and local officials, and the pull of clan relations, which inform how they as foreign persons are received and how they should react. They employ a variety of strategies vis-a- vis these local civilian actors— material exchange, appeal to or respect for symbolic displays of power, being present and conveying willingness to dialogue, among others. Commanders at the tactical level engage formal and informal civilian leaders alike, putting importance on tribal leaders, rebel commanders, religious notables and families/clans particularly in remote places where the reach of national government is limited. Administrators and bureaucrats are also included because they make projects happen and be completed. They manifest an expansive view of their job as commander to include building social capital (i.e. confidence building, generating good will), no matter how incremental, given the limited duration of their mission or the rapid turnover of host country government officials. This extends to attending religious celebrations and events, and providing services to the locals even if such is not a core part of their mission. There is a healthy dose of security caution in dealing with local authorities and with the local population, often informed by experience in prior missions.

There appears considerable interdependence with local authorities in terms of resources, communications and rules that warrants more substantial coordination, as theorised by [6]. Commanders must rely on the good will of local leaders for troop safety, abide by social conventions that frame engagements, and on the services of local interpreters and interlocutors. The engagements are pragmatic in line with [5] argument and more in line with getting missions accomplished, whether it be obtaining information or starting/completing a project.

The commanders' relationship with local security forces is strongly mediated by a mismatch between what they consider as professional standards of behaviour (e.g. rules of engagement and standard operating procedures) and "local way of doing things." There are plenty of negative accounts of how local security forces fall short of training standards, and the insidious influence of tribal and family allegiances militating against the formation of a professional force. More so than with civilian actors, commanders display optimism that improvements towards professionalism of the security force will be made with further training and joint activities like checkpoints and patrols.

The commanders have limited engagements with civilian humanitarian actors. Where present, the interaction is framed by assumptions of incompatible mandates and organizational culture. The humanitarian actors' presence is acknowledged but as they are doing separate things, there is no imperative beyond coordination for matters of security or force protection. Both mainstream media and social media are also peripheral players, engagements with whom are strictly governed by pre-set conditions (assigned publicists, script, etc.) given the commanders' concern about how their activities while deployed may be portrayed to audiences at home, confirming [6] argument about increasing cognisance of the importance of operational level dynamics to government policies.

References

1. Clemmensen JR, Archer EM, Barr J, Belkin A, Guerrero M, Hall C, Swain KEO (2012) Conceptualizing the civil-military gap: a research note. Armed Forces Soc 38(4):669–678
2. Egnell R (2013) Civil–military coordination for operational effectiveness: towards a measured approach. Small Wars Insurgencies 24(2):237–256
3. Franke V (2006) The peacebuilding dilemma: civil-military cooperation in stability operations. Int J Peace Stud 11(2):5–25
4. Rietjens S, Soeters J, van Fenema PC (2013) Learning from Afghanistan: towards a compass for civil–military coordination. Small Wars Insurgencies 24(2):257–277
5. Wong L, Bliese P, McGurk D (2003) Military leadership: a context specific review. Leadersh Quart 14:657–692
6. Ruffa C, Dandeker Christopher, Vennesson Pascal (2013) Soldiers drawn into politics? The influence of tactics in civil–military relations. Small Wars Insurgencies 24(2):322–334
7. Ruffa C (2013) Introduction: coordinating actors in complex operations. Small Wars Insurgencies 24(2):206–210

8. Zaalberg TB (2008) The historical origins of civil-military cooperation. In: Bollen M, Riet-jens S (eds) Managing civil-civil-military cooperation: 24/7 joint effort for stability. Ashgate Publishing, Hampshire, UK
9. Angstrom J (2013) The changing norms of civil and military and civil-military relations theory. Small Wars Insurgencies 24(2):224–236
10. Scheltinga TAM, Rietjens SJH, Boer D, Sirp J, Wilderom CPM (2005) Cultural conflict within civil-military cooperation: a case study in bosnia. Low Intensity Confl Law Enforcement 13(1):54–69
11. Bangari RS (2014). Establishing a framework of transformational grassroots military leadership: lessons from high-intensity, high-risk operational environments. Vikalpa 39:3 (September):13–24
12. Laurence JH (2011) Military leadership and the complexity of combat and culture. Mil Psychol 23:489–501
13. Nobel O, Wortinger B, Hannah S (2007) Winning the war and the relationships: preparing military officers for negotiations with non-combatants. Research Report 1877. U.S. Army Research Institute for the Behavioral and Social Sciences, Arlington, VA
14. Abiew FK (2003) NGO-military relations in peace operations. Int Peacekeeping 10(1):24–39
15. Goodhand J (2013) Contested boundaries: NGOs and civil–military relations in Afghanistan. Cent Asian Surv 32(3):287–305

Operational Experiences in Missions: Country Case of the Cameroonian Army

Blaise Nkfunkoh Ndamnsah

Abstract Cameroon has a modest record of deploying peacekeepers in UN and African-led missions. In recent years, Cameroon's major deployments have focused on the Central African Republic (CAR).

1 Introduction

Cameroon has a modest record of deploying peacekeepers in UN and African-led missions. In recent years, Cameroon's major deployments have focused on the Central African Republic (CAR). In September 2014, a Cameroonian major-general, Martin Chomu Tumentah, assumed the role of Force Commander. Also in September 2014 MISCA was transitioned into a UN peacekeeping operation, MINUSCA. General Chomo remained the Force Commander and Cameroon maintained nearly 1,300 peacekeepers in the mission.

> Speaking at a send-off ceremony in the capital city, Yaoundé, Cameroon's Defence Minister Joseph Beti Assomo highlighted the peace efforts of Cameroonian troops in Central African Republic that Cameroon is always determined to fulfil its regional and international commitments as concerns collective security in an honourable, decent and effective manner, the troops have provided the CAR with multifaceted support in order to enable the country to get its institutions which have already been damaged for several years now back on its feet, Assomo said.[1]

To fight effectively, the Cameroonian armed forces must be manned, equipped, and trained to operate under dangerous, complex, uncertain, and austere conditions—often with little warning. They require the right personnel operating the right equipment with the right training to win but often commanders complain of insufficient personnel, equipment, and training.

---

[1] http://www.bernama.com/en/news.php?id=1763939.

B. N. Ndamnsah (✉)
Faculty of Social Sciences, University of Ljubljana, Ljubljana , Slovenia

© Springer Nature Switzerland AG 2021
M. Nuciari and E. Olivetta (eds.), *Leaders for Tomorrow: Challenges for Military Leadership in the Age of Asymmetric Warfare*, Advanced Sciences and Technologies for Security Applications, https://doi.org/10.1007/978-3-030-71714-8_12

The personnel, equipment, and training need to be balanced and to support the load. The most modern equipment is useless without highly trained personnel to operate and employ it. Conversely, outmoded or unreliable equipment can hamper the effectiveness of the most highly motivated and skilled personnel. To fight effectively, personnel must train with their combat equipment, practicing their combat missions under realistic, demanding conditions. Quality personnel, equipment, and training are the essential dimensions of combat.

Understanding the personnel, equipment, and training dimensions of combat readiness requires some understanding of the operations that military organizations perform. Combat operations of almost any scale are exceptionally complex, requiring integration and synchronization of myriad activities ranging from individual actions to coordinated movements by large, geographically dispersed organizations.

At the basic level of combat operations, individuals and crews must operate their equipment, ranging from individual weapons to combat vehicles, aircraft, and ships. This involves operating all the systems for communications, situational awareness, etc. Then they must employ their equipment as part of larger unit teams, executing their part in tactical operations. Each smaller unit is part of an even larger team that incorporates many different functions ranging from fire support to intelligence, surveillance, and reconnaissance to logistical and medical support. As required, these can be combined into joint task forces that include all these functions in land, sea, air, space, and even cyberspace dimensions.

All these organizations, from the smallest units to joint task forces, must be tied together by command, control, and communications networks that provide them with awareness of the friendly and enemy situations and orchestrate their individual activities to achieve the commander's intended objectives. At the same time, they all require support, including transportation, refuelling, rearming with ammunition, maintenance, and medical evacuation and care. Because of their complexity, combat operations are often vulnerable to single points of failure.

The present paper is the result of research carried out in the field in the far northern areas of Cameroon, in three different regions bordering Nigeria, Chad and the Central African Republic, as well as university research aimed at developing a theoretical framework, carried out at the University of Ljubljana, Slovenia, which has included observation of EU-MLF battle group military exercises[2], ERGOMAS[3] (European Research group on Military and Society biennial conference Israel) research, interviews and private conversations with European officers and one of the European Battle Groups, various African Union ministers and military officers as well as the War College of Cameroon.

---

[2]Maribor Slovenia (Observer to the EU-MLF battel group military exercise, operation "Clever Ferret 2014").

[3]13th Biennial conference of ERGOMAS held at The Open University of Israel, Ra'anana, Israel.

2 Research Focus

The scope of the paper is to survey the experience and resources of Cameroon's military as it confronts its greatest challenge in decades. So peaceful has Cameroon been over the decades since the Second World War (and before) that the national military is not heavily armed or possessing much combat experience. The emphasis is now on proper training for asymmetric warfare and the improvement of weapons systems and logistics.

In the meantime, Cameroonian officers now have increasing experience with peace-keeping operations in the African Union and United Nations, as well as deployments within the national territory. According to UN statistics, Cameroon increased its peacekeeping troops from 100 in 2013 to over 500 in 2014 to reach a total of 1,285 in 2015. Cameroon has also contributed troops to the Central African regional force (ECCAS Standby Force/FOMAC) since 2006, which has since been absorbed into the African Standby Force (ASF). Douala has served as the African Union's Continental Logistics Base since 2011.[4]

Local research was conducted in 2015, with the kind permission of the Cameroonian Défense Ministry and the General Chiefs of Staff, by interviewing about 40 local commanders of the Cameroonian Army. These ranged from lieutenants to colonels. Data was collected on the officers' years of service, number of missions abroad, languages spoken, specific training received, and training not received but desired.

The overall picture that has emerged was quite good, but useful in indicating needed areas of improvement. Officers were asked to relate their field experiences, experience with their soldiers/units, logistics, linguistic experience/issues, Rules of Engagement and level of morale within their unit. The conclusions are summarised at the end of this paper.

3 Method and Techniques

The main research question is: *what are the changes in the command action in an environment of asymmetric warfare and how and how much they affect the professional preparation of commanders?*

In order to answer these questions, our main objective was to check the answers that commanders with concrete experience in the field give to this challenge, their remarks to the existing doctrine and directions, their proposals, suggestions, experiences.

The three factors in this chapters are: *Training and Specific training, logistical Issues and relationships with other actors in the area.* These are factors that could impact the mission operational environment and local populations in the course of post-conflict stabilization operations at the tactical level in the framework of

---

[4]http://www.providingforpeacekeeping.org/2015/08/18/peacekeeping-contributor-profile-cameroon/.

asymmetric conflict. The field work was mainly conducted through semi-structured interviews with the Cameroonian military personnel. The military that have been in an asymmetric war fare. Interviewing an adequately sized group of officers with concrete command experiences at every level: platoon, company, and battalion (or equivalent). In total forty interviews were conducted in 2014.

While conducting interviews, some important conflictive factors were also obtained asking directly to the interviewees about: *Training and Specific training; logistical Issues and relationships with other actors in the areas of operation.* what they deemed to be the most relevant hindrance causing frictions in missions. In this way we had a double-check to detect and elaborate the final list of conflictive factors to keep in mind. The elements noted by the military personnel in the interviews and discussions groups have been numerous and varied, which shows their relevancy for the military forces' routines.

Insufficient Training and Specific training; logistical Issues and relationships with other actors in the areas of operation, which is the main task for many military members, becomes a constant obstacle for mission success. Example, flow of information about new topics that sometimes can have an impact on military actors. This is particularly true for CIMIC members, who are the channel of communication between the civil population, the local authorities, the international organizations, the NGOs and the military contingent in order to make inform decisions at the tactical level. Such interactions have provided knowledge and experience about the local population.

3.1   Training and Specific Training

The Cameroonian military has seldom fought against forces from other states. Thus, their strategic acumen and operational capacity to respond to evolving threats and conflicts may be limited. Experience is becoming less of an issue as better training programs are implemented, such as the EIFORCES School or through training partnerships with other countries, such as China. Cameroonian military personnel require individual training and specific training throughout their careers. Initially, junior officers are taught basic tactics and leadership skills. As they become more senior and assume higher-level responsibilities, they learn advanced skills ranging from organizational management techniques to national-level strategy. Enlisted personnel also progress to become effective and mature leaders at higher levels.

As military operations and their enabling technologies become increasingly sophisticated and complex, the training required to be mastered, and demands even more time and resources. Thus, it is more effective and efficient to retain trained personnel by motivating them to remain in the service than it is to recruit and train replacements. Lack of resource becomes the key player in as a result less efficiency at military operations. Recruiting and training activities are both resource and time intensive, and limited assets are available to perform them one hand. On the other hand, old personnel are tired and less efficient in some cases:

- Mastery of languages (what languages?), good training before mission, language problems during the mission, the mission influence of such mastery,
- Received basic training, his correspondence, proposals,
- Specific training received (governance, cultural, socio-political training), its correspondence, the mission influence on your ability in these fields, proposals.

In 2008, Cameroon created a training program, referred to as the International School for Security Forces (EIFORCES), for police and law enforcement contingents for peacekeeping missions. The school is modelled after the Bamako peacekeeping school in Mali and the Kofi Annan International Peacekeeping Training Centre in Accra, Ghana.

3.2   Mastery of Languages (What Languages?), Good Training Before Mission, Language Problems During the Mission, the Mission Influence of Such Mastery

When speaking of CA training, we must face the problem of linguistic barriers. Cameroon is bilingual in French and English, although French dominates 80% of the country. Some areas of Cameroon are English-speaking, and many other troops in other missions use English. Therefore, this can be an obstacle. Likewise, native English-speaking Cameroonian commanders may have problems in French-dominated operational areas.

3.3   Received basic Training, His Correspondence, Proposals

3.3.1   Management of War-Children

The immense problems of war-children, both as young, abandoned orphans, and as child soldiers at a slightly older age, are not really treated in any training courses for Cameroonian commanders. This problem is encountered by both officers and soldiers. What training courses have been attended, seems to regard mostly senior officers, and not necessarily field commanders. In some cases, the problem cases are handed over to NGOs, but only if an NGO specifically equipped to handle this problem exists close by.

3.4 Specific Training Received (Governance, Cultural, Socio-political Training), its Correspondence, the Mission Influence on Your Ability in These Fields, Proposals

This training should include topics such as Cultural Awareness, Linguistic barriers, Civilian-Military interaction, security sector reforms, Child Protection, Monitoring and Rehabilitation, Leadership & Gender.

3.4.1 Cultural Awareness

Cultural Awareness training in military operations normally means preparing both officers and soldiers for the context in which they will operate, including both the territory and the other troops with which they will be interfacing. Most of the surveyed Cameroonian commanders complained that they had never received such training, either for the destination country of operations or for other troops in the mission. A small percentage had worked in UN missions before, and had had a few meetings in this sense, ff not with the UN, then with the AU, although these were described as "briefings" and not real training.

3.4.2 Civilian-Military Interaction

Civil-military interaction is mostly a question of the soft power of the country, each unit should have an officer dedicated as contact person, but in many cases, the commanders interviewed complained of no preparation in this sense. What experience in this field exists, seems to have come mostly from UN mission participation—but not all UN missions offered the possibility to acquire CIMIC training.

In the developed world, there are currently three major approaches to civil-military interaction: that of the UN, that of NATO and the EU. NATO tends to favour a comprehensive approach. The UN has the Multidimensional approach and the EU is currently seeking a middle ground between the two others integrated approach, being mostly in a development stage, now.

What CIMIC training has been received to date by some Cameroonian commanders comes from the UN only. No other approaches have been represented.

The United States maintains an "African Command" out of Stuttgart, Germany. This command centre administers also military exercises with various African Defence Ministries including Cameroon[5] and an operational Army unit in Vicenza, Italy, and an Air Force unit in Ramstein in Germany.

---

[5] https://www.africom.mil/.

Other social training courses, for example on child protection, leadership or gender issues/molestation, have not existed for the commanders. For example, operations with integrated female soldiers can be problematic in some specific cultural/territorial areas, where female equality is questionable. As another example, not entirely expected, can be the problem not of molestation, but rather in an entirely voluntary sense, soldiers falling in love with female counterparts, married soldiers falling in love, children of non-registered unions between soldiers and/or with local citizens, all of which can create problems for commanders, also within the context of civilian-military relations.

3.5   Logistical Issues

Cameroonian defence Officers were surveyed regarding logistical issues. Their responses were not pessimistic but pointed to needs for improvements. They also mentioned a difference between operations in Cameroon, which were much less problematic, than missions abroad, where logistical supply, etc. were more of a challenge. A difference also exists in foreign missions among UN, the AU, and the regional ECCAS missions (Economic Community of Central African States).

As early as 2009, ECCAS member states agreed to set up a logistics and supply warehouse in Douala to support peace operations requiring rapid deployment. The facility, located near the airport, is intended to serve the entire continent. Moreover, Cameroon is strategically positioned to act as a staging point for peace operations in the region. Douala, a port and the largest city in Cameroon, acted as the main departure point for convoys resupplying peace operations elsewhere in the region, such as the MINURCAT mission in Chad/CAR that ended in 2010. This is indicative of the broader role Cameroon can play in supporting regional stability. Cameroon has also been able to expand the scope and scale of its peace operations with support from regional partners. Currently, there are few women involved, mostly serving as police, representative of approximately 4% of the country's UN peacekeepers. Cameroon's aging military equipment needs greater investment going forward.

The list of technical training not received is very long and includes not only weapons and vehicle training. Just to mention some of the relevant issues: Power Engineering: Cybernetics, Mechatronic and Industrial Engineering: Materials, Science and Technology: Heating and Process Engineering: General Mechanics; Optodynamic and Laser Applications; Tribology and Technical Diagnostics; Fluid Dynamics and Thermodynamics; Heat & Mass Transfer and Environmental Studies; Working Machines and Technical Acoustics and Radio communication systems.

Finally, due to resource constrains, the air force space command officials have very little materials and technological knowledge on modern Surveillance systems; Battlefield Management Systems; Water purification; Armoured Warfare Training Systems; Mobile Training System and Small Arms Simulators; Remote Weapon Station Training and Artillery Simulators.

(a) **Equipment**

Based on the missions, Cameroon's military are authorized to have specific quantities of types of equipment. For example, Armor battalions in the Army are authorized to have a certain number of tanks and the necessary support equipment, such as refuelling and maintenance vehicles. Air Force fighter squadrons are authorized to have a certain number of fighter aircraft of specific models and associated ground support equipment.

Equipment readiness depends on two factors: the number and types of equipment in organizations and the operational status of that equipment. Service regulations authorize the military to have specific numbers and specific models of equipment. However, the equipment they have depends upon inventories of existing equipment and the procurement of new, usually more modern equipment to replace equipment that wears out, is destroyed, or becomes obsolete. As procurement accounts decline, procurement of new equipment can be delayed, affecting readiness in two ways: First, older generations of equipment are less effective than the newer generations and secondly, delayed modernization means using older existing equipment, which is less reliable and more difficult and expensive to maintain. This tends to lower the operational status of equipment fleets.

(b) **Maintenance and repair**

Maintenance and repair of equipment are essential to combat readiness. They are also tremendously time and resource intensive, requiring large numbers of highly skilled personnel, technically sophisticated tools, and a steady, reliable supply of replacement parts. The scope of maintenance and repair ranges from the daily checks and services performed by operators and crews to repairs by unit maintenance personnel to detailed refurbishing done by depots, shipyards, and commercial corporations.

As available funding declines in the Cameroon defence budget, equipment maintenance and repair have been one of the first bill payers. As such, it is often an early indicator of collapsing combat readiness. For example, reduced funding for repair parts can lead to a vicious downward spiral in equipment operational readiness rates. Without replacement parts, units are tempted to cannibalize parts from equipment that is already non-operational. Removing parts to keep other equipment operating or flying not only places additional demands on maintenance manpower, but also creates "hangar queens" missing so many parts that they become very expensive to repair.

Because most military equipment is designed for a long service life, it usually is scheduled for depot, shipyard, or commercial refurbishment several times during its "career." This is essential for corrosion control in aircraft and ships and replacement of major sub-assemblies, such as suspensions in ground vehicles. It is also economically smart because it can significantly extend the useful service life of the equipment. As budgets tighten, such maintenance may be deferred, creating large backlogs and leaving military with less reliable equipment that is prone to breakdown. In this sector, we would mention the following issues.

1.   **Weapons & ammunition, both personal and unit**

Weapons and Ammunition were cited by the interviewees as representing a problem in some cases. For example, not all Cameroonian weapons come from the same country of origin, and they then use different ammunition. Occasional problems develop with the type of ammunition being supplied not being correct for that unit's weapons. In other cases, soldiers receive their training on one type of weapon, and then are supplied with other types in the field. Like all African countries, and unlike NATO countries, there is no real standardisation of what ammunition and weapons are used.

2.   **Vehicles**

Vehicles exist, but there is always room for improvement. More and better protected vehicles were requested, particularly against improvised explosive devices, and technical training of course should include general mechanics. Mention was made by commanders of the particularly bad roads in areas of operations, and the need to have vehicles equipped for such roads. Their complaints included lack of fuel in many situations.

3.   **Aircrafts & accessories**

Air Force commanders were also interviewed and complained about the lack of equipment. Cameroon's military equipment is limited. For example, the Air Force has few attack helicopters. This is insufficient for the scope and scale of the campaigns Cameroonian peacekeepers participate in. As of early 2015, most Cameroon's helicopters were deployed to fight Boko Haram in the north of the country. This leaves the rest of Cameroon in theory vulnerable to attack, and results in a low likelihood that Cameroon will engage in aerial peacekeeping efforts away from its borders. Moreover, Cameroon's military does not have adequate surveillance aircraft, preventing intelligence gathering, a crucial component of fighting insurgent groups.

Few helicopters for both attack and rescue missions exist, the number could be improved. A specific request was communicated for helicopters (or drones) with cameras to improve surveillance and reconnaissance capabilities. The use of scarce aircraft also becomes a bureaucratic problem to get limited resources into the air. These resources must also be used on a practical basis for civil protection/evacuation purposes, limiting their engagement in military and anti-terrorism operations.

4.   **Personal equipment**

Personal equipment like uniforms, boots and flak jackets are sometimes problematic. Mostly complaints regarded the need for new boots and more personal equipment expressly for combat zones. To note, once again, that Cameroon has known many decades of peace, so sometimes war-zone equipment is lacking.

5. **Engineering and NBC equipment, tools, services**

This area would need improvement. This would also include road and bridge construction tools, such as bulldozers, caterpillars, wheel-loaders, etc.

Civil engineering is generally the preserve of the Army Corps of Engineers in most developed countries. This work is potentially very valuable in Civilian Military relations. "winning the Hearts and Minds" as the Americans say, is much influenced positively if the military can contribute to the local infrastructure. A general lack of tactical/logistical vehicles has been noticed.

Finally, nuclear, biological and chemical warfare equipment seemed non-existent. This does not seem to be a problem now.

6. **Medical, Pharmaceutical & Humanitarian Equipment and Products**

In missions abroad there were complaints regarding the lack of hospital equipment and services, including doctors and nurses. This shortage included ambulance vehicles. To note that many developed countries, when participating in international missions, medical supplies to local populations is important.

Mention was also made of a need for more psychological assistance to soldiers and civilians in war zones. Battle stress, nightmares, low morale would be better addressed with professional psychological personnel. What is offered at this level is usually civilians attached to the military. In certain war zones there are no civilians around. In this case commanders are in crisis without professional military figures who can fulfil these roles.

3.6   Interaction with Other Actors

Relationships with other actors in the area includes:

- Local communities and local civil authorities
- International organizations, NGOs,
- Command and control of Cameroonian army in Multinational Operations.

1. **Local communities and local civil authorities**

Woking with local communities as a military is always challenging and requires a great skill. Most community problems are problems that are not solvable by the military, but the military require some basic knowledge on how to handle or behave in such situation. A good example of such community problems is the experience in Central African Republic(CAR) which where generally: Adolescent pregnancy, access to clean drinking water, child abuse and neglect, crime, domestic violence, drug use, environmental contamination, ethnic conflict, health disparities, HIV/AIDS, hunger, inadequate emergency services, inequality, jobs, lack of affordable housing, poverty, racism, transportation and violence.

When analysing these real community problems, the analysis may show multiple reasons behind the problem. They persist despite efforts and are real challenges according to some officers we interviewed:

- Analysing community problems is hard work. It took real mental effort that most low-level Cameroonian military are not used to sitting down and thinking deeply about the problem.
- Real community problems are complex. Economic development depends on the global economy, a force you can't have much effort on. You may have opposition, either from within the community itself, or from powerful forces trying to protect their own interests.
- When we went looking for reasons and underlying causes for significant community problems, we found more than one. Several different reasons may be influencing the problem, in different ways, all at the same time. It was not an easy task to untangle all the reasons and their relative strengths, but it was necessary in order to reach a solution.
- The problem did not only have more than one reason; It had more than one solution too. Many different types of actions might be necessary for revitalization.

Analysis, including the analytic methods we have described, could take us a long way. With good analysis, some resources, and enough determination, we believe even the most troublesome problems can be addressed and solved.

The military plays a vital role in the security and defence of the community thus working together with local authority is fundamentals. The local authorities usually maintain a wide array of capabilities and resources that can be made available upon request.

2. Governmental organizations and NGO

The different cultures in the military and NGO's present a major challenge to effective interaction. The NGO community is described generally as a loosely configured system or network of actors which coalesce around common funding sources and voluntary standards, without an effective chain of command. Both sets of actors have spent time trying to understand each other's structures and ways of working. Most NGO's in Central African Republic (CAR) have often been openly hostile to foreign military forces. The tensions between these actors are not simply to do with cultural differences, but also stem from fundamental differences in motivations, goals and approaches.

NGO's operating in Central African Republic (CAR) together with Cameroonian military as a component of a coalition offers some reflections on the relationship between national military actors and the international community.

3. Command and control of cameroonian army in multinational operations

As Commander in Chief, the President always retains national command authority over Cameroonian forces. Command authority for a multinational force commander is normally negotiated between the participating nations and can vary from nation to nation. In deciding regarding any appropriate command relationship for a multinational military operation, national leaders carefully consider such factors as mission, nature of the operational environment, size of the proposed Cameroonian force, duration, and rules of engagement.

Cameroonian forces usually establish liaison early with forces of other nation, fostering a better understanding of mission and tactics, facilitating the ability to integrate and synchronize operations, assisting in the transfer of vital information, enhancing mutual trust, and developing an increased level of teamwork.

4 Conclusion

With its 2016 GDP estimated at just under USD30 billion, and its military budget estimated at USD 370 million in 2017, or around 1.2% of GDP, Cameroon is a peaceful country in the Economic Community of Central African states without a greatly armed military. More outside assistance is needed, as there is some, but limited, margin to increase government defence spending.

The Economist Intelligence Unit estimates 4.8% growth for 2017, and an average 4.5% growth for 2018–2021. These numbers are completely respectable but increases in military expenditures should follow and not precede GDP trends, so as not to jeopardize the positive economic health of the country as it seeks to attract new investment. And yet, military success in fighting off the Boko Haram threat is essential for Yaoundé to maintain its reputation as a peaceful, trading nation with a talent for economic development. Particularly as the current decade is shaping up to be very positive for growth in Sub-Saharan Africa.

The key, of course, is the further professionalization of military officers, which led to the determination of the focus of this research paper. This can only be achieved realistically through ties to developed-world, democratic military organisations, especially through the UN and perhaps the EU and the AU, although not in such a way as to encourage the Great Power or Superpower competition of the past. This author's conviction is that this may be most easily achieved through avoidance of liaisons to the world's largest militaries, in favour of ties with smaller, but well-financed professional armies, for example, of Europe's smaller and medium-sized countries.

The Cameroonian Defence Ministry gave its kind permission to visit restricted areas near (but not quite in) combat zones. The almost 40 officers interviewed in local research in the field in Cameroon gave a general impression of being welcoming, professional and generally optimistic (their interviewer was also a Cameroonian citizen).

Regarding policy recommendations for the future, this author would limit himself to observing that most first-world countries have engineering faculties that collaborate in some way with national militaries in many technical areas that are not directly related to weapons and lethal systems. Like many other African and developing countries, Cameroon's state universities has its engineering faculties that produce excellent quality candidates, who upon graduation sometimes find gainful employment in the country, and sometimes are forced to seek gainful employment outside the country. Such are the conditions of any developing country. The issue is delicate. This author is not advocating full-scale militarisation of universities or faculties. But there is room for increased cooperation between local faculties and the defence ministry of Cameroon, based upon limited budgets to sponsor competitive programmes to link Engineering graduates with local companies supplying technical support to the military, such collaboration would go far in boosting the professional and technical capabilities of the Cameroonian land, air and sea forces.

This collaboration might also be aimed at training officers in service and/or on missions, about technical support issues. Superior weapons, tactics and discipline are key elements for any victorious military in any context. But the reliability and capabilities of weapons systems cannot be emphasised to the detriment of the human resource element, and like any modern corporation, a successful business formula must include development of human resources—a key factor in the maintenance of morale, officer recruitment and retention, and the general professionalisation of democratic militaries. To this end, social training in such areas as Cultural Awareness and Civilian/Military relations, cooperation and communication, especially in battlefield regions, has been an increasing focus of Cameroons defence.

The most cost-effective way to boost this training would be to develop a CIMIC training centre in Cameroon in conjunction with such centres as the NATO CIMIC Group South in Motta di Livenza (province of Treviso) outside Venice,[6] Italy or the NATO CIMIC centre of excellence in -the Netherlands,[7] To note that such centres would be open to both military and civilian staff of the Defence Ministry.

The NATO CIMIC North centre in the Netherlands has in the past sponsored courses in the politico-military decision-making process, military organisations and structures, and especially the NATO military concept for defence against Terrorism.[8]

The latter course included such topics as: Counterterrorism, Compliance with International Law, Support for Allies, Non-duplication of efforts and complementarity of strategies, awareness of the threat and prevention, and crucially, sharing best practice, expertise and information relating to capabilities relevant to CT. For example, NATO's work on airspace security, air defence, maritime security, Special Operations, response to CBRN, non-proliferation of Weapons of Mass Destruction and protection of critical infrastructure is well established and may be useful to an effective CT.

---

[6]https://www.cimicgroup.org/.

[7]https://www.cimic-coe.org/.

[8]https://www.nato.int/cps/en/natohq/topics_50349.htm.

Bibliography

1. Cronin PM Irregular Warfare: New challenges for civil-military relations
2. Bagayoko-Penone N (2008) Cameroon's security apparatus: actors and structures. GO/0717, African Security Network
3. "Sub-Saharan Africa" (2015) In: International institute for strategic studies, The Military Balance 2015, Taylor & Francis, pp 435–36
4. NATO (2013) NATO glossary of terms and definitions. NATO Standardization Agency, Brussel
5. Ben-Shalom U, Shamir E (2011) Mission command between theory and practice: he case of the IDF. Défense Sec Anal 2:101–117
6. Armistead L (2004) Information operations: warfare and the hard realities of soi power. Brassey's Inc, Washington DC
7. Luthans F (2010) Organizational behaviour: an evidence-based approach. 12th edn, New York
8. Yukl G (2013) Leadership in organizations global edition, 8th edn. Pearson Education Limited, Essex, England
9. Cannon J, Cannon J (2003) Leadership lessons of the Navy seals. McGraw Hill, New York
10. Hughes RL, Ginnett RC, Curphy GJ (1999) Leadership, enhancing the lessons of experience, 3rd edn. McGraw-Hill, Boston, MA
11. NATO (2013) Allied joint doctrine for operational-level planning. NATO STANDARDIZA-TION AGency, Brussel. 17. US Army (1986) US Army training manual. FC 100–20

Experiences of Dutch Junior Leadership in Uruzgan (Afghanistan) between 2006 and 2010

'Only the Dead Have Seen the End of War' (Plato)

Jos Groen and René Moelker

Abstract The outcome of this research provides fundamental information, knowledge, and facts how Dutch junior officers applied their leadership skills during this counterinsurgency mission and how they experienced their assignment, not only as a military professional but also as a person. The interviews showed that these junior leaders were well prepared for their tasks. They were competent leaders who were cultural aware, which is a critical competence in counterinsurgency environments. The interviews also showed these junior leaders were not perfect, but competent enough to reflect on their experiences and decisions, ready to learn from them. To develop military leadership skills, the Dutch Army needs missions like these to keep up a sufficient level of professionalism. Missions of the size like the one in Afghanistan between 2006 and 2010 are probably not possible anymore, not now or in the near future and not in the long run because of the number of budget cuts since 2010. This will surely have a negative effect on the level of professionalism of our soldiers, for when there aren't challenging missions, military professionalism can hardly prosper.

J. Groen (✉)
Dutch Veterans Institute, Doorn, The Netherlands
e-mail: jmh.groen@nlveteraneninstituut.nl

R. Moelker
Netherlands Military Academy, Breda, The Netherlands

© Springer Nature Switzerland AG 2021
M. Nuciari and E. Olivetta (eds.), *Leaders for Tomorrow: Challenges for Military Leadership in the Age of Asymmetric Warfare*, Advanced Sciences and Technologies for Security Applications, https://doi.org/10.1007/978-3-030-71714-8_13

1 Introduction

The International Security Assistance Force (ISAF) is a NATO-led security mission in Afghanistan established by the United Nations Security Council on 20 December 2001 by Resolution 1386[1] as envisaged by the Bonn Agreement.[2]

Dutch military personnel were deployed to Afghanistan from the end of 2002. Several units were deployed and many individual staff officers also held posts at ISAF headquarters over the years. From November 2002 to August 2003 the Netherlands initially contributed multiple rotations of small, 250-strong units during ISAF phase 1. From July 2004 up to and including September 2006 Dutch military personnel were deployed to the northern Afghanistan province of Baghlan. During this period, several Dutch Provincial Reconstruction Teams (PRT's) worked from the provincial capital of Pol-e Khomri. In autumn 2005, a battalion of the Netherlands Marine Corps with a field dressing station was sent to Mazar-i-Sharif in northern Afghanistan to supervise the elections.

From 2006 onwards, the focus of the Dutch military shifted to southern Afghanistan. The Netherlands twice commanded the ISAF mission in the southern region from RC(S)[3] ISAF headquarters (from November 1, 2006, to May 1, 2007, and from November 1, 2008, to November 1, 2009). During these two periods, a substantial number of posts within the staff were held by Dutch personnel.

The main Dutch mission was conducted in the province of Uruzgan from the spring of 2006. Uruzgan is to the north of Helmand province, the main focus of the fighting in southern Afghanistan. This is the province in which Mullah Omar, the spiritual leader of the Taliban, spent part of his youth and its geographical position means that the province acts as a strategic hinterland for Helmand.

Following initial, essential national logistic preparations, operation Task Force Uruzgan commenced on August 1, 2006. The original plan was for the Dutch to be the lead nation in Uruzgan for two years, but in the interim, it was decided to extend this period by another two years. The Task Force Uruzgan mission ended on August 1, 2010, with the handover of military responsibilities to Task Force Stryker, a U.S. unit.

---

[1]United Nations Security Council resolution 1386: adopted unanimously on 20 December 2001, after reaffirming all resolutions on the situation in Afghanistan, by the Council which authorised the establishment of the International Security Assistance Force (ISAF) to assist the Afghan Interim Authority in the maintenance of security in Kabul and surrounding areas (Source: https://en.wikipedia.org/wiki/United_Nations_Security_Council_Resolution_1386).

[2]The Bonn Agreement (officially the Agreement on Provisional Arrangements in Afghanistan Pending the Re-Establishment of Permanent Government Institutions) was the initial series of agreements passed on December 5, 2001 and intended to re-create the State of Afghanistan following the U.S. invasion of Afghanistan in response to the September 11, 2001, terrorist attacks (Source: https://en.wikipedia.org/wiki/Bonn_Agreement_(Afghanistan)).

[3]The ISAF has a command structure which has divided the country into five regional commands which are under operational control of HQ ISAF: Regional Command North, East, South, West and Capital.

During these four years, the Dutch conducted what was for them a major military mission in terms of personnel and (material) logistics. Throughout this period, operations by large units such as the Provincial Reconstruction Teams and the Battle Group within Task Force Uruzgan were supported by logistic units, engineers, artillery, signals units, medical personnel, SF-units, marines and the Royal Netherlands Air Force. In total, about 20.000 Dutch military personnel worked in Afghanistan over this period. The overall effort was much greater, as just as much work for this mission was conducted within the armed forces in the Netherlands: not just within the framework of preparations, but also with regard to the sustainment of the mission.

The ISAF mission in Afghanistan, including the four years in Uruzgan, cost the Netherlands a total of one and a half billion Euros. This is only the tangible cost, however. In their article 'Burden sharing in Afghanistan' Bogers et al. [5] describe that over the period 2001–2010 on the dimension population size as of one million of the country's population Denmark suffered the most casualties (6.0), followed by the UK (4.9), Canada (4.0), the U.S.A. (3.6), Norway (1.9), the Netherlands (1.1) and Australia (0.8). Over the four years in Uruzgan, twenty-four Dutch military personnel were killed during operations, casualty numbers the Dutch had not suffered since the Korea war in the 50's. Nearly 140 personnel were wounded, many of them seriously.

1.1 The Objectives of the Project

The original project aim was to record the experiences of Dutch platoon commanders with a view to setting out the lessons learned and experiences gained for the benefit of the armed forces. This opinion and objective changed over the course of the project, which was executed in 2011.

Initially, only infantry junior leaders were to be involved in the project. However, from the interviews and knowledge gained from operating in Afghanistan, it was realised that, in addition to (combat) experience, a great deal of other relevant knowledge and interesting aspects could be learned: the experiences of engineers, for instance, or junior leaders who had served in Provincial Reconstruction Teams, Operational Mentor Liaison Teams or Psyops Support Elements. It was decided that attention also ought to be paid to the experiences of these colleagues.

On the other hand, it was realized that the stories told by these colleagues were significant in ways other than purely the operational aspect of lessons learned. The interviews made the breadth of these experiences clear: the personal and emotional perceptions and their effects. It is also important to record all these impressions for the benefit of society and future generations. By publishing these personal stories of the Afghanistan mission, there is a greater chance of appreciation and respect, which in addition to greater self-respect for veterans can also aid coping with possibly serious incidents [33]. The importance of this for veterans has been demonstrated in the coping process regarding previous missions to which the Netherlands had contributed. The objective of the project, therefore, broadened substantially: it was no longer simply a matter of recording factual experiences, but also themes such as personal perception, appreciation, recognition, and coping. This information could only be obtained by conducting a qualitative study; this strategy ultimately led to a total of 23 in-depth interviews.

1.2 Results

The interviews were analyzed through the open coding method [4]; this led to the themes outlined in the result section. This section describes part of the themes that through open coding were identified for each phase in the chronology of the mission. For each period these themes are illustrated with a number of quotations.

2 Part I: Preparations for Deployment

'The goals and methods of educating young men on their way to becoming warriors are broadly similar at all times and places'. [39]

2.1 Team Building

Because of its expected positive effects, one of the main aspects of the preparation period was team building. A meta-analysis [32] that examined the relationships between team training interventions and team functioning suggested these positive effects: team training can enhance team performance and is useful for improving cognitive outcomes, affective outcomes, teamwork processes and performance outcomes. French and Bell [9] or Putko [29] also stressed the importance of team building. The Japanese proverb 'A single arrow is easily broken, but not ten in a bundle' is another clear indication of the importance of this aspect.

All the platoon commanders who participated in this study devoted a great deal of time to this issue, as they recognised that a close-knit team would be essential to the mission. A unit which works together properly and operates like a well-oiled machine is generally better able to conduct the difficult tasks expected of it during a mission.

Faith in each other is very important and I tried to achieve this through team building. It is essential here that you get to know your personnel and that they know you. I believe it is very important to invest in your personnel. I tried to get to know about everyone's family circumstances during personal interviews. I would then know in future what they were talking about when they told me things about the situation at home. Or I would then be able to ask with genuine interest about how things are at home with the partner or the children.

This type of conversation and attention ensures closer mutual ties. When you invest in these mutual ties, work becomes much easier. I did so via personal chats or by organising all kinds of activities in an informal setting outside working hours. (Erik, Battle Group (BG) 5)

I found communications within the group very important. I, therefore, spent a great deal of time talking to the platoon. I told them what we had done and why. How actions had gone during an exercise and that everyone knew what each other's contribution had been. I wanted everyone to be aware of the overall platoon picture. In doing so, I also tried to work on creating team spirit and faith in each other. I thought that team building was very important and I deliberately devoted attention to this. (Stellan, BG 4)

2.2 Mental Component

With psychological injuries accounting for between 10 and 50% of operational casualties, there is consistent evidence that adequate psychological preparation for deployments is a vital operational requisite. Beyond the psychological costs to soldiers, empirical results also indicate that the stressors found in military contexts can contribute to errors in judgment and performance, reducing operational effectiveness. Thus, the development of training programs that successfully prepares personnel for the psychological rigors of operations, in addition to the physical and technical demand, is important for operational effectiveness and maintaining the well-being of individual military personnel [37].

According to the Dutch military doctrine, military power comprises three components: conceptual, physical and mental. The mental component is a major part of the preparation for a mission, not only for the above-mentioned effects but as this component also contributes to the (intrinsic) motivation to carry out the assigned tasks during the mission. Several platoon commanders, therefore, included specific mental training aspects in their preparations program.

Mental training was very important to the platoon. We invested in this continuously. As a unit, it is not just about things you do well or the skills you have. The key to success is mental attitude: the unit works best when people are in good condition in mental terms. (Maarten, Engineer)

Training the mental component was just as important. Just before deployment, in conjunction with the police, I arranged for a number of police dogs, as I thought it was important to create a period of increased tension. I had arranged various interesting activities with dogs as a serious threat. The Deputy Platoon Commander and I had kept this a secret.

Everyone had a great and instructive day. The platoon cadre had seen enough to know how the men coped in stressful situations. On the basis of the individual responses, we had a great starting point for the evaluation, focused on our mission. Because that was the objective: what can you get out of this as a person and how might you be able to use this in a comparable situation in the near future? (Gerwin, BG 6)

For me, the priority was not purely group operations but also working on the mental aspect. One of the group commanders had spent time in the Special Forces. He had some great ideas about training the mental component. I ordered him to arrange an exercise for this. It was a fairly tough programme.

Before the physical component actually started, you could already see the effect of the first part of the programme on the men. Being in a stressful position for several hours is uncomfortable and unpleasant. In the evening, with the help of the sports instructors, we conducted a programme on the climbing tower, including the 'leap of faith'. We then had the men march for a while, followed by a good session in rowing boats. You could tell that some of the men really only got into their stride then, including one of the deputy group commanders. He had completely shut out everyone else and was only concerned with himself. We evaluated this with him afterwards. The exercise was an instructive experience, for the men and for us. As platoon cadre, we had gained thorough insight into the mental resilience of the men. (Rob, BG 4)

2.3 Time

A great deal is often demanded of personnel during the preparation period. Within a relatively short period of time, military exercises are held in addition to participation in various courses, some of which are mandatory. Furthermore, a great deal of time is invested in important procedures, such as operating according to drills or gathering relevant information on the deployment area and future opponent. Consequently, there is rarely a good balance between work and leisure time during the preparation period for a mission. In military jargon, this is known as 'a deployment before a deployment'. The feeling that the mission has already begun is also called 'psychologically deployed' by Pincus et al. [27].

> By setting priorities, in consultation with the company, we attempted to avoid having a deployment before a deployment. We regularly discussed this with each other. In spite of this, I think that the home front experienced the preparations for the deployment quite differently. As a group, we were doing something new, a project which had generated a lot of interest and this motivated us enormously. We felt we couldn't do enough to prepare ourselves as thoroughly as possible for our tasks. The home front thought that we were away so much doing all kinds of activities that everyone within the group was told at some point that it was if the mission had already begun. (Dennis, Engineer)

This can be done differently. In the interviews, the important role fulfilled by the next level of command up is often cited, as can be seen from the following quotation:

> Almost everyone, including our commander, had indicated that they did not wish to create a deployment before a deployment. The commander ensured that there was sufficient off-duty time to go home. He realised that he could fill the entire five months with all kinds of exercises and lessons, but that he wouldn't gain anything by that. I did not, therefore, experience the preparation period as tough and busy. (Dennis, Operational Mentor and Liaison Team (OMLT))

2.4 Departure

The departure and absence of their loved ones during deployment places a heavy burden on the home front, especially where children are involved. The response of children to an extended deployment of a parent is very individualized and also depends on their development age [27] or sex [19]. It also often proves difficult for outsiders to understand the home front's acceptance of the partner's long-term absence.

My own home front has always supported me in the decisions I have made and the same applied to this deployment. However you look at it, it was not an easy time for my girlfriend as our son was just a couple of months old. It is sometimes hard to explain this support to some people, usually people who have no ties with military personnel. She did come up against that. The military profession is not an easy one, and that applies to the home front too. However, she knew what to expect, as we already knew each other during my previous deployment. (Mark, BG 11)

My wife has experienced me being sent on a mission before. She knows what it's like. She knows me very well, so she knows what to expect of me. Of course, she doesn't necessarily want another deployment because she will have a very busy time on her own with four children at home. In the evenings in particular when the children are tired, you miss your partner's contribution.

I always make clear arrangements about how we keep in touch. No news is good news. Only when someone from the Defence Social Service is at the door do you know something is wrong. I have promised my wife she will never hear it on the car radio. Such procedures always work properly when they are needed (Steven, BG 10).

The imminent departure is often a period of ambiguity, in many ways. This was an issue for several of those interviewed. This feeling sometimes abates after the departure, but experience shows that the sense of fear almost never dissipates for the home front as the interviews showed.

There was a contradictory feeling at home. My parents are very proud of the work I do and can see that I am very happy in my job. You can see that quite clearly and in that respect, my departure caused a conflicting feeling. They were very happy for me, but they were of course also worried. Unfortunately, nearly twenty colleagues had already been killed by the time I left. That naturally got them thinking. (Geert, Psyops)

3 Part II: The Mission

3.1 Arrival

At the times of year when temperatures in Uruzgan were the hottest, an acclimatisation programme was held in Minhad (United Arab Emirates). Delves et al. [6] evaluated the operational acclimatisation during deployment to a hot-dry environment and found direct evidence of the positive effects in all physiological variables.

The journey then continued to Uruzgan, where the Handover-Takeover period (HOTO) with their predecessors was initiated. The relevance of a thorough HOTO is emphasized by Kilcullen [15] and it should be a face-to-face in situ HOTO to be effective [2].

We flew first to Minhad and underwent an acclimatisation programme there. It was very hot and incredibly humid. Temperatures sometimes reached 63^0 Celsius (145^0Fahrenheit) with 97% humidity. I thought I would go mad, but luckily the programme was well thought-out. The balance between work and relaxation was fine and was increased over the week. I noticed that my body responded well. (Geert, Psyops)

Together with my Deputy Platoon Commander and other platoon cadre I left one week ahead of the platoon. We first spent a week acclimatising in Minhad. That was well-organised. We then left for Camp Holland. We went to Chora for a week with the platoon cadre, to the White Compound. Following a brief introduction, we patrolled the region every day. The patrols were well-prepared by our predecessors. The platoon cadre and I were therefore given a good idea of the region.

The handover went smoothly. The HOTO did not just focus on the region. The group commanders (GPCs) were able to consult thoroughly with their counterparts at the same level. We also made time to discuss all the other tasks and operations at the White compound. This was also well-prepared. (Barry, BG 7)

In general, everyone was well cared for over the four years. There was almost always a well-prepared programme, which included plenty of time for sharing experiences and conducting joint patrols. What was noticeable was the heavy physical and mental effect on predecessors due to the high operational pace of the mission.

My predecessors were clearly exhausted and looking forward to the end of the mission. They had experienced a tough deployment. I saw that in the tired faces of my colleagues and I got the sense that they saw us as saviours. (Dennis, Engineer)

I was met by a Deputy Platoon Commander with huge bags under his eyes, who had given a final salute to his PC two weeks previously. (Stellan, BG 4)

I noticed that my predecessors had had a very tough time. They were happy that their deployment had come to an end. (Dennis, OMLT)

One of the interviewees indicated that it was difficult for him to support the newcomers.

At the end of my deployment, I had virtually no energy to look after my successors. I had already seen nearly three-quarters of the company depart and in my head, I was already on the way home. I found that very tough. (Erik, BG 3)

3.2   The Takeover

According to Kilcullen [15], early successes will have a positive effect on the rest of the tour. A positive effect with respect to creating confidence among the personnel can therefore be achieved by having a unit accustom itself gradually to its new operational environment during its first independent operational task, at least if this is possible after the HOTO.

We had a calm operational build-up. The company had thought it through properly. We started, for instance, with minor operational tasks during the day. Later, we also conducted night patrols. My first assignment was a fairly simple task lasting a half-day. We had to move through the desert to a high ridge and adopt an overwatch position. From there, we had to provide protection for an operation by another platoon. This allowed us to get used to local conditions, to become accustomed to working in this terrain and to driving around in it. (Peter, BG 1)

Things occasionally turn out differently, but that can also have a positive effect.

On patrol, on our third day in the region, we were supposed to move to a position. We were conducting our patrol, but we never reached the position. We were fired on quite accurately and were more or less surrounded. I learned a lot from that situation (....). What I saw that day has stayed with me. I was able to use the lessons I learned that day throughout the remainder of the mission. (Eric, BG 3)

3.3   Counterinsurgency (COIN)

COIN warfare is a subject which is studied by a lot of scholars who described different key factors considering this type of conflict.[4] A key aspect of COIN warfare is to build a protector-protégé relationship with the local population, according to Krieg [16]. Herman Kahn [14] argued in 1968 that 'the two most important political factors in 'winning hearts and minds' are looking like a winner and providing security.' Porch [28] highlights the often-overlooked danger of a population-centric approach, in that it causes the soft target population to suffer attacks and retribution when insurgents begin to view the people to be conspiring with the government or COIN forces. Certain elements of these COIN approaches were reflected during the interviews.

> I realized the platoon would be deployed in a counter-insurgency operation. It is very attractive for a military unit if it can use its resources maximally for what it has trained for: combat. Combat, however, is not an essential element of a counter-insurgency. You cannot beat the insurgents by fighting alone. A counter-insurgency is a people-oriented approach, and the protection of the population is a priority in that. The information that is obtained from the population, for instance, is essential.

> It was difficult though to build up a relation, which resulted in the platoon being able only to identify with the local population to a limited extent. That relation, however, is what it is all about in a COIN operation. The best approach is for a unit to stay in an area instead of coming back there from time to time. The problems which a population faces become the problems of the unit to a certain extent. We talked about these things in the platoon during the classes we had on this subject in the preparation phase. In practice, we did not manage to build up this relationship with the local population due to our changing deployment in various areas. (Ralph, RC(S))

> I found it very interesting to talk to the local population. I was really considered as an interlocutor. In the beginning, it was clear people were fathoming me. I looked rather young and did not have a beard. Some of my colleagues grew a beard on purpose. I saw that that was nonsense, as the Afghan men would see through that immediately. As a man, I had to make sure I met the profile they had of men and I noticed that respect simply had to grow. During the mission there grew a situation in which they realized that I was a man true to my word. Of course, it is helpful when, in the meantime, some credits have already been built up in the area. Surely the men knew I was that commander who had been in fights regularly in their area over the past few weeks and who had held his own. The Afghan culture is a warrior culture and when a man has proven he can fight, he will command respect. In their eyes, I would come to their meeting with thirty armed warriors and that is why they listened to me. Sometimes life is very simple indeed!

> I did not have the impression that the people were very actively trying to improve their situation. Their hands seemed only set for receiving. They did not dare to make a fist. Up to

---

[4]Military historian Martin van Creveld [38] has an interesting opinion about all the research and publications surrounding COIN though: 'The first, and absolutely indispensable, thing to do is throw overboard 99% of the literature on counterinsurgency, counterguerrilla, counterterrorism, and the like. Since most of it was written by the losing side, it is of little value.'

an extent, I could understand them. The platoon would be around in the area every few days and there were actually too few people to guarantee the security in our sector. The platoon, and in fact the company, could not live up to expectations. This meant that when the platoon had left, our opponent would have a free hand. I knew that sometimes the local population was threatened by the Taliban. When someone in his own quala[5] gets a weapon pushed in his mouth, he, of course, becomes more careful. The Dutch gave stickers and were friendly, the Taliban used brutal violence and terror. I realized full well which had a deeper impact.

In any case, it will never get any better if you are not prepared to take any risks at all. People must be prepared to take risks mutually. There were enough opportunities for the population to give information about the Taliban unheard and unseen. It is quite understandable that they would not openly reveal in a shura[6] who belonged to the Taliban. That made sense. But there were plenty of opportunities to talk. In my view, the local population did not take those chances and that is why I found it difficult to begin a conversation fully motivated each time. (Stellan, BG-4)

I learned a lot from my contacts with the local population: how to deal with people from another culture; how to get information from them in difficult situations. Before the mission, we were pressed upon to adjust to the local culture. This is partially true. Thus, we were told that for the first half-hour or so we would have to make small talk. I learned that you could do things differently and that I could explain why I did not do certain things, based on my own culture, and people would understand. I could do this by motivating why I did not do certain things. I never took off my shoes when I entered people's houses. I would sometimes tell that I was pressed for time and that therefore I wanted to come to the point quicker. That never caused problems. Afghans understood I came from a different culture and no one was surprised when I said that. Not everything needed to be done their way and I sometimes explained to them that certain things were important for me. Approaching someone with respect was appreciated very much, but that did not mean I would have to adapt to all their customs. (Bart, BG-2)

'Smile and Wave', previously applied by Dutch Forces during the SFIR mission in Iraq as a part of the hearts and minds campaign, was a phrase commonly used by military personnel throughout the mission. A professional, ethical and sufficient open-minded attitude is important during counterinsurgency missions [11, 15, 25], such as the ones in Afghanistan and Uruzgan, with the intent to win the hearts and minds of the locals. This is not easy, however, when you have just been fired at or lost a colleague. At such times, platoon commanders need to keep their heads, display understanding for the dominant emotions, but also issue clear and unambiguous guidelines.

I could clearly see the sorrow and emotions on their faces after the IED strike. However, I also saw the frustration, which could potentially be aimed at the locals. I immediately talked to them about it. I didn't expect them to make thumbs-up signs to the locals that day, but I would not accept any negative gestures. I asked the GPCs to keep an eye on this too. They had to have a clear head. If on the way back we were to antagonize the local people because of these emotions, this could jeopardize our safety and security in the region in the long run. (Kevin, BG 12)

---

[5]Quala: Afghan house.

[6]Shura: meeting with local Afghan leaders.

3.4   Leadership

Over the years an incredible amount of published books about leadership have described many different theories on the subject. But when it comes down to act as a leader, circumstances and the kind of people you have to work with play an important role in leadership choices, as some of these examples show.

> I do not believe in one specific way of leadership. Leading differs per person and situation. In one situation task-based leadership is required: the intent is stated and the men are free to act within the context of the intent. When they experience problems, they will no doubt come to you with them. In another situation perhaps a more directive style is required and people have to listen, for instance, under time pressure. Whenever the circumstances allow it, one can lead in a more social way and the men can think along. Leadership is a mix of the various available tools. I could move one man with a carrot, while the other needed to be kicked in the butt. This is how I worked as a leader. (Bart, BG-2)

> Leadership consists of fathoming people and taking the capacities of your people into account. As a commander, you have to be able to work with the people who have been assigned to you. You have to accept people as they are and to act accordingly. You can point out someone's shortcomings to him, but you cannot always enforce the desired behaviour. At a certain moment, you will see that you can demand something of people, but everyone has their own individual limitations.

> I had a very good section commander who only lacked some social skills. His men accepted this of him, and they had a blind trust in him at other moments, except that he was less versatile in the socio-emotional field. I am sure he became somewhat more open to his men, but only to a certain extent. During the mission, his men would sometimes go to another section commander for a good talk. I had to help him with this aspect from time to time, but I accepted that. Leading is giving as well as taking. (Anonymous)

> At a certain moment, there was a turning point in the cooperation within the platoon. In the beginning, I thought it was quite important that everyone liked me until I understood that that was not important at all. I had to see to it that everyone did their job well, in order to perform optimally during the mission. The men agreed to this. When I came to realize this, I changed my attitude. I think I was fairly strict but just. That is an attitude that most leaders do not have immediately because they still lack the necessary self-confidence. It is a process of growth. More and more, I grew into my role and I managed to put my mark on the platoon. Eventually, this gave me the ability to tell the men that I wanted things done in a particular way and not any different. It worked as long as I did not do this in an unreasonable manner. In general, I would not avoid a discussion. Relations were good in the platoon, and everyone knew that, up to a certain extent, they could say what they thought of a certain decision or choice. After we had discussed it, I would map out a certain course and my choice was carried out. That is why I was the platoon commander. (Stellan, BG-4)

> I had made clear arrangements with my 2iC in order to mark out our responsibilities. Together we talked a lot about this. Thanks to these mutual arrangements I could focus more on my key tasks as PC, which I found very appealing. The same held good for my 2iC who could focus on the section commanders, which was his role.

> By giving the section commanders some leeway, I tried to create a free environment, in which they would feel confident enough to share their problems, feelings, and uncertainties in all openness. I created this space for the section commanders to indicate to me and my 2iC where things did not go smoothly or where more time was needed. I wanted the section commanders to be able to talk to us about these matters so that my 2iC and I would be able to lay a finger on the sore spot and make a decision. We had to give the section commanders the feeling that they were taken seriously.

It worked, for they regularly came to see us. When they disagreed with a certain approach they would say so. They would offer alternative solutions, which was an approach that appealed to them very much. Or they would discuss the manner in which we communicated within the platoon. I was open to this. It was one of the lessons I had learned while studying at the Royal Academy. This gave me the opportunity to adapt my manner of operating and style of leadership on the basis of constructive criticism of others. (Mark, BG-11)

I received many complaints from within the platoon about the lack of information. Then I had a brilliant idea, if I may say so myself. I put everyone in a classroom and handed out blank world maps. I told them that this was a test, like at secondary school. So there was to be no peeking. I wanted every man for himself to indicate Afghanistan on the map. I think there were only three men who had the right answer! That was exactly my intention. I told them that they were continually harping about a lack of information, but they did not even know where Afghanistan was on the map. I thought they were right to complain about the scarce information, but you can find a lot of information on Afghanistan on the internet. Apparently, nobody made use of that. I told them that they could expect of me: I would share every relevant bit of information I had or I would try to find it. This, in my view, did not mean they could not search for it themselves. I did not hear very much about this lack of information anymore after this 'lesson'. Since that day many privates and corporals would give me all sorts of websites where they had found interesting data, for instance, on the most commonly used mines in Afghanistan. I had got the men thinking. (Geerten, Engineers)

Inspirational leadership is no guarantee of success, but in the case of leadership under extreme operational conditions, it is essential that commanding officers are willing to lead from the front (FM 6–22; [21, 35]). This is always expected of military commanders in the Israeli armed forces, see for instance Herzog [12]. If commanding officers are willing to run the same risks as their subordinates, they not only gain their respect but also faith in their decisions.

Leading by example is essential: you cannot simply issue difficult orders and then go and sit safely in your command post. At that moment, you also have to stand at the head of your unit. If you don't, then your men will start to think: 'go figure it out yourself.' (Dirk, BG 8)

I always made sure that I was at the front because leading by example is really important in my view. I accompanied every foot patrol and was therefore always with my men when there was a problem. They really took note of that. The PC was also always included in the sentry duty rota. However, sometimes I would wake up in the mornings and they had let me sleep in. Then it turned out they had altered the rota so that 'their PC' could have some extra rest. I thought that was amazing. (Stellan, BG 4)

3.5 Command Relations

While deployed in Uruzgan, Dutch junior leaders were confronted with all sort of aspects regarding command relations, both negative as well as positive. Some negative examples are adversity to risk, doubts about the given assignment or intent, micromanagement activities or a lack of trust. All military leaders need to recognize these issues and have to be willing to act upon them because true breakthroughs on the battlefield will often arrive through 'a willingness to accept risk and do things differently' [7].

During my mission with BG-2, I had the perfect company commander. I, as well as the other PCs or the platoon NCOs, could approach him anytime. He left us very free so that we could determine our own way, and he supported us towards the upper echelons. I notice at the beginning of the mission that the S3 section of the BG was working at the micro-level, by planning at the level of the platoon. The company commander brought this up for discussion and the result was a change of approach. When the platoon passed on specific issues, he would take them along to the level of the BG. After this meeting, he would give feedback to the PCs. He joined the patrols on a regular basis and at such moments he would function as a full member of the platoon. He did not take charge of the platoon when he came along but did the things that were expected of every platoon member. For instance, when he was asked to observe a certain sector, he did so. I thought that was an example of an excellent mentality. When there was a company action he would take the lead, and I thought he showed himself a tactically gifted commander at such moments. (Anonymous)

During the mission, I certainly received a number of assignments that troubled me. For myself, I had a very clear idea of how I wanted to operate, what I thought was an acceptable risk for my unit. And I was fully convinced of that. Whenever I received an assignment which I thought was not sound, for instance, because of the objectives we had to attain with it, I did not accept it just like that. I experienced this several times in Uruzgan. That led to some discussions, not so much within the platoon but with the company commander. I spent a lot of time analyzing the assignment and I think I did it well. The result was that sometimes I thought a different manner of operating was more sensible given a particular situation, and it would differ from what the company commander had in mind. I was an experienced PC who knew the trade of operating with a mechanized unit, and who knew about operating with the various vehicles. I certainly knew how to deal with that. If the company commander set me too many preconditions for an assignment, which were too limiting to my liking, I would discuss this with him. (Anonymous)

You cannot always avoid frustrations, and there were a few that bothered me. They would occur, for instance, if I was put in a position as a commander in which I was unable to carry out a certain assignment as ordered. At a certain moment, I executed an assignment differently from the way I had been ordered by my commander because I felt the assignment was not sound. I attained the objective, but in a different way: by not doing what I had been ordered. In the end, that proved to be sensible because it made it impossible for our opponent to attack us. (Anonymous)

I experienced my cooperation with the company commander as extremely pleasant. He was quite clear towards his PCs. He indicated that he was the commander and not the company staff. As it was, there were regularly situations that the staff gave all sorts of assignments to a platoon. I would sometimes indicate that I could not do a certain assignment. The staff thought that was nonsense and did not agree with me. I would then tell them that I had only one commander, the company commander. Let's wait and see who the commander will support, the reaction would usually be. Well, it was not the staff by definition. The company commander regularly supported the PCs. He told his staff that the PC was the one in the best position to assess whether a platoon could do a given task. In his view, a PC would not refuse an order for no good reason. And in that way, he was an immense support for us. (Anonymous)

I am not in the position to give a judgement about my company commander. He may have taken decisions on the basis of arguments that I am not aware of. What I did see, though, is that we both had different leadership styles. As a leader, he was more task-oriented and less relation-oriented. I saw the effects of that on the people within the company and that has made me more conscious of what is important in a leader for a soldier. Incidentally, that is not what you can learn in theory at the Royal Academy. Our company commander supported me and the company very well during the preparation and the training and he deserves praise for that. It ensured that we started the mission as a well-trained unit. (Anonymous)

3.6   Responses Under Extreme Conditions

'Success or failure will rest, increasingly, with the individual Marine on the ground– and with his or her ability to make the right decision, at the right time, while under extreme duress' [17].

Everyone responds differently under extreme (environmental) conditions, such as military combat or the imminence of death [18]. As a military commander, you need to take this into account, in the case of coming under fire for instance or in stressful situations.

At that point, we were under heavy fire. The prescribed drills for fire engagement had to be carried out. It was great to see the individual reactions from the men. For some, it seems to be in their blood to fight back, to attack in the direction of the fire. Others wait patiently in a covered position near a Bushmaster, in a safe environment. One soldier behind the Bushmaster felt he had to lie down to fire at the opponent. Another was fine as he was, behind the Bushmaster. (Mark, BG 11)

I play tennis and when my game is lousy I regularly smash my racket. Therefore, I was afraid I would also react like this in Uruzgan at such a moment: whenever things did not go the way I wanted them to go. I was afraid I would forget why I was there, that I would not be able to control my emotions and that that would prevent me from making the right the decision. I was afraid of that before I left for Afghanistan. In Uruzgan, I saw a different side of myself. I could stay calm and collected when I had to, although I had not changed a bit. And I have not since I returned. Of course, I have some more experience under my belt to which I can refer, but I do not view life any different. In the meantime, I still smash my racket from time to time on the tennis court. (Anonymous)

People sometimes respond automatically, which is not always ideal during an exchange of fire.

One soldier had a jammed casing in his Minimi rifle and tried to solve this using a cleaning rod. At the same time, however, he had to run quickly towards new cover, during which he was covered by his sergeant. Just before he reached the new cover, he dropped his cleaning rod. So what did he start to do? He wanted to turn and pick up the cleaning rod while still under fire. The sergeant realised this and was able to grab him by the collar and pull him behind the wall. 'What do you think you are doing?' 'I wanted to pick up the cleaning rod,' he explained. 'Get down, and forget the cleaning rod,' the sergeant replied. (Bart, BG 2)

Fear is a common and crucial emotion in such situations. When fear does not take over, this can be a useful means for continuing to function correctly. And by not showing fear, fear will not spread amongst the troops, for fear is contagious [20].[7]

I noticed that I never felt fear during combat. I was not scared of being hit. I didn't even think about it. The realisation came later. This was positive. I was able to keep a cool head, in spite of the adrenaline. In the case of enemy activity, I usually needed five to ten seconds to realise what was going on and then I was able to act. (Kevin, BG 12)

---

[7]In his book 'Look out below', published in 1958 by the chaplain (Lt. Col.) Francis Sampson, who served with the 501st Parachute Infantry Regiment (101st Airborne Division) during WW II, Sampson already made a similar remark when a soldier was evacuated for his hysterical fear of artillery fire: 'for fear and hysteria are contagious'.

I had a section commander who would always be the first to do everything. No assignment was too much for him. Until he was personally involved in an IED strike. In his view, he was driving precisely in the tracks of the preceding vehicles, but unfortunately, that was not the case. Fortunately, he was driving in a Bushmaster and there was hardly any damage. After the strike, his behaviour changed. He had had it. Then he became the perfect section commander for me: his conduct was more balanced and he dealt with his responsibility in a more conscious way. He was more thoughtful and did not always want to be the cock of the walk anymore. (Anonymous)

I never knew any real fear in 2007, also not at moments where this might have been possible. Somehow I became very calm when the bullets struck next to me. I am a quiet person anyway, but I was always very calm. During my second mission, my sense of fear was quite different. By that time I had had plenty of IEDs exploding around me, and during my second mission I also drove in an MB, an open vehicle. I would regularly sit in such a way during a move that my knees did not come underneath the dashboard compartment. I did this to prevent my lower legs from staying behind in the vehicle if I was catapulted out of the vehicle in an explosion. This is how I would sit in the MB when we moved through a gully. When we had come out again, I would literally sigh of relief. When I think about it, it is really bizarre. Incidentally, my driver had the same feeling about all this. He had struck an IED in a previous mission when he was in Chora. My gunner had driven behind an MB that had struck an IED, killing two men. All three of us had a past with IEDs and we had rather driven in a different vehicle. Sometimes we were really tense, and therefore I would become very angry when the armoured vehicles in front of us did not make a good track for us. (Stellan, BG-4)

When under fire, people are generally well aware that they are in danger.

We came under heavy fire. I saw the bullets hitting the wall about thirty centimetres away from me. I was too visible, so my position was obviously not good. I therefore improved my position so that the direct fire ceased. (Bart, BG 2)

But this example shows this is not always the case, as one of the interviewed platoon commanders had to be told by others that he was in danger as he was too busy doing other things.

One of my soldiers approached me during the battle. I was so busy sending radio messages while sitting against the quala, that I didn't realise bullets were hitting the wall just above my head. It was interesting to hear the individual stories of the soldiers on this point. They also talked about me. Several of the men in my group said that they had seen what was happening and that they had fired in the direction from which the shots aimed at me were coming. I hadn't even noticed. (Barry, BG 7)

3.7 Ethical Dilemmas

Clearly, ethics is an aspect of leadership and not a distinct approach that exists along-side other approaches to leadership. This holds especially true for the military, as it is one of the few organizations that can legitimately use violence. Military leaders have to deal with personnel who have either used or experienced violence. This inter-twinement of leadership and violence separates military leadership from leadership in other professions. Even in a time that leadership is increasingly questioned, it is still good leadership that keeps soldiers from crossing the thin line between legitimate force and excessive violence [23].

> I really had to decide about life and death in Uruzgan. For me, it was always clear how I had to act in situations when I had to make that choice. Do I see any weapons or not? Are there civilians about or not? When I was fired upon from a certain quala: can I attack the quala with heavier weapons or is there a chance that there are civilians in there? Those were the ethical dilemmas, but in fact, it all came down to one thing: is it him or me? We did not fire until there was an immediate threat. This rule also applied to my men, but it was always the human being who used the weapon system and who had to make a choice whether to fire or not. I have always tried to avoid collateral damage, but when I fired, I did not know where a bullet might ricochet. So, in some cases they were hard choices. (Bart, BG-2)

> I was confronted with several dilemmas during the mission, which in certain cases had nothing to do with my assignments. One day I visited a Kuchi family who had two sick children. One of these two children had already died and had been buried next to the tent. The people could not travel to a medical facility. I then contacted the company commander and told him that we had to do something about this. I told him I would not leave the family until I could make a firm promise. We arranged for a doctor to come and see the child the following day. Later I was told that that kind of initiatives did not belong to my work, but certainly in the case of children, I had great problems with that. I found it very hard to accept when I knew that those children were abused by someone with some power. When I saw someone abusing a child, I would always interfere. I would stop immediately and show in my own way that I did not accept that.

> I am 100% certain that I have made the wrong choice on occasion. Unfortunately, I cannot undo that, but I never did it on purpose and those were never easy choices. There were decisions which I sometimes had to take in a split second. I think that I, and the company, made reasonably discrete and well-considered decisions. (Erik, BG-3)

> There is actually one thing that really bothered me and that was the way in which young boys were abused as sex objects. These situations I found personally very hard, the way the local men treated these children. It was a phenomenon of which everyone could see that it had permeated the Afghan culture to the very core. It was something that no one would accept in the Netherlands.

> From time to time, I saw how an ANP officer would negotiate with a father of a small boy, who an hour later would be delivered again to daddy. The boy would walk around in the police post in nice clothes, with makeup on his face and everyone knew that he was probably drugged. Sometimes such a boy would sit on an ANP officers lap, and I still had to do business with him.

> I could not apply my own principles to that, for I was a guest in this country or would visit someone in his own quala. If I tried to do something about this, I would destroy that relation. It was the reality in Afghanistan, but not something I liked seeing. The Koran dictates a lot, but apparently not where it concerns sex with little boys. This phenomenon is actually the only thing. Furthermore, I did not experience any difficult dilemmas. (Rob, BG-4)

> All too often problems were solved too quickly by the members of the OMLT, the result of which was that the ANA were confronted too little with planning problems. When the ANA themselves do not solve their own mistakes enough, there is no learning process. If I had not interfered, I would regularly not have been able to start an operation. Or, I would have gone out with men who had taken the wrong type of ammunition. Should I not interfere? It would frustrate the joint operation with the Dutch unit and that is what I wanted to avoid. Such situations have always formed difficult dilemmas for the entire OMLT: to interfere or not to interfere? (Dennis, OMLT)

3.8 Frustration

Frustration is an emotion that occurs in situations where a person is blocked from reaching the desired outcome. Frustration can often provoke feelings of insecurity, discouragement or disappointment. Typically, the more important the goal, the greater the frustration and resultant anger or loss of confidence [1, 36]. ISAF commanders have repeatedly expressed frustration that NATO and their capitals have not given them their mandate or resources to accomplish their mission [31]. In 2009 General David McKiernan (ISAF commander: June 3, 2008–June 15, 2009) expressed his frustration with the limitations placed on ISAF forces. In a February 2009 briefing at the Pentagon, Gen. McKiernan stated, 'we have an advantage with our military capabilities, with speed, with mobility, with intelligence, with firepower, with logistics. When we place caveats on our military contributions, we tend to reduce those advantages.'[8] During the interviews, these Dutch junior leaders expressed some of their own frustrations while they were deployed in Uruzgan.

> I would always get a lot of confidence from my company commander. What frustrated me was the lack of confidence in the platoon commanders at the Battle Group and Task Force (TFU) level. All release authorities for the deployment of heavy means were shielded off frantically. When something happened everyone would have to give his opinion about it before we would get permission to deploy heavy means. The people in Camp Holland first had to build up a situational awareness of a situation with which the platoon commander was confronted in the area.
>
> Only, there has never been an upscale to see whether it was sensible to send a platoon commander on operations with eighty men and fifteen vehicles. Apparently, I am capable enough to bear that responsibility and to take decisions on which so many lives depend. Nobody ever woke up a commander for this, but when I wanted one round of the Panzer Howitzer, I was not deemed capable to take my own decision. I thought that was a very awkward situation. I found the lack of confidence at the highest echelon of the executive level embarrassing. It is good to build in certain checks, but in this case there were simply too many.
>
> In my view, colleagues within the TFU tried to keep grips on the situation at all costs. With all due respect for them, they were not raised within a system in which the platoon commanders or company at this level is capable of taking such far-reaching decisions at such moments. As it was, that was the reality in Afghanistan. (Stellan, BG-4)
>
> At one moment, halfway through the mission, the BG got the order to be more careful with the machine gun ammunition, as we used up too much. When ammunition is spent in these quantities, there is bound to be an operational reason for it, I thought to myself. Still, would we please be more economical with this kind of ammunition!
>
> I was also frustrated by the way in which the mission had been presented by the politicians, and by the reporting about the mission in the Netherlands. In the media, the reports were always positive with regard to the reconstruction. The mission was going well, the message was, although there were incidents like firefights and IED strikes on a weekly basis. When something happened or people got hurt, this was underrepresented in the papers, hardly causing a ripple. They kept up this kind of reporting in the media throughout the entire mission and that frustrated me. In the telephone calls from home or the e-mails from friends

---

[8]U.S. Department of Defence, 'Briefing with General McKiernan from the Pentagon', February 18, 2009.

everyone was always talking about the reconstruction or writing, how is the reconstruction coming along there? The daily practice was completely different. *(Anonymous)*

Logistically speaking, we were in a good period in 2007. We still had enough ammunition, for instance. In 2009, during my second mission, this was much worse: we were really in trouble with the 81MM shells. How could it be otherwise: during my first mission in 2007 our mortar section fired 3000 (+) shells in four months, not counting the flares. They kept an accurate count. That is an average of 25 shells per day. And then I am not even talking about the quantities of 5.56MM and .50 calibre ammunition which was spent during the firefights. These quantities were not reckoned with for our 'reconstruction' mission, I believe. (Anonymous)

3.9 Debriefing

Debriefing and evaluations are an important part of learning and coping with incidents. Not only because processes can be improved, as O'Toole and Talbot [24] describe: 'formal learning systems such as after-action reviews captures the knowledge and determines a uniform interpretation.' Looking back is just as important after people have experienced serious incidents because of coping mechanisms. After such incidents, it is important for military personnel to be able to talk about them, to be able to give free rein to their emotions, as Raphael et al. [30] report: 'debriefing may be perceived so positively because it meets many needs: the need of those not directly affected to overcome their sense of helplessness and the guilt of surviving, to make restitution, and to experience and master vicariously the traumatic encounter with death; the needs of those directly affected to speak of what has happened, understand it and gain control; and the symbolic need for workers and the management to assist those who suffer and show concern.'

Back at base, we were cared for as requested. I had said that I wanted to let off steam with the platoon between the inner and outer ring of Deh Rawod base. I had also asked the Company Sergeant Major (CSM) to arrange some food and drink, some beers (low-alcohol, of course) for the men. After letting off steam, we went to the base itself. The CSM had arranged for the minister, social workers, the psychologist and all kinds of people who could talk properly to our men. I had asked them to meet in the dining room so that we could at least get things off our chests. At times you could hear a pin drop in between the conversations in the dining room. (Marcel, BG 9)

4 Part III: Reflection

4.1 Return Home

Families worry about the physical and mental health of the military family member upon return, especially after combat situations [8]. The safe return of military personnel is an event full of joy and emotion, but 'although reunion may be joyously anticipated, it can be as challenging as the separation' [40].

Only after the end of the mission did I realise how difficult it had been for my parents. They had been really worried. My parents don't usually display their emotions, but when I walked into the arrivals hall at Eindhoven, their eyes filled with tears. I only heard later from others how much the mission had occupied their thoughts. They had never let on in conversations and correspondence during the mission itself. (Maaike, Provincial Reconstruction Team (PRT))

My mother was very happy that I was home. Like any mother, she had been very worried about me. She was very contented that I was back. (Barry, BG 7)

It was not easy to get back into home life. My daughter really had to get used to my presence. One day, my wife had gone to work and I was on my own in the house with my daughter. I wanted to do things for her, but she just wanted her mum. That was one of the hardest things. It took over six months for our relationship to return to more or less normal. (Erik, BG 5)

The interviews show that a large part of the returning men and women had to re-accustom themselves to normal conditions at home and during their daily work. The tension of the mission seems to have stayed with some military personnel for a while.

Once I even experienced a colleague and myself ducking down when, on the way to an exercise, a tyre burst at a petrol station on the highway A27. We looked at each other and I asked whether he had also thought it was an IED strike. We had both had the same thought and it was quite funny. It's not a problem and has nothing to do with fear. You have to get rid of some tension in your body and it takes time. (Gerwin, BG 6)

The leader's role in situations like this is important to overcome the stigma associated with admitting a mental health problem and seeking help for that problem [10]. The same interview with Erik showed the importance of leaders communicating openly about this with their troops.

I talked about this with my platoon. I remember that we were all sitting around and a few of them said that they wouldn't participate in the interviews with the Defence Social Services after returning home. It was a load of rubbish and there were no problems, they said. I told everyone to think about it long and hard. I told them about the emotions I was experiencing, the things that troubled me and what I had problems with. You could see them thinking, 'oh, so the lieutenant also has problems with certain issues.' Only then did they start to talk. (Erik, BG 5)

4.2 Looking Back on the Mission

One noticeable aspect is the positive comments from all those interviewed, in spite of the fact that some of these young officers had faced very difficult assignments. This is a promising signal, for 'construing positive meaning from war and peacekeeping experiences, especially related to combat exposure or high perceived threat, is associated with better psychological adjustment' [33].

I look back very positively on my mission. It was a great time because I was surrounded by all kinds of great people. I worked with lots of very different people in a very pleasant manner. It was an unforgettable experience. My personal contribution was minor, but I felt that I was doing something worthwhile. I gained a huge amount of experience, as a person and as a soldier, which I can use for the rest of my life. (Anke, General Practitioner)

I look back on the mission with a great sense of satisfaction and a positive feeling. I think that as a relatively young PC, with little experience and quite a lot of responsibility, I personally came out of it well. Those things I could influence turned out well. I looked back on this period so positively that I wanted to go on another mission. (Geerten, Engineer)

Personally, I think it was a period in my life which I shall always view as very important. A period in which I learned several major life lessons which will stay with me for the rest of my life. (Peter, BG 1)

4.3 Coping

When the soldiers come home they need to reconstruct a civilian or no-longer-deployed reality so as to fit back in with the Dutch military, their family, and society. Sharing experiences with others is one method of coping with the negative experiences of a mission. Not everybody is capable to talk about their combat exposure and experiences. In a research done by O'Brien and Hughes [22] Falkland veterans who admitted to full PTSD symptomatology five years after the event were significantly more likely to state that on their immediate return to the UK they suffered problems, including talking about their experiences. It is something which is not always easy to do so, however.

I find it a huge effort to talk to people about the mission. I have to explain so much and I don't want to. I prefer to talk to my brother, who is also in the military, or one of my best mates. To both of them, I have talked that much I don't have to explain to them everything from the start. I feel I can tell them anything. I, therefore, talk about my missions very little with others. (Erik, BG 3)

With respect to coping, recognition and appreciation depend greatly on those around you. My family and friends want to listen and understand what it's all about in dealing with events. It is not that we deliberately sat down to do so, but they were interested in what I had to say. For other soldiers from the platoon, I noticed that the home front didn't always know how to react. Their friends had a totally different frame of reference. Those friends were more interested in a new motorbike, for instance. I noticed this difference after I got back from leave. During their leave, the soldiers were able to talk about things to varying degrees. This meant that a great deal of coping with incidents had to occur back at the base within the platoon after the leave. Some soldiers in my platoon thought the disembarkation leave lasted far too long. They wanted to be back with their mates. They missed that sense of belonging to a group and the idea that everyone understood them 100%. They didn't get that from their families and friends. (Stellan, BG 4)

About six months after the two missions, I saw signs that the soldiers needed to talk to their platoon cadre or the Spiritual Welfare Service or Defence Social Services personnel. I didn't pick up these signs during actual missions. I think that this was linked to the operational pace. You move from one operation to the next, so you don't really have time to reflect. And of course, you have colleagues around you to whom you can talk 24/7. Once you're home, you can talk about it, but they don't really understand. The partial disintegration of the unit meant that some of the men found it more difficult to talk to someone about their experiences. (Bart, BG 2)

4.4 Lessons Learned

Lessons identified can improve operations, as many researches emphasize [3, 13, 26, 34]. A large number of individual lessons were, of course, learned during the TFU mission. Here, you can see overlap between those interviewed: on the role of commanding officers with respect to, among other things, leadership, team building, communications, planning and conducting operations, combat and to work with interpreters and the local population. All those interviewed, however, provided interesting information into many aspects on the basis of their own experiences and backgrounds.

> At each presentation following my mission, I name what I believe to be my most important weapon as a platoon commander: my men. Any investment in them always pays itself back many times over. And that was the case here too. I have always put a great deal of effort into my relationship with my men. I was always available for the soldiers. They could phone me at any time of the day or night, even at the weekend. I helped them if they wanted to study etc. I think that that contributed to the high morale within the platoon and the men's motivation. I believe that is why the mission went so well. (Dirk, BG 8)

> This is one of my main lessons for others. Once you learn to make use of the knowledge of others, you can tackle the most complex situations. Use your platoon cadre and your specialists. Train with them and learn to work with them. Use what is offered and deploy it in such a way that it is used to the full. Then you can manage all the vehicles and personnel for which you are accountable for. (Bart, BG 2)

> Physical and mental resilience is essential. Both these elements are required. This needs to be sorted before departure. You may be well-drilled, have a great atmosphere in the unit and be well-trained in tactics: if you don't know your own physical and mental limits and haven't experienced being able to function properly after exceeding those limits, then you are missing out on essential training and opportunities. (Marcel, BG 9)

> 'Begin with the end in mind.' This is one of the seven habits of effective leadership according to Steven Covey. I missed this leadership habit among many of those in my immediate vicinity: a clear end objective, with an action plan which has been formulated using SMART (Specific-Measurable-Acceptable-Realistic-Time bound). This starts during the preparation period, during which you set the main and derived objectives for the mission. This remains just as important during the mission itself, however. During the mission, you have to clearly formulate what you want to achieve with your unit in your area of responsibility. Next, you need to continue communicating this clearly to your men. Too many key officials didn't apply this strategy during the mission. (Maarten, Engineer)

5 Part IV: The Key Question

In political circles, the Dutch mission was always described as a reconstruction mission. In practice, however, there was occasional and in some areas regular heavy fighting. However, this last aspect, the actual fighting, was not sufficiently communicated in the media; the Ministry of Defence was sometimes ambiguous about this in the opinion of those interviewed. In spite of the restricted picture, a public debate quickly arose on the nature of the mission: what were we dealing with in Uruzgan, a reconstruction mission or a combat mission? As those interviewed had experienced the situation at first-hand, it was interesting to hear their view concerning this discussion.

> I was never just in the fighting. It was a mix of everything and that's what made my mission so interesting. I know for certain that you can only lose if you focus entirely on combat. Within the company, we devoted just as much attention to reconstruction. We always recognised the importance of that and that is what we planned our tasks around. This is important in a counterinsurgency operation. When you know you have 100 warriors in the region, you haven't won the battle when you've eliminated all 100. The problems have not gone away. (Erik, BG 3)

> I find it odd that people see this as a surprise. The creation of security (Defence) is something that military personnel are excellently suited to doing! Anyone can do the other two Ds, Diplomacy & Development.[9] I thought the political response was very strange, i.e. that if we were involved in combat there could by definition be no reconstruction mission. The main basis for reconstruction is precisely to create a stable basis and security in a region. When you create security, you are conducting a crucial task in a reconstruction mission. You can construct all kinds of things, but if it all goes up in flames then you have nothing left to show for it. I didn't understand the debate. I thought it was more of a non-debate. (Stellan, BG 4)

6   Results and Discussion

6.1   Review

This kind of an interview project amongst junior leaders so shortly conducted after a mission is quite unique. Its results are very relevant for future operations. The outcome provides fundamental information, knowledge, and facts how these young officers applied their leadership skills during this counterinsurgency mission and how they experienced their assignment, not only as a military professional but also as a person. The interviews showed that these junior leaders were well prepared for their tasks. They were competent leaders who were cultural aware, which is a critical competence in counterinsurgency environments. The interviews also showed these junior leaders were not perfect, but competent enough to reflect on their experiences and decisions, ready to learn from them. The publication of the book in the Netherlands in April 2012, based on these interviews, will surely meet the other aims, for instance, the aim of more respect and appreciation for the ones who have contributed to the ISAF-mission. So, the objectives of this project were certainly met.

To conclude, a content analysis was applied to select what is seen as the most important lessons learned as stated by the young officers in the interviews:

During the preparation period, try to work as much as possible on the basis of fixed structures. This saves a great deal of time during the mission. Leaders must first know themselves, otherwise, they can never be capable of recognising others' strengths and weaknesses. This is essential to forming as strong a team as possible.

---

[9]3D security is a framework promoting development, diplomacy, and defence as security strategies, an approach the Dutch government has used in their ISAF campaign in Uruzgan.

Invest constantly in your men, so that they can evolve as people. This makes them perform better, which in turn automatically leads to the team you have created being stronger. Physical and mental resilience is essential to a team being able to perform under extreme conditions. You must therefore never include soldiers in your unit who do not meet these criteria. In this respect, it is more important to have a good team than to have good control of all your tasks as a unit. You will automatically grow into your tasks and role as a team once the team is fully up and running. The greater the team's span of control, the more you must delegate and rely on the advice of your specialists. You cannot manage everything. Leading your unit by example is crucial here: as the leader, you must lead from the front and in doing so also maintain the initiative.

6.2   The Future

The army needs missions like the ISAF mission to keep up a sufficient level of professionalism. Missions of the size like the one in Afghanistan between 2006 and 2010 are probably not possible anymore, not now or in the near future and not in the long run because of the number of budget cuts since 2010. This will surely have a negative effect on the level of professionalism of our soldiers, for when there aren't challenging missions, military professionalism can hardly prosper.

The Dutch Army, like other armies, has been subject to severe budget cuts that led to major changes, reductions and logistical problems like a lack of ammunition and spare parts which hampered the ongoing operations and training severely in the past years. Because the Army also lacked both interesting exercises and missions it did not appeal anymore to both young men and women from civil society to join the Army as well as serving young soldiers. Many of the latter, including promising junior NCO's and officers, therefore left the Army. This recruitment problems and personnel reduction are shown in a substantial shortage of boots on the ground with some units having to deal with only 75–80% of its positions being filled, and sometimes even less.

Due to these financial, logistical and personnel problems the operational level of the Army is well below acceptable standards. Because of the described current situation, some of these promising junior leaders which were interviewed have also left the Army to find new and more interesting challenges in the civilian environment. Let us hope that the ones who are currently still serving are able to turn the tide and can help to meet and cope with all of the challenges that lie ahead of us, because they may not have seen the end of war but they certainly have an important role to fulfil in the future of the Army, the Defence Department and any possible ensuing conflicts.

References

1. Adegbore AM, Adeniji OS, Adeshina K (2015) Stress and frustration effects on use of ICT for research by undergraduates in Ogun State Nigeria. J Ergon 5:143
2. Ali I (2011) Coexistence or operational necessity: the role of formally structured organisation and informal networks during deployments (ICCRTS paper)
3. Biddle SD (2002) Afghanistan and the future of warfare: implications for army and defense policy. Strategic Studies Institute, U.S. Army War College, Carlisle
4. Boeije H (2005) Analyseren in kwalitatief onderzoek. Denken en Doen. Boom onderwijs, Amsterdam
5. Bogers MP, Beeres RJM, Lubberman IG (2011) Burden sharing in Afghanistan. Mil Spect 180(11):487–501
6. Delves S, Fallowfield J, Milligan GS, Owen J, Middleton M (2007) Evaluation of operational acclimatisation to a hot dry environment. Med Sci Sport Exerc 39(5 suppl):S206
7. Doll Y, Miller B (2008) Applying the kotter model: making transformational change in a large organization. Int J Knowl Cult Chang Manag 8(1):53
8. Figley CR (1993) Coping with stressors on the home front. J Soc Issues 49:51–71
9. French WL, Bell CH Jr (1999) Organizational development—behavioural science interventions for organizational improvement. Prentice Hall, Englewood Cliffs, NJ
10. Greene-Shortridge T, Britt T, Castro C (2007) The stigma of mental health problems in the military. Mil Med 172:157–61
11. Hajjar RM (2010) A new angle on the U.S. military's emphasis on developing cross-cultural, competence: connecting in-ranks' cultural diversity to cross-cultural competence. Armed Forces Soc 36(2):247–263
12. Herzog C (1984) The Arab-Israeli wars, 2nd edn. Arms and Armour Press, London
13. Hyams KC, Riddle J, Trump DH, Wallace MR (June, 2002) Protecting the health of United States military forces in Afghanistan: applying lessons learned since the Gulf War. Clin Infect Dis 34(5):S208–S214
14. Kahn H (1968) On the possibilities for victory or defeat. In: Armbruster F et al (ed) Can we win in Vietnam? The American Dilemma. Pall Mall, London
15. Kilcullen, D. (2006). Twenty-eight articles: fundamentals of company-level counterinsurgency. Mil Rev May–June: 103–108
16. Krieg A (2016) Commercializing cosmopolitan security: safeguarding the responsibility to protect. Palgrave Macmillan, London
17. Krulak CC (1999) Cultivating intuitive decision-making. Marine Corps Gazette 83(May):18–22
18. Lazarus RS, Folkman S (1984) Stress, appraisal, and coping. Springer, New York
19. Lester P, Peterson K, Reeves J, Knauss L, Glover D, Mogil C, Duan N, Saltzman W, Pynoos R, Wilt K, Beardslee W (2010) The long war and parental combat deployment: effects on military children and at-home spouses. J Am Acad Child Adolesc Psychiatry 49:310–320
20. Miller WI (2000) The mystery of courage. Harvard University Press, Cambridge Massachusetts
21. Mutch A (2006) Organization theory and military metaphor: time for a reappraisal? Organization 13:751–769
22. O'Brien L, Hughes S (1991) Symptoms of post-traumatic stress disorder in Falklands veterans 5 years after the conflict. Br J Psychiatry 159:135–141
23. Olsthoorn P (2017) Military ethics and leadership. Koninklijke Brill NV, Leiden
24. O'Toole P, Talbot S (2011) Fighting for knowledge: developing learning systems in the australian army. Armed Forces Soc 37(1):42–67
25. Perez C (2012) The soldier as lethal warrior and cooperative political agent: on the soldier's ethical and political obligations toward the indigenous other. Armed Forces Soc 38(2):177–204
26. Perito RM (2009) The U.S. experience with provincial reconstruction teams in Afghanistan. United States Institute of Peace, Washington DC
27. Pincus SH, House R, Christensen J, Adler LE (2001) The emotional cycle of deployment: a military family perspective. J Army Med Dep 615–623

28. Porch D (1986) Bugeaud, Gallieni, Lyautey: the development of French colonial warfare. In: Paret P (ed) Makers of modern strategy: from Machiavelli to the Nuclear Age. Princeton University Press, Princeton, New Jersey, p 394
29. Putko J (2006) Teambuilding: a strategic leader imperative. US Army War College
30. Raphael B, Meldrum L, McFarlane AC (1995) Does debriefing after psychological trauma work? A time for randomised controlled trials. Br Med J 310:1479–1480
31. Rubin BR (2013) Afghanistan from the cold war through the war on terror. Oxford University Press, New York
32. Salas E, Diaz Granados D, Klein C, Burke CS, Stagl KC, Goodwin GF, Halpin SM (2008) Does team training improve team performance? A meta-analysis. Hum Factors 50:903–933
33. Schok ML, Kleber RJ, Elands M, Weerts JMP (2008) Meaning as a mission: a review of empirical studies on appraisals of war and peacekeeping experiences. Clin Psychol Rev 28:357–365
34. Soldaat PB, Broks DJ (2009) Observaties rond operaties in Afghanistan. Mil Spect 178(5):252–266, (6):340–349
35. Solomon Z, Mikulincer M, Hobfoll SE (1986) The effects of social support and battle intensity on loneliness and breakdown during combat. J Pers Soc Psychol 51:1269–1276
36. Soule SA (2017) The writer's guide to character emotion. FWT Publishing, Stockholm
37. Thompson MM, McCreary DR (2006) Enhancing mental readiness in military personnel. In: Military life: the psychology of serving in peace and combat, vol 2. Operational demands and adjustment. Praeger Press, New York, pp 54–79
38. Van Creveld M (2006) The changing face of war: lessons of combat, from the Marne to Iraq. Presidio Press, New York
39. Van Creveld M (2008) The culture of war. Presidio Press, New York
40. Woods S, Scarville J, Gravino KS (1995) Waiting wives: Separation and reunion among army wives. Armed Forces & Society 21:217–236

Printed in Great Britain
by Amazon